Beyond The Shadows

Divergence and Opportunity

Tim Bost

With Additional Commentary By
Jim Cummins

FinancialCyclesWeekly.com

Harmonic Research Associates

Beyond The Shadows
Divergence and Opportunity

Submit all requests for reprinting to:
Harmonic Research Associates
611 Riviera Dunes Way, Unit 702
Palmetto, FL 34221 USA

The astrological and market charts in this publication were prepared with the Fibonacci/Galactic Trader software from PAS Inc. (www.galacticinvestor.com), the Win*Star program from Matrix Astrology Software (www.astrologysoftware.com), the Kepler and Sirius programs from Cosmic Patterns Astrology Software (www.astrosoftware.com), and the Solar Fire, Solar Maps, and Nova Chartwheels programs available from Astrolabe (www.alabe.com).

Published in the United States of America by Harmonic Research Associates.

www.HarmonicResearchAssociates.com

First Print Edition

ISBN-10: 1-933198-55-9
ISBN-13: 978-1-933198-55-2

EAN: 9781933198552

Cosmic Dichotomies and Global Affairs

To even the most casual observer, it seems apparent that our planet is in a time of unprecedented stress and strife. Social and economic inequities abound. International alliances are unsteady, and in some cases untenable. Populism, nationalism, and isolationism have become the guiding principles of widespread political movements. Hardly a day goes by without news reports of mass shootings, refugees in crisis, or horrendous terrorist attacks. More than ever before, individuals seem to be driven by fear and distrust in their personal relationships, in their professional lives, and in their social and political choices.

That's why astrological perspectives are so important. When we can look beyond our nagging fears and our most pressing and immediate concerns, we have an opportunity to view ourselves in a new light. As we connect with planetary rhythms and cosmic cycles, we not only get a sense of just how finite our own petty cares actually are; we also gain the reassurance that an ordered universe has to offer us – we can understand that our lives are not random and we are not condemned to be victims. Our lives can have purpose and meaning, just as surely as day follows night and the seasons progress in a predictable order.

But just what kind of purpose and meaning can we expect to find? Here again, the rich lore provided by the accumulated astrological wisdom of the ages can offer us comfort, direction, and the potential for deep and rewarding understanding. From an individual perspective, we can learn a lot from our natal horoscopes, which reveal the unique imprint of cosmic energies that make us the remarkable individuals that we are, with all our latent capabilities and all our potential for happiness and fulfillment.

At a global level, we can also use the power of astrology to enrich our experience and comprehension. Through the study and application of mundane astrology – the branch of the cosmic science that connects geopolitical and economic affairs with planetary cycles – we can gain a much more sanguine attitude toward world events. We no longer have to succumb to fear or submit ourselves to demagoguery, but can choose more reasoned and tolerant assumptions instead.

And that's where the power of eclipses comes in. Of all the many astrological configurations and planetary dynamics that influence world affairs, eclipses are the most potent. Each eclipse offers us new circumstances to ponder, new lessons to learn, and new paradigms for our individual role in global affairs. Along the way, we can strengthen our own individual character, discover fresh opportunities to exploit for enhanced well-being, and open ourselves up to unexplored paths of service and social contribution.

That's exactly why we take the time to devote some special study to each solar eclipse, and to prepare a monograph that provides observations and commentary intended to be helpful in getting the biggest benefits from this significant astrological event.

Solar Eclipses and Market Activity

Whenever they appear, solar eclipses provide us with prominent sign posts that can give us a sense of direction in otherwise confusing and frustrating times. They can signal shifting social trends, coalescing cultural patterns, and significant breakthroughs in business,finance, and technological innovation.

By paying attention to solar eclipses and their effects, we gain insights that offer us a unique perspective, even if we typically pay attention to other astrological phenomena. We can prepare ourselves spiritually, financially, and psychologically for the challenges and opportunities that lie ahead.

The solar eclipse on September 1, 2016 is no exception. As we approach this cosmic event, we are at the point of culmination for some major astrological cycles that have dominated world events and the public consciousness for several years. They have taken us to notable extremes in the polarization between political, religious, and cultural factions, and we have suffered the consequences, not only in our private lives as individuals, but also in our public institutions and in our connections with the entire world around us.

In geopolitics, in governmental affairs, in business and commercial development, and in our family and community connections, we have seen these rivalries reach new heights of acrimony, bitterness, and self-serving hypocrisy. And as political campaigns have have commanded public attention, not only in the U.S., but in other nations as well, those extremes have been amplified with ego-driven showmanship that has taken on surreal proportions in the media echo chamber.

In short, the intensity and passion of ideology and the willingness to provoke no-holds-barred confrontations on all levels have reached staggering proportions. But the fact is, under the current circumstances we have to learn to deal with that kind of overwhelming energy whenever we start to examine the real-world implications of major cosmic alignments.

Astrology is serious business. When we look at solar eclipses we are definitely always dealing with matters of global consequence, and international events like the ones that have taken place in the past few years can serve as as a salutary reminder of just how powerful eclipses really are.

At the same time, we never want to forget that big change brings big opportunity. That's true for us not only if we are actively involved in speculations or investments, but also in our personal lives and in a broader context as well.

As we look to the markets as bellwethers of emerging trends in the broader social and geopolitical arena, we have an occasion not only to enrich our understanding of the real power of eclipses and of the huge potential that lies ahead, but also to create new visions of solutions to the problems and challenges that the world faces.

As is so often the case, as we anticipate the coming of the next solar eclipse in the weeks and months prior to the event itself, we are already experiencing the kind of tension, stress, and turmoil that can so often be triggered by high-impact astrological events.

In our personal and professional relationships, many of us are still grappling with financial traumas and unfulfilled priorities, with fantasies and hopes about our prospects for the future, and with massive uncertainty provoked by global tensions, social unrest, and the hysterical sensationalism of the mass media. At best we are likely to feel confused and frustrated by the circumstances around us; at worst we may be depressed or panic-stricken.

This sensational focus simultaneously manages to trivialize the true significance of cooperative initiatives and technological advances while fanning the flames of myopic xenophobia in a maelstrom of preoccupation with personalities and petty scandals. The negative energy begins to feed on itself, and more and more outrageous distortions begin to color the reality of our experience, and increasingly fantastic assumptions are conjured up to justify the escalation of alarm and hysteria.

It's undoubtedly a dangerous and disturbing situation, and since solar eclipses act as intense focal points for the full range of our experience, we can inevitably expect many of our world's major dissonances, injustices, and other problematical circumstances to get increasing emphasis during the coming months.

We are likely to feel the effect at all levels, from our homes and communities to the realms of international commerce and geopolitical posturing.

In spite of that prevailing stress, however, the solar eclipse of September 1, 2016, promises us the prospect of radical changes in our circumstances. That kind of change may not always be entirely comfortable for us to deal with, but it does offer us an an opportunity to explore fresh ideas and creative solutions, both at a personal and a global level.

At the same time, the solar eclipse of September 2016 provides us with a transcendent context for world events and economic developments that resonates powerfully with eternal truths. This intensely focused manifestation of fundamental relationships on a planetary scale presents us with potential insights that are anchored in ancient wisdom, and as it does so, we have an opportunity to move past the shadows of fear and illusion to claim and proclaim a bold new vision for the future.

It is, after all, in the midst of mundane stress and striving, in the swirl of chattering preoccupation with life's most superficial concerns, that the most surprising and most potent expressions of all-pervading grace and creative intelligence so often make themselves known. We have only to reconnect ourselves with the latent power of our Silent Source to share in their transforming potential in our own lives.

As the sages and seers remind have reminded us throughout the ages, with great power comes great responsibility. As we open ourselves up to an ever more enlivened expression of grace and intelligence in our lives, we automatically accept the mantle of stewardship. No matter what our cultural or religious background may be, and no matter what our political affiliations or sympathies, we have an unassuming opportunity to make an unspoken pledge to the fullest possible expression of spiritual activism in our lives.

Like the total solar eclipse that made its influence felt so profoundly earlier in the year, this eclipse is essentially a call for opening up a full expression of spiritual activism in our lives. If we are willing to dedicate ourselves to selfless service, and if we are truly receptive to what is being offered, we will find that the solar eclipse in September rises up to provide the support of nature in endorsing and backing up that pledge of spiritual engagement. In fact, it offers us an extraordinarily reassurance that we can and must embrace the responsibilities that lie before us.

As we consider this opportunity and as we assess the spiritual resources that are at our disposal, however, we must not succumb to complacency. We are not being called to a role of passive acceptance of the circumstances that we are confronting. In fact, we may need to take action in ways that may seem extreme, or at the very least unprecedented.

In some cases, our spiritual responsibilities may oblige us to take on confrontational roles, not necessarily in a spirit of combat or aggressiveness, but as a steadfast expression of wisdom, kindness, tolerance and compassion in the face of bigotry, fear, and duplicity. That kind of combative role may of course require some physical engagement on our part, since being a force for good in the world typically implies a willingness to “show up” in situations that can feel threatening or uncomfortable.

Even so, we must remember that the real battle is usually within ourselves. If we are to fulfill our true role in the world, we must remain fully grounded in the clarity of pure consciousness while we engage wholeheartedly in the challenges and opportunities that so often come disguised as a crisis, whether is in the realm of economic well-being, of world affairs, or of our personal connections and relationships.

It is on that inner battlefield that the solar eclipse of September 2016 confronts us most unequivocally. We need to summon the energies of our emotional bodies, focus our spiritual intentions, and apply all the resources of our intellects to accomplish the task of stepping out of the shadows of our past misconceptions and limitations. That inner determination takes genuine discernment, an ability to distinguish reality from illusion, as well as a sincere willingness to allow true Grace to flow through our lives in increasingly refined expressions.

It's definitely a bold move that is called for, but what better time to implement it than a solar eclipse? Eclipses are, after all, times of shadows moving across the face of the Earth. Whether or not we are physically under the path of the eclipse's shadow, we experience its shadowing influence as a transit to our natal horoscopes, bringing into focus the areas in our lives that require the most work and that offer us the biggest opportunities. As we engage personally and globally with the energies of this solar eclipse, we can transform our own lives in significant ways, and we can share that transformation with the world around us. The eclipse comes to us in a time of major stress, to say the least.

But like any important event in a time of severe stress, the things that create big conflicts can also create big chances for advantageous or resourceful activities. With an atmosphere of extreme tension and potentially dangerous confrontation continuing to be a dominant theme in social and political interactions, we have a volatile situation that can produce big swings in the movements of the markets, surprising opportunities for traders and speculators, and the potential for developing astro-trading strategies that can be extraordinarily profitable. And as we shall see as we look at the September total solar eclipse in greater detail, there are specific factors at work at the time of the solar eclipse that can offer us some remarkable benefits in the midst of a great deal of stress, conflict, and negativity.

Essentially, then, this eclipse deserves some highly-focused consideration, and that's the purpose of this monograph—to provide useful perspectives that we can put to work in our planning, not only at the time of the eclipse itself, but for the months ahead as well, especially when it comes to our personal well-being and our involvement in the markets.

The fact is, we really can't escape eclipses and their potent impact on our lives. Throughout human history, these cosmic events have been surrounded with a unique mystique that has inspired superstitions, given birth to myths and legends, and energized folklore, popular culture, and spiritual traditions around the world.

Among the various celestial phenomena which are observable from earth, eclipses are perhaps the most commonly recognized by the general public. They are certainly easy enough to observe with the naked eye, as long as you're in the right place at the right time and you aren't dealing with cloudy or overcast skies.

But the widespread awareness of eclipses is also at least partly due to the fact that when eclipses are visible in a particular locality they typically receive a considerable amount of special attention in local newspapers and on the television news. Usually the news stories and commentaries about eclipses play them up as extraordinarily rare events, sometimes in ways that generate more misunderstanding than useful information.

But eclipses are not only mysterious and fascinating events; when properly understood from an astrological perspective and then skillfully used in an active engagement with the markets, they can provide us with unique understanding and perspectives that we simply can't get in any other way. As a result, solar eclipses can be powerful money-making tools, too!

The Challenges of Using Eclipses in Astro-Trading

Throughout my many years of working with astrology and the markets, I have repeatedly found that eclipses are the single most significant celestial phenomena that we need to reckon with in financial forecasting and market timing. Even so, using eclipses in forecasting presents a unique set of complexities for astro-traders and for market analysts who want to add astrology to their set of tools for prognostication.

Nearly 30 years ago, when I began a systematic study of solar eclipses as key factors in stock market forecasting, I naively thought that a simple list of procedural rules and interpretive guidelines would be sufficient to provide the basis for profitable eclipse trading strategies.

Ultimately, however, that proved to be far from the actual case.

A set of rules and guidelines and a well-orchestrated approach to analysis are certainly useful, but during the years that I've been working with eclipses in the markets those rules have gradually evolved, transforming themselves into something quite different from my original guidelines. As a result I've had to rethink my assumptions about eclipses and their effects repeatedly, which overall has been a good thing.

I've repeatedly had to challenge my own prejudices and have been obliged to reexamine traditional astrological texts in the light of more modern empirical studies. While there have been times when I've been left with more questions than answers, for the most part I've actually found those occasions uniquely satisfying.

At least those experiences have helped me stay more conscious of exactly what I'm doing while making my own trading decisions, and along the way my forecasts have become more accurate and my trading has become more profitable. I've shared those results with my students and clients, as well as with the members of our online community at http://www.financialcyclesweekly.com.

The real challenge is that the original rules and guidelines that I developed in this study, along with the assumptions behind them, were based on a limited range of real-world practice. When I first started out I was new to the markets, and there were many things I simply didn't understand. But the more I have had to deal with diverse experiences in the markets, and the more those real-world experiences have challenged my preconceptions, the more I have come to understand that while eclipse interpretation rules may be important for evaluating behavior and for clarifying our expectations about the potential outcome of events before and after solar eclipses, those rules are not necessarily universally applicable.

Eclipses occur regularly and with great predictability, but each eclipse has its own unique characteristics, and in spite of the fact that there may some fundamental similarities among them, not all eclipses have the same effects on society and on trading activities in the markets.

While the nuances and variations among eclipses certainly make for interesting study and reflection for scholars intrigued by the subtleties of astrological theory, they also present some very real challenges for market astrologers and astro-traders.

Naturally enough, the impulse of most individuals who start to apply astrological considerations to market analysis is to believe that they should simply look for key astrological signatures that connect with the markets in significant ways—after all, if there is a clear relationship between a particular event in the heavens and a corresponding event in the markets, and if that correlation takes place without exception regardless of the specific market trends and circumstances, we will not only have validated astrology as an essential part of technical analysis; we will have discovered the Holy Grail of market forecasting!

Unfortunately, though, things aren't quite that simple in market astrology. Inevitably we must have some knowledge of market fundamentals, and of the mathematical cycles that correspond with significant market movements, if we are to be fully competent in our search for trading advantages.

And even with that kind of solid foundation, there are many nooks and crannies to be explored and many rabbit trails to follow when we start trying to figure out how planetary alignments relate to market action, with inevitable challenges along the way. In my experience, nothing reveals the obstacles and inconsistencies more quickly than the study of solar eclipses and their impact on the markets.

While different eclipses do have some factors in common, and while there are also eclipse series that link individual eclipses through extended periods of time, each individual eclipse also has its own distinctive characteristics—its own path of visibility, its own position in the zodiac, and its own particular relationship to previous eclipses and to the pattern of planets in the sky at the time the eclipse takes place.

In my own work I have found that it is through an examination of these unique features, especially from an astrological perspective, that we can gain some of the best insights into the potential effects of a particular eclipse. And it's those insights that can help us position ourselves appropriately as astro-traders for optimum profits from our trading in equities, options, and commodities.

Looking At The Track Record

Before specifically examining the September 2016 solar eclipse in detail, however, I think it's worthwhile to review briefly some of the results of the forecasts and trading implementations based on the previous solar eclipse, which took place in March 2016.

While forecasting market action based on eclipses is inevitably more an art than a science, it's nevertheless interesting to use an analytical eye in taking a retrospective look at the accuracy of what those forecasts revealed.

I must confess, though, that sometimes that kind of examination is quite humbling because of the errors and misconceptions it reveals—astrologers are human, too, after all, and I've certainly made my share of mistakes (some of them quite embarrassing!). Those errors have been due in most cases to the limits of my own vision and imagination rather than to any shortcomings of astrology itself.

At other times, of course, reviewing previous forecasts and the track record of events that followed them offers some delightful surprises-- every once in a while, the forecasts are actually right! But regardless of whether the track record itself is positive or negative, reviewing it is always instructive, and the insights gleaned from looking at past forecasts always help the current forecasting process as we move ahead to consider the next eclipses that are coming up.

The primary focus in reviewing the forecasts in the last eclipse report, of course, is its accuracy in describing conditions in the stock market. But even more importantly, we were once again able to identify profitable trading opportunities associated with the solar eclipse.

After all, the real reason we publish these special reports just prior to each solar eclipse is to help you devise effective trading and investment strategies for the coming months, so what we are most concerned about is how helpful we have actually been in creating tangible trading results.

The Eclipse Trade Track Record

In addition to the analysis of the solar eclipse impact and the solar eclipse Lunar Returns during the March 2016 eclipse cycle, there were also four specific stocks mentioned in connection with that solar eclipse that I thought offered good trading prospects: Avalonbay Communities Inc. (AVB); Cincinnati Financial Corporation (CINF); Infosys Limited (INFY); and Photronics Inc. (PLAB).

In each case, the proposed trading strategy was to "put on a long position soon after the eclipse takes place. This is typically within a couple of weeks following the eclipse (in some cases waiting for price pull-backs where appropriate for optimum purchasing opportunities). Our plan is to set an initial stop on each trade to minimize risk exposure, to trail a stop if a trade turns profitable, and then, if we are still in the trade, to reevaluate our positions around June 4, 2016, when we will get the Sun's conjunction with the March/September two-eclipse midpoint, and on June 8, 2016, when the transiting Sun squares the March Eclipse Point."

In each case we chose to enter these trades immediately after the March solar eclipse, on March 9, 2016. Our solar eclipse trading strategy produced a 100% winning trade percentage. Our winning trades returned an average of 5.74% in 20.5 trading days.

Here's a quick review of all four of the trades for these "eclipse picks" for the solar eclipse in March 2016, detailing the entry and exit points, along with the results for each of the trades.

Avalonbay Communities Inc. (NYSE - AVB)

This trade brought us the net return that was closest to the average result of any of the four eclipse trades, both in profits it produced and in the duration of the trade itself. We bought AVB on March 9 at 179.00, with an initial stop set at 171.75. On March 11 it closed at 183.21 and we raised the stop to 177.50. After a close at 187.04 on March 18, we raised the stop to 182.50 to lock in profits for the trade. Our stop was elevated to 163.50 after AVB closed at 185.09 on March 24. It closed at 169.87 on April 1, and we raised our stop to 188.00. That's where we were stopped out of the trade a few days later, selling AVB at 188.00 on April 7, for a 5.03% gain in 20 trading days.

Cincinnati Financial Corporation (NASDAQ – CINF)

This eclipse trade was the shortest of the four trades we took, and also brought us the smallest return. We bought CINF on March 9 at 63.60, with an initial stop set at 62.00. On March 11 CINF closed at 65.90 and we raised the stop to 63.50. After a close at 67.78 on March 18, we raised the stop to 64.90 to lock in a small profit for the trade. That's where we were stopped out of the trade on the next trading day, selling CINF at 64.90 on March 21, for a 2.04% gain in 8 trading days.

Infosys Limited (NYSE – INFY))

This trade brought us a solid return. We bought INFI on March 9 at 17.75, with an initial stop set at 17.25. On March 11 the stock closed at 17.96 and we raised the stop to 17.50. After a close at 18.52 on March 18 we raised the stop to 18.00 and locked in profits for the trade. Our stop was elevated to 18.30 after INFI pulled back to close at 18.31 on March 24. With a close at 19.25 on April 1, we raised the stop to 18.90. That's where our stop was hit and we closed the trade on April 5, selling INFY at 18.90 for a net profit of 6.48% in 18 trading days.

Photronics Inc. (NASDAQ – PLAB)

Our longest-duration eclipse-based trade, with a position in PLAB, began on March 9, when we bought the stock at 9.90. Our initial stop for the trade was set at 9.30. On March 11 PLAB closed at 10.06 and we raised the stop to 9.60. After a modest pullback and a close at 9.85 on March 18, we raised the stop to 9.65. Our stop was raised to 9.85 when PLAB closed at 10.00 on March 24. PLAB closed at 10.55 on April 1, and we raised our stop to 10.10 at that point, locking in a profit for the trade. With a slight pullback and a close at 10.48 on April 8, we raised the stop to 10.15. PLAB moved up to close at 10.62 on April 15, so we raised the stop to 10.50. On April 22 it closed at 10.97, and we responded by raising the stop to 10.83. That stop was hit on April 29, taking us out of the position at 10.83 for a profit of 9.39% in 36 trading days.

Our Overall Trading Results

Once again a study and analysis of the solar eclipse provided an excellent focal point for identifying potential trading opportunities. During the last 16 times that we have published a group of prospective eclipse trades in our series of books and monographs, we have had only six losing trades, with all of the other trades for the various eclipse cycles turning out to be winners.

For the solar eclipse of March 2016 the mean duration of our trades was 20.5 trading days, a period that was about 43% shorter than the duration of the trades in the previous eclipse cycle. While not all eclipse cycles produce trading opportunities of the same duration, we have found that the considerable advantage of trading with eclipses more than makes up for the discrepancies.

The Second Solar Eclipse of 2016

The first of the two solar eclipses of 2016 came on March 9 in most of the world, but late in the day on March 8 in the U.S., with the Sun and Moon meeting at 18°56' Pisces for the event. The second solar eclipse of the year will arrive on September 1, with the meeting of the Sun and the Moon coming at 09°21' Virgo.

Because our primary bias in this report is toward the impact the eclipse will have on market activity, especially the activity in the U.S. markets, most of our financial charts in this report are set for New York City, with the eclipse occurring at 05:03:02 p.m. EDT on Thursday, September 8, 2016,.

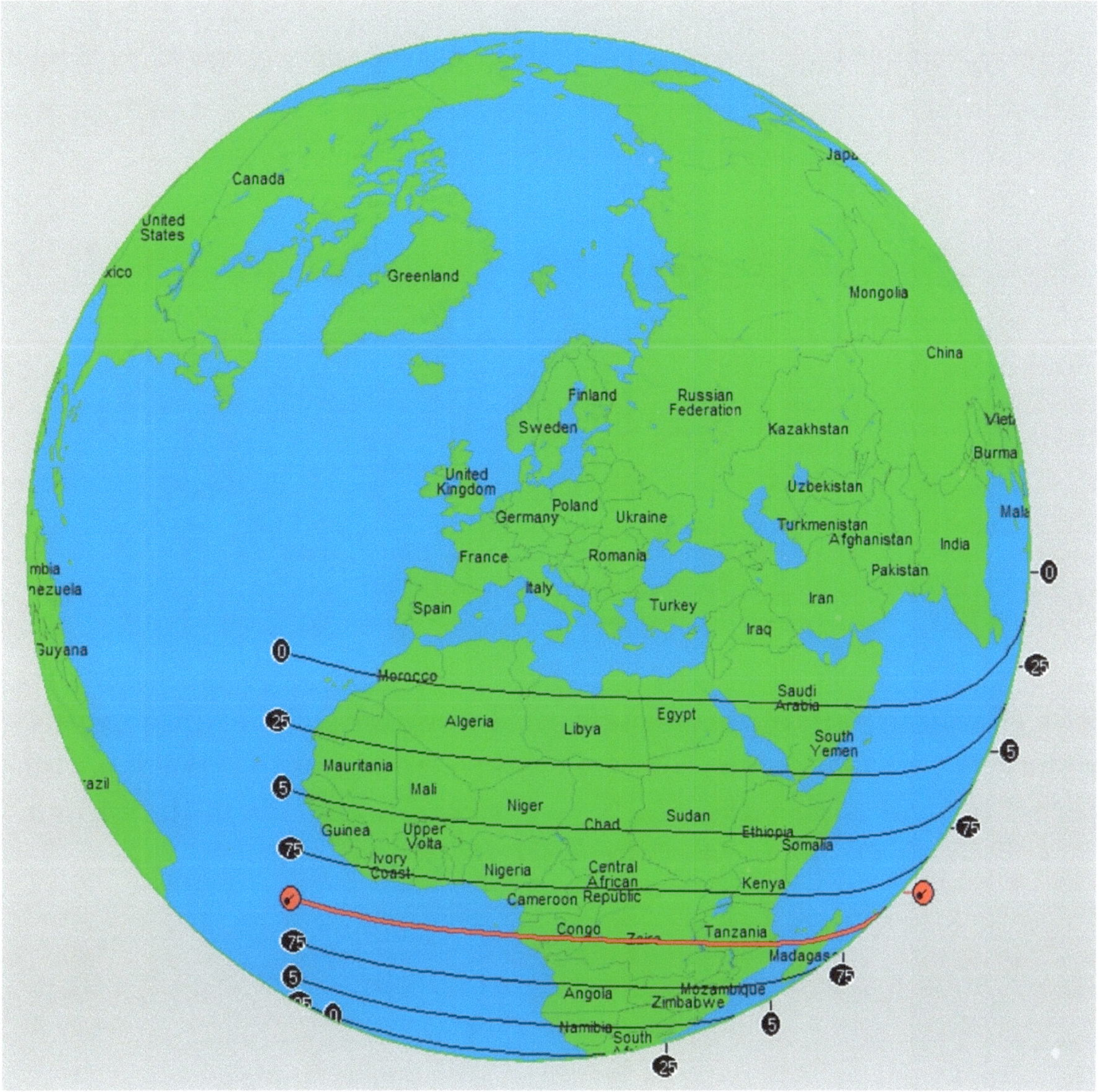

The eclipse in September is an annular solar eclipse, a "ring of fire" eclipse in which a ring of the Sun's light remains visible around the dark mask of the Moon, so it's not a total eclipse bringing complete darkness. This solar eclipse will be visible from the Atlantic Ocean, all of Africa except for the northernmost part of the continent, the southern half of Saudi Arabia, Oman, Yemen, Madagascar, the Indian Ocean, and the northwestern fringe of Antarctica.

The September 1 annular solar eclipse begins at 06:13:06 GMT, with the central eclipse starting at 07:18:58 GMT. The central eclipse ends at 10:54:06 GMT, with the entire event concluding nearly six hours after it began, at 12:00:42 GM. The time of the greatest eclipse comes at

09:18:06 GMT, but as astrologers we focus on the New Moon point of Sun/Moon conjunction, at 09:03:02 GMT on September 1, which is 05:03:02 EDT.

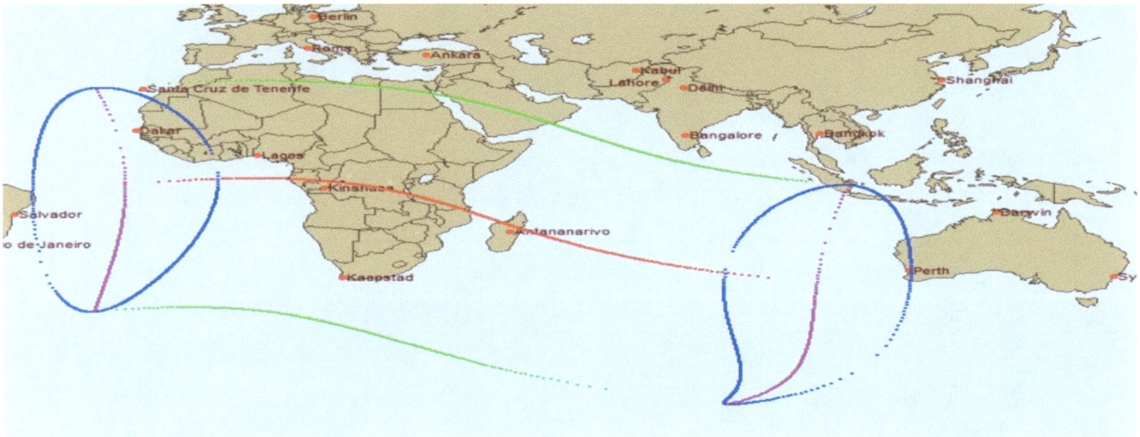

The complete path of the September 1 annular solar eclipse begins in the Atlantic Ocean, just off the eastern tip of South America, cuts across central Africa and Madagascar, and then ends in the Indian Ocean west of the Australian continent.

When we examine the horoscope for the solar eclipse of September 1,

2016, we set our chart for New York City, since this is the financial center for the US and indeed, for the world as a whole. With our analyses of solar eclipses during previous years, we have consistently found that calculating our charts for New York City provides us with useful insights into the potential impact of eclipses on market trends and economic developments. We recognize, of course, that there are many other hubs of economic and financial activity around the globe. We encourage readers to calculate the charts in this volume for other locations that they may be interested in, especially if they are focused on trying to track market activity in a specific part of the globe.

The chart as calculated for New York City has fixed signs of the zodiac on the angles of the horoscope, but this highly focused dynamic is not echoed very much in the chart as a whole. In fact, only the transneptunian factors Apollon and Poseidon are also in fixed zodiac signs. There is plenty of cardinal energy being demonstrated at the time of the solar eclipse, but the overwhelming emphasis here is on the mutable signs of the zodiac.

That emphasis on mutability underscores the fundamental message that the eclipse brings to our planet as a whole, and specifically to us as traders and investors. The message is a simple one: this is a time of profound and radical change. There is no way to avoid massive shifts in geopolitical alignments, in social relationships, in climatic conditions, in economic paradigms, and in our personal lives and relationships as well. If we resist change, and try to cling to old ideas and outmoded institutions, we risk irrelevance and dysfunction at best, and utter annihilation at worst.

The solar eclipse presents us with an opportunity to embrace change, to welcome it not only for what it may add to the enrichment of our lives and the fulfillment of our hopes and dreams, but also in gratitude for the harsh lessons that change can bring. When we are obliged to confront our own fears and apprehensions, and when we have no choice but to deal with our own tentativeness in assimilating new ways of thinking, we are being offered circumstances that can open us up to new vistas of understanding and experience.

The fundamental energy in this solar eclipse horoscope breaks down in an intriguing way. With one exception, all of the planets in this horoscope are disposited by Mercury, which is in retrograde motion in the second house of the horoscope, applying to a conjunction with Jupiter.

The implication here is that there are important lessons to be learned and key messages to be conveyed at this time. But those lessons and messages can be easily misunderstood, and efforts to communicate effectively right now are likely to involve more and more grandiose schemes and plans, which manage to miss the mark just enough to create confusion and frustration along the way.

The only planet in the horoscope which is not disposited by Mercury is Venus, which sits in the midst of a stellium in the second house of the horoscope while remaining unaspected. This separated expression of planetary energy gives Venus an extremely important role, essentially creating a fulcrum point that can be used to balance times of confusion with refined insights patiently steering a course toward harmony, balance, and beauty.

It's helpful for us to remember that the September solar eclipse comes after a series of eclipses and outer planet alignments which have added substantially to the increasingly dramatic levels of stress for our planet as a whole over the past couple of decades. Those stressful times have not completely vanished, but even so have been considerably diminished as we move into this new eclipse cycle and prepare for a transformed world.

One of the fundamental expressions of this stressful energy is revealed through the alignment of the solar eclipse itself at 9° Virgo in a T-square pattern with Neptune at 10° Pisces and Saturn at 10° Sagittarius. This is a challenging dynamic for the planet and for economic institutions as well, with hopes of wealth and abundance being seen as increasingly delusional thinking as harsh realities confront social structures and challenge individual financial initiatives.

While this planetary configuration does not necessarily mean that the outlook is entirely negative, it does give us an important warning about the need to take seriously any issues regarding shared resources, cultural values, power structures, and the rules and regulations which can potentially quash the human spirit while ostensibly trying to create safer and more secure structures for creative endeavor. We are likely to see the implications of this T-square play out in the coming months in natural disasters, in divisive political contests, in global struggles, and in the pressures of everyday living as well.

But as challenging as this T-square pattern may be, it is only part of the picture at the time of the September solar eclipse. The eclipse horoscope also features a Grand Trine pattern between Neptune and the transneptunian factors Kronos and Poseidon. This planetary configuration speaks to the potential for completely transformational dynamics at a cultural and spiritual level, presenting compelling alternatives to outmoded structures in a way that opens up new horizons for spiritual development, for creative new ideals, and for administrative structures that can hold up the highest values and most noble expressions in our lives.

In short, the solar eclipse presents us with some major divergences. When divergences occur within the financial markets or in the trading environment, they always help us identify potentially profitable circumstances that can be exploited in one way or another to gain leverage, to enhance wealth, or to accomplish bigger goals. But at a more fundamental level, the divergences that are likely to be revealed in the coming months will present us with ethical and spiritual choices, not only in our personal lives but in our social interactions and even on an international scale as well. It is our ability to see past the illusions of duality so that we can grasp the core consciousness that unites all life on this globe, that can turn a simple awareness of divergence into a supreme opportunity for permanent transformation.

That kind of thinking may seem bombastic if we are unaccustomed to viewing our lives from a heroic perspective.

But if we are willing to acknowledge our own true capabilities, if we are able to see ourselves as uniquely qualified agents of a sorely-needed planetary evolution, then that bombastic thinking can become truly humbling. Whether we are dealing with short-term financial advantage or are embracing our role in transforming the planet at large, it is the contrasts and divergences that confront us which are truly important at this time. They give us opportunities to rise to the occasion, and in doing so help us prepare for the major planetary transformations which are still to come.

The solar eclipse of September 2016 is a truly significant event, but it does not operate in isolation. The solar eclipses coming up in the years just ahead will act in ways that redefine geopolitical dynamics and human relationships on a truly incomprehensible scale. If we are wise, we will look to the energies offered us through the solar eclipse of September 2016 as a training ground, as a chance to practice the skills and perceptions that we need to master in order to build the intellectual, spiritual, and emotional muscles required for active participation in the global transformation that lies ahead.

When we examine the horoscope for the solar eclipse of September 1, 2016, we set our chart for New York City, since this is the financial center for the US and indeed, for the world as a whole. With our analyses of solar eclipses during previous years, we have consistently found that calculating our charts for New York City provides us with useful insights into the potential impact of eclipses on market trends and economic developments. We recognize, of course, that there are many other hubs of economic and financial activity around the globe. We encourage readers to calculate the charts in this volume for other locations that they may be interested in, especially if they are focused on trying to track market activity in a specific part of the globe.

The chart as calculated for New York City has fixed signs of the zodiac on the angles of the horoscope, but this highly focused dynamic is not echoed very much in the chart as a whole. In fact, only the transneptunian factors Apollon and Poseidon are also in fixed zodiac signs. There is plenty of cardinal energy being demonstrated at the time of the solar eclipse, but the overwhelming emphasis here is on the mutable signs of the zodiac.

That emphasis on mutability underscores the fundamental message that the eclipse brings to our planet as a whole, and specifically to us as traders and investors. The message is a simple one: this is a time of profound and radical change. There is no way to avoid massive shifts in geopolitical alignments, in social relationships, in climatic conditions, in economic paradigms, and in our personal lives and relationships as well. If we resist change, and try to cling to old ideas and outmoded institutions, we risk irrelevance and dysfunction at best, and utter annihilation at worst.

The solar eclipse presents us with an opportunity to embrace change, to welcome it not only for what it may add to the enrichment of our lives and the fulfillment of our hopes and dreams, but also in gratitude for the harsh lessons that change can bring. When we are obliged to confront our own fears and apprehensions, and when we have no choice but to deal with our own tentativeness in assimilating new ways of thinking, we are being offered circumstances that can open us up to new vistas of understanding and experience.

The fundamental energy in this solar eclipse horoscope breaks down in an intriguing way. With one exception, all of the planets in this horoscope are disposited by Mercury, which is in retrograde motion in the second house of the horoscope, applying to a conjunction with Jupiter.

The implication here is that there are important lessons to be learned and key messages to be conveyed at this time. But those lessons and messages can be easily misunderstood, and efforts to communicate effectively right now are likely to involve more and more grandiose schemes and plans, which manage to miss the mark just enough to create confusion and frustration along the way.

The only planet in the horoscope which is not disposited by Mercury is Venus, which sits in the midst of a stellium in the second house of the horoscope while remaining unaspected. This separated expression of planetary energy gives Venus an extremely important role, essentially creating a fulcrum point that can be used to balance times of confusion with refined insights patiently steering a course toward harmony, balance, and beauty.

It's helpful for us to remember that the September solar eclipse comes after a series of eclipses and outer planet alignments which have added substantially to the increasingly dramatic levels of stress for our planet as a whole over the past couple of decades. Those stressful times have not completely vanished, but even so have been considerably diminished as we move into this new eclipse cycle and prepare for a transformed world.

One of the fundamental expressions of this stressful energy is revealed through the alignment of the solar eclipse itself at 9° Virgo in a T-square pattern with Neptune at 10° Pisces and Saturn at 10° Sagittarius. This is a challenging dynamic for the planet and for economic institutions as well, with hopes of wealth and abundance being seen as increasingly delusional thinking as harsh realities confront social structures and challenge individual financial initiatives.

While this planetary configuration does not necessarily mean that the outlook is entirely negative, it does give us an important warning about the need to take seriously any issues regarding shared resources, cultural values, power structures, and the rules and regulations which can potentially quash the human spirit while ostensibly trying to create safer and more secure structures for creative endeavor. We are likely to see the implications of this T-square play out in the coming months in natural disasters, in divisive political contests, in global struggles, and in the pressures of everyday living as well.

But as challenging as this T-square pattern may be, it is only part of the picture at the time of the September solar eclipse. The eclipse horoscope also features a Grand Trine pattern between Neptune and the transneptunian factors Kronos and Poseidon. This planetary configuration speaks to the potential for completely transformational dynamics at a cultural and spiritual level, presenting compelling alternatives to outmoded structures in a way that opens up new horizons for spiritual development, for creative new ideals, and for administrative structures that can hold up the highest values and most noble expressions in our lives.

In short, the solar eclipse presents us with some major divergences. When divergences occur within the financial markets or in the trading environment, they always help us identify potentially profitable circumstances that can be exploited in one way or another to gain leverage, to enhance wealth, or to accomplish bigger goals. But at a more fundamental level, the divergences that are likely to be revealed in the coming months will present us with ethical and spiritual choices, not only in our personal lives but in our social interactions and even on an international scale as well. It is our ability to see past the illusions of duality so that we can grasp the core consciousness that unites all life on this globe, that can turn a simple awareness of divergence into a supreme opportunity for permanent transformation.

That kind of thinking may seem bombastic if we are unaccustomed to viewing our lives from a heroic perspective.

But if we are willing to acknowledge our own true capabilities, if we are able to see ourselves as uniquely qualified agents of a sorely-needed planetary evolution, then that bombastic thinking can become truly humbling. Whether we are dealing with short-term financial advantage or are embracing our role in transforming the planet at large, it is the contrasts and divergences that confront us which are truly important at this time. They give us opportunities to rise to the occasion, and in doing so help us prepare for the major planetary transformations which are still to come.

The solar eclipse of September 2016 is a truly significant event, but it does not operate in isolation. The solar eclipses coming up in the years just ahead will act in ways that redefine geopolitical dynamics and human relationships on a truly incomprehensible scale. If we are wise, we will look to the energies offered us through the solar eclipse of September 2016 as a training ground, as a chance to practice the skills and perceptions that we need to master in order to build the intellectual, spiritual, and emotional muscles required for active participation in the global transformation that lies ahead.

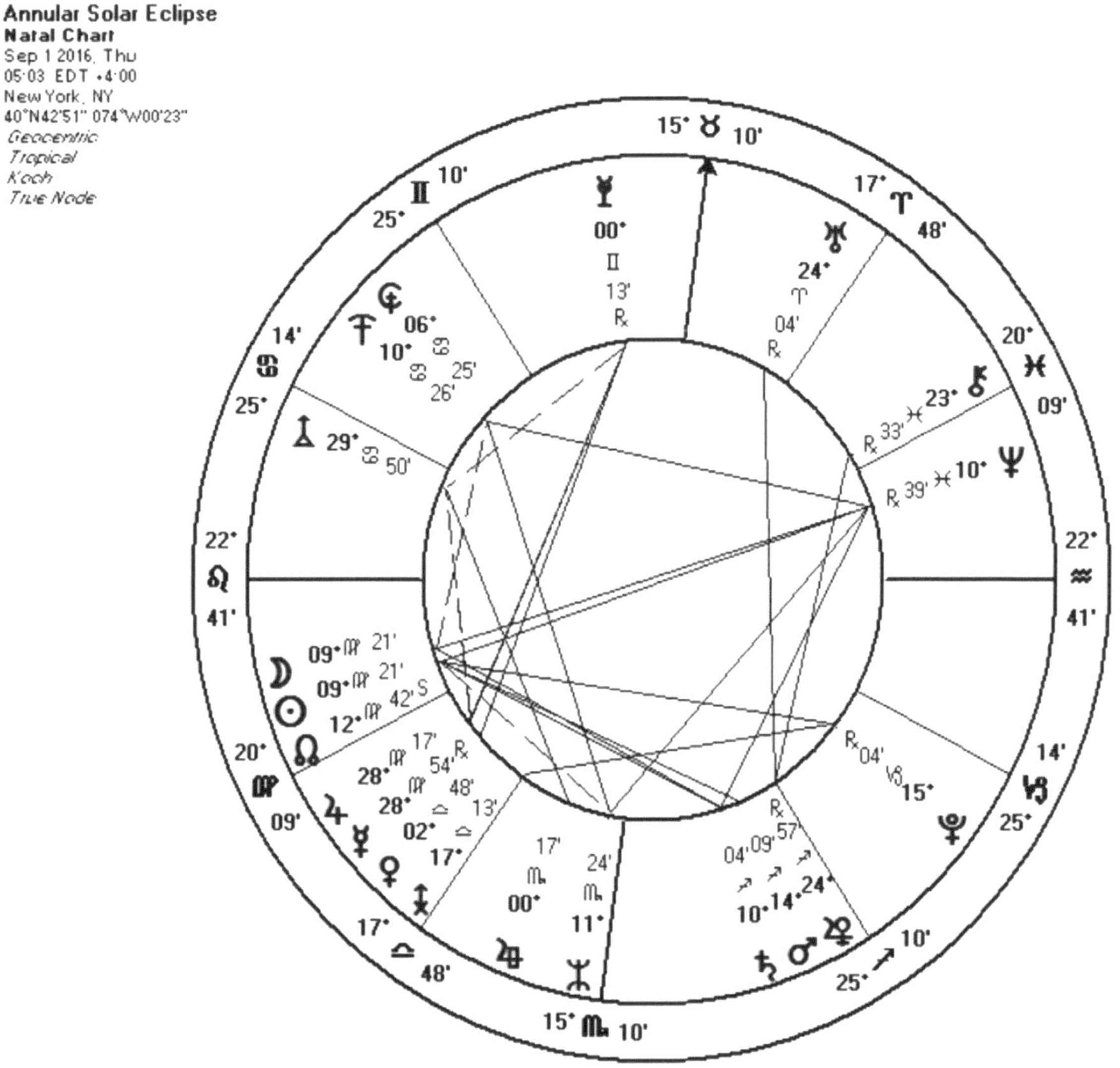

When we examine the horoscope for the solar eclipse of September 1, 2016, we set our chart for New York City, since this is the financial center for the US and indeed, for the world as a whole. With our analyses of solar eclipses during previous years, we have consistently found that calculating our charts for New York City provides us with useful insights into the potential impact of eclipses on market trends and economic developments.

We recognize, of course, that there are many other hubs of economic and financial activity around the globe. We encourage readers to calculate the charts in this volume for other locations that they may be interested in, especially if they are focused on trying to track market activity in a specific part of the globe.

The chart as calculated for New York City has fixed signs of the zodiac on the angles of the horoscope, but this highly focused dynamic is not echoed very much in the chart as a whole. In fact, only the transneptunian factors Apollon and Poseidon are also in fixed zodiac signs. There is plenty of cardinal energy being demonstrated at the time of the solar eclipse, but the overwhelming emphasis here is on the mutable signs of the zodiac.

That emphasis on mutability underscores the fundamental message that the eclipse brings to our planet as a whole, and specifically to us as traders and investors. The message is a simple one: this is a time of profound and radical change.

There is no way to avoid massive shifts in geopolitical alignments, in social relationships, in climatic conditions, in economic paradigms, and in our personal lives and relationships as well. If we resist change, and try to cling to old ideas and outmoded institutions, we risk irrelevance and dysfunction at best, and utter annihilation at worst.

The solar eclipse presents us with an opportunity to embrace change, to welcome it not only for what it may add to the enrichment of our lives and the fulfillment of our hopes and dreams, but also in gratitude for the harsh lessons that change can bring. When we are obliged to confront our own fears and apprehensions, and when we have no choice but to deal with our own tentativeness in assimilating new ways of thinking, we are being offered circumstances that can open us up to new vistas of understanding and experience.

The September 1 solar eclipse comes just 44 hours after a retrograde station by Mercury on August 30. Mercury, as we shall see, plays a very important role in the eclipse horoscope. Because the solar eclipse comes so soon after that retrograde station, Mercury is still virtually stationary at the time of the solar eclipse.

Mercury makes its retrograde station on August 30 at 29°04' Virgo, continues its retrograde motion until September 22, when it makes its direct station at 14°49' Virgo, and then begins to move forward again through the zodiac.

It will not be until October 6, however, that Mercury will return to its original point of retrogradation at 29°04' Virgo. There is thus an extremely strong connection between the solar eclipse horoscope and this particular Mercury retrograde cycle.

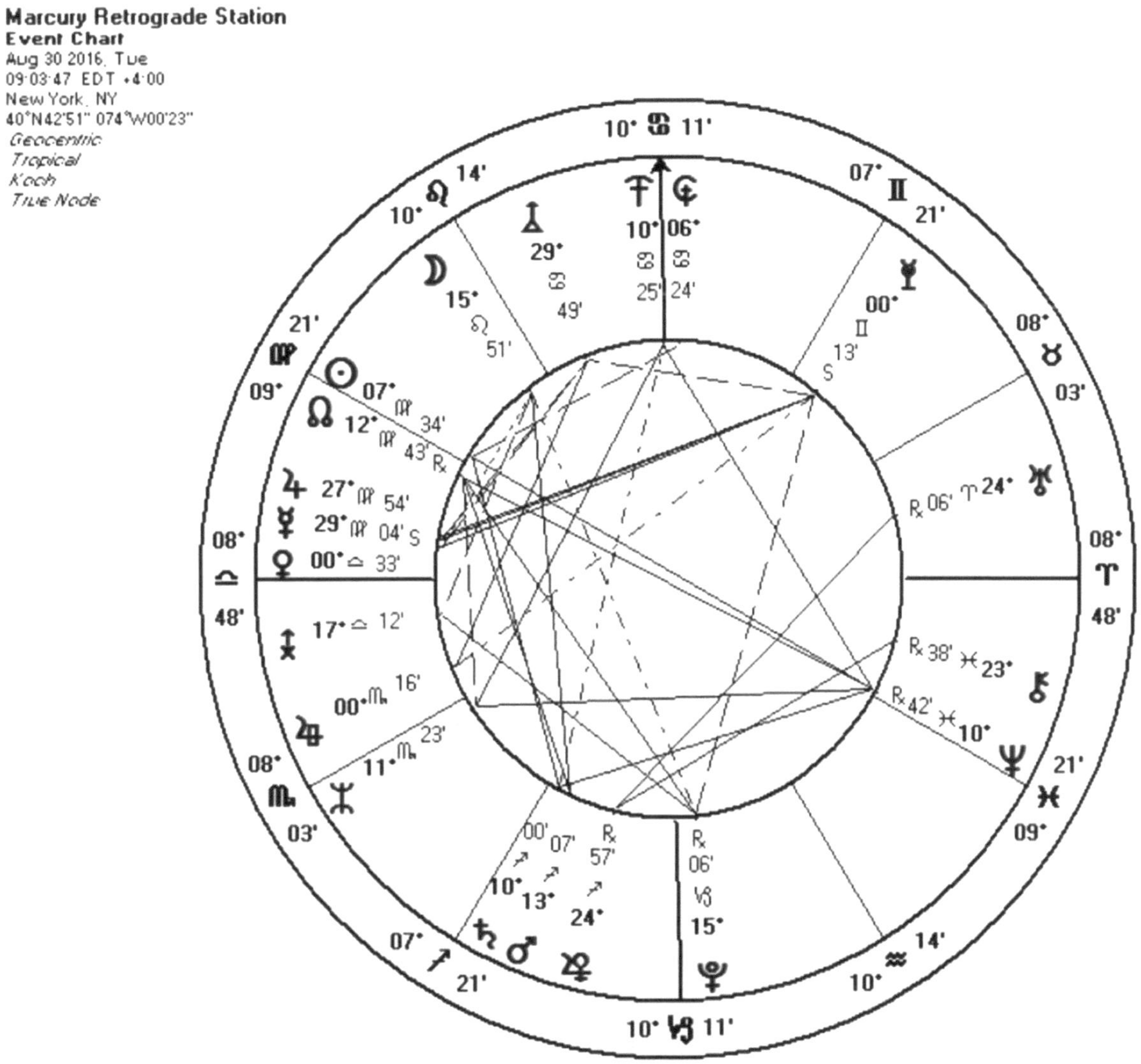

As we begin our analysis of the solar eclipse, then, it's worth taking a look at the horoscope for the Mercury retrograde station that occurs two days prior to the eclipse on September 1. This chart is especially significant because Mercury makes its retrograde station at the tight midpoint of Venus and Jupiter, which are the traditional money planets in classical astrology. Note that this configuration occurs in the 12th house of the Mercury retrograde horoscope, suggesting that concealed activities or ulterior motives may be dominant in financial communications just prior to the time of the solar eclipse.

This Jupiter/Mercury/Venus configuration expresses a desire for positive outcomes, financially and otherwise. For those involved with the markets, that desire is likely to be intensified by the application of retrograde

Mercury to a sextile with Vulcanus, a transneptunian factor which adds intense energy to the mix. But note as well that retrograde Mercury is also in a powerful square with Admetos, which tends to inhibit the possibilities for fulfillment at this time.

While Admetos may not prevent positive financial outcomes altogether, it at least suggests that the opportunities for financial gain at this time are likely to be limited to very specific channels. Any speculator or investor who seeks to profit from this eclipse cycle would do well to keep this narrowing of possibilities in mind, not only during the entire Mercury retrograde cycle between August 30 and October 6, but during the entire solar eclipse cycle as well.

The fundamental energy in the September 1 solar eclipse horoscope breaks down in an intriguing way. With one exception, all of the planets in this horoscope are disposited by Mercury, which, as we have just noted, is in retrograde motion. Retrograde Mercury is in the second house of the eclipse horoscope, applying to a conjunction with Jupiter.

The implication here is that there are important lessons to be learned and key messages to be conveyed at this time. But those lessons and messages can be easily misunderstood, and efforts to communicate effectively right now are likely to involve more and more grandiose schemes and plans, which manage to miss the mark just enough to create confusion and frustration along the way.

The only planet in the horoscope which is not disposited by Mercury is Venus, which sits in the midst of a stellium in the second house of the horoscope while remaining unaspected. This separated expression of planetary energy gives Venus an extremely important role, essentially creating a fulcrum point that can be used to balance times of confusion with refined insights patiently steering a course toward harmony, balance, and beauty.

It's helpful for us to remember that the September solar eclipse comes after a series of eclipses and outer planet alignments which have added substantially to the increasingly dramatic levels of stress for our planet as a whole over the past couple of decades. Those stressful times have not completely vanished, but even so have been considerably diminished as we move into this new eclipse cycle and prepare for a transformed world.

One of the fundamental expressions of this stressful energy is revealed through the alignment of the solar eclipse itself at 9° Virgo in a T-square pattern with Neptune at 10° Pisces and Saturn at 10° Sagittarius. This is a challenging dynamic for the planet and for economic institutions as well, with hopes of wealth and abundance being seen as increasingly delusional thinking as harsh realities confront social structures and challenge individual financial initiatives.

While this planetary configuration does not necessarily mean that the outlook is entirely negative, it does give us an important warning about the need to take seriously any issues regarding shared resources, cultural values, power structures, and the rules and regulations which can potentially quash the human spirit while ostensibly trying to create safer and more secure structures for creative endeavor. We are likely to see the implications of this T-square play out in the coming months in natural disasters, in divisive political contests, in global struggles, and in the pressures of everyday living as well.

But as challenging as this T-square pattern may be, it is only part of the picture at the time of the September solar eclipse. The eclipse horoscope also features a Grand Trine pattern between Neptune and the transneptunian factors Kronos and Poseidon. This planetary configuration speaks to the potential for completely transformational dynamics at a cultural and spiritual level, presenting compelling alternatives to outmoded structures in a way that opens up new horizons for spiritual development, for creative new ideals, and for administrative structures that can hold up the highest values and most noble expressions in our lives.

In short, the solar eclipse presents us with some major divergences. When divergences occur within the financial markets or in the trading environment, they always help us identify potentially profitable circumstances that can be exploited in one way or another to gain leverage, to enhance wealth, or to accomplish bigger goals.

But at a more fundamental level, the divergences that are likely to be revealed in the coming months will present us with ethical and spiritual choices, not only in our personal lives but in our social interactions and even on an international scale as well. It is our ability to see past the illusions of duality so that we can grasp the core consciousness that unites all life on this globe, that can ultimately turn a simple awareness of divergence into a supreme opportunity for permanent transformation.

That kind of thinking may seem bombastic if we are unaccustomed to viewing our lives from a heroic perspective.

But if we are willing to acknowledge our own true capabilities, if we are able to see ourselves as uniquely qualified agents of a sorely-needed planetary evolution, then that bombastic thinking can become truly humbling. Whether we are dealing with short-term financial advantage or are embracing our role in transforming the planet at large, it is the contrasts and divergences that confront us which are truly important at this time. They give us opportunities to rise to the occasion, and in doing so help us prepare for the major planetary transformations which are still to come.

The solar eclipse of September 2016 is a truly significant event, but it does not operate in isolation. The solar eclipses coming up in the years just ahead will act in ways that redefine geopolitical dynamics and human relationships on a truly incomprehensible scale. If we are wise, we will look to the energies offered us through the solar eclipse of September 2016 as a training ground, as a chance to practice the skills and perceptions that we need to master in order to build the intellectual, spiritual, and emotional muscles required for active participation in the global transformation that lies ahead.

Midpoint Activation

We can gain a deeper level of insight into the true implications of this solar eclipse by examining the midpoint structures in the eclipse horoscope.

The eclipse point itself activates the midpoint of the Ascendant in New York City and the transneptunian factor Cupido, suggesting that there will be a strong impact on social and cultural sensibilities during the months following the solar eclipse. This attention to refined values and artistic concerns is reflected in the eclipse activation of the Venus/Midheaven midpoint as well.

While these cultural indications have the potential for working out in positive ways as well as negative ones, there are other midpoint activations which seem to suggest more stressful outcomes. The eclipse point provides a direct activation of Uranus, adding a tremendous amount of volatility and potentially explosive energy into the mix during the weeks and months following the eclipse, with the possibility of a big impact socially, geopolitically, and personally, as well as in the market environment.

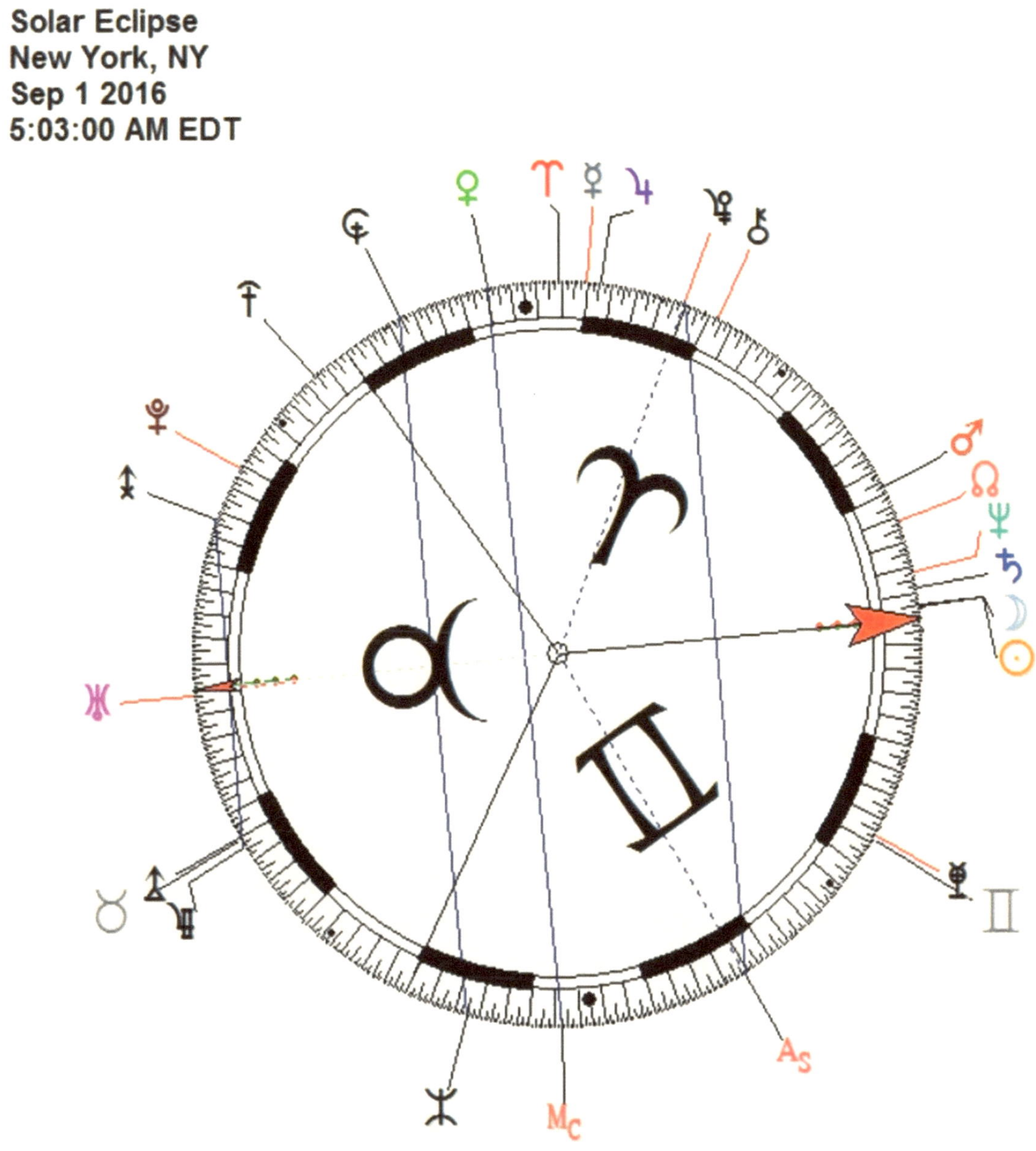

The Zeus/Apollon midpoint activation by the eclipse indicates the potential for dramatic expansion of commercial activities and market influences at this time, while the Hades/Poseidon midpoint trigger gives us an indication that new ideas and market paradigms which emerge after the eclipse may have decidedly negative implications.

That negative potential is reflected in other midpoint structures at the time of the solar eclipse as well. Eclipses are global events, after all, and the key to understanding global implications in any horoscope is the Aries Point. This particular point, as depicted on the 90° dial with the glyph for Aries, represents all of the cardinal points of the zodiac, those places where the Sun's passage marks the beginning of the seasons of the year and gives structure to world events in a predictable pattern.

In the eclipse horoscope the Aries Point triggers the midpoint of Chiron and Hades, hinting that our willingness to deal with the most repressive circumstances, social dynamics, and political personalities may actually hold some potential for positive outcomes in rather surprising ways, if we are only willing to engage in the nasty business that confronts us.

That potential comes into even sharper focus by the Aries Point activation of the Zeus/True Lunar Node midpoint in the eclipse horoscope. This planetary picture is the signature for elections, and the election campaigns in the United States, with their recent excesses of vitriolic political posturing, will definitely be a point of major focus in the time immediately following this solar eclipse. In spite of the overly-theatrical nature of the political campaigns themselves, the solar eclipse makes it very clear that activities at the ballot box during the months ahead will have a critical role in global affairs for quite some time to come.

The net result may be represented best of all by the Aries Point activation of the Vulcanus/Admetos midpoint in the solar eclipse horoscope. This is a planetary indication of times of new beginnings, particularly those which require a return to core values or essential reliance on basic resources. But this planetary combination also suggests that this is likely to be a time of potential crisis, representing a need to start over in order to address a new set of challenges in somewhat dire circumstances.

An examination of the midpoint structures in the horoscope for the September 1 solar eclipse can give us valuable insights by itself, but it is also useful to review this eclipse in the context of a precursor event. That was the solar eclipse that occurred during the summer of the year 1331. It offers us a glimpse of a factor which can provide an important influence today.

In most cases planetary midpoints act in a horoscope on their own, providing sensitive points that can be activated by other planets, but which don't always coincide with the positions of other planets in the chart. In some cases, however, we can also look to other sensitive points as potential triggers of midpoint structures, essentially providing “invisible activations” of the midpoints in the chart.

That's the case with the horoscope for the solar eclipse of September 1, 2016. Even though there are no planets in the chart at 20°32' Cancer, we can define that particular degree of the zodiac as an active sensitive point in this horoscope, because it marks the location of the very first eclipse in the Saros series of which this current eclipse is a part.

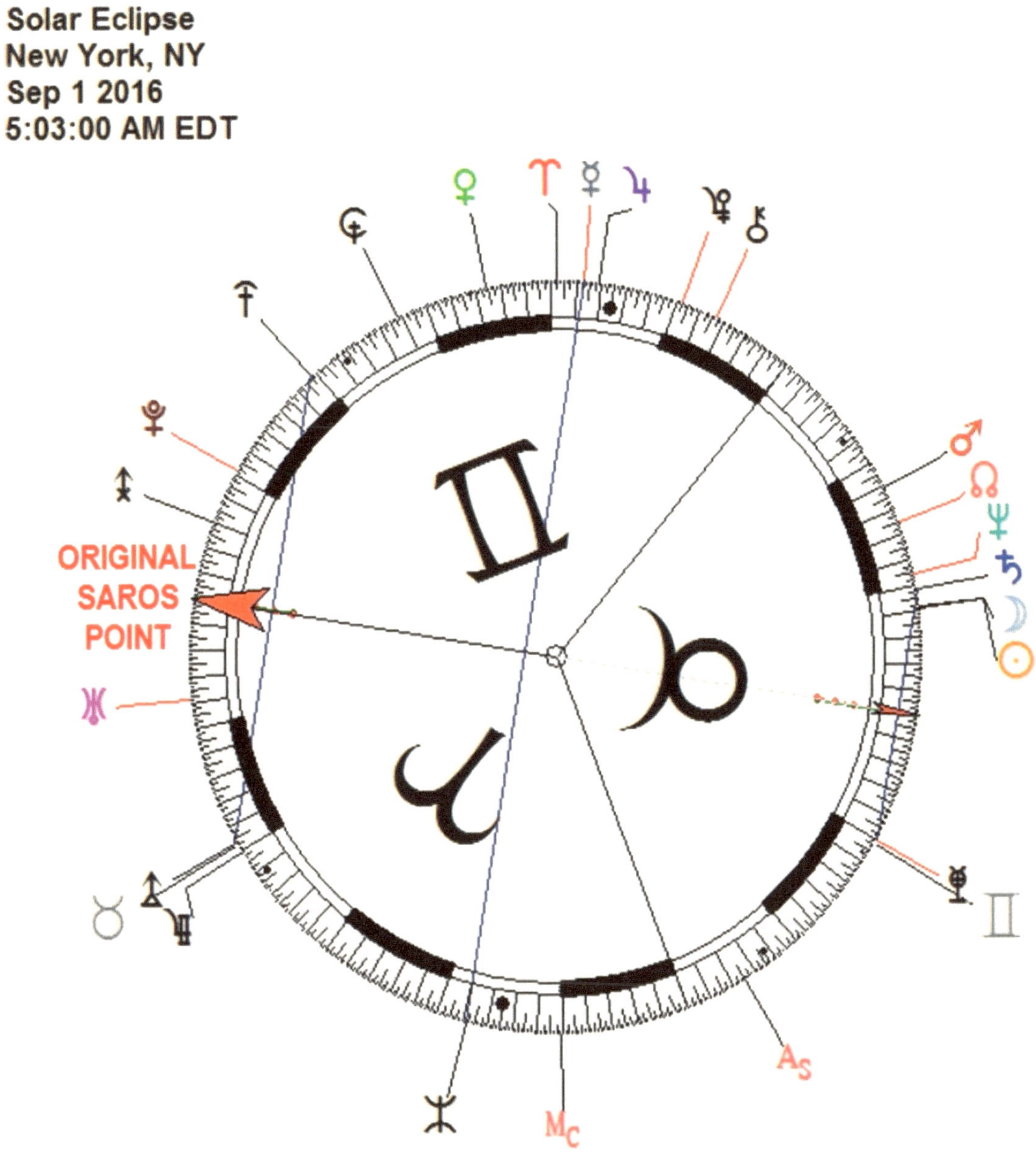

That eclipse took place in the year 1331 but its position still provides a powerful activating influence today. When we superimpose that original Saros point on the 90° dial for the current solar eclipse, we can see the midpoint activations that would otherwise be hidden from us.

The solar eclipse from July 5, 1331 activates the current

Mercury/Poseidon midpoint, giving us a reminder that this is indeed a time in which spiritual thinking is required, especially if we are to create new and more creative models for social interaction and economic progress.

The original Saros point also triggers the Kronos/Vulcanus midpoint in the September 1 eclipse horoscope. This is the core formula for the rise of a despot, an individual who expresses huge influence by wielding extreme political power and by embodying the total authority of the state.

The Saturn/Admetos midpoint in the current eclipse horoscope is also triggered by the original Saros point of 1331. This configuration suggests the likelihood of a major economic slowdown being precipitated by the events immediately following the solar eclipse. There's the potential for a major depression, but even if that extreme degree of economic restriction does not occur, there is a strong likelihood of work stoppages, commercial bottlenecks, and stubborn obstructions to commercial activity and market success.

Although it is imperative for us to create new visions of cooperation and shared prosperity, this eclipse activation makes it abundantly clear that we must also be particularly sanguine about the potential challenges that we will face in bringing such ideals into manifestation.

But why should we even be thinking about a solar eclipse that took place 685 years ago? As always, one of our goals with this report is to provide a broader perspective for astro-traders, one that takes into account a more comprehensive range of historical and cultural implications accompanying the current planetary dynamics that are likely to impact the markets. By understanding the astrological mega-trends which operate in the background to shift cultures and consciousness, we can be more finely attuned to the day-to-day opportunities presenting themselves in the markets in our current time.

One of the key factors in understanding the historical perspective of the current eclipse is an awareness of the role of a sequence of eclipses known as a Saros cycle.

The solar eclipse on September 1, 2016 is a part of Saros Series 135, a sequence of eclipses that began in the year 1331 with a series of partial solar eclipses that continued through 1493, followed by annular solar eclipses fom 1511 through 2305, hybrid solar eclipses in 2323 and 2341, total solar eclipses from 2359 through 2449, and a final series of partial solar eclipses starting in 2467 which will conclude with the final eclipse in Saros Series 135, on August 17, 2493. And, as the eclipse map from 1331 indicates, the initial partial eclipse in the series had limited visibility – it was situated near the North Pole.

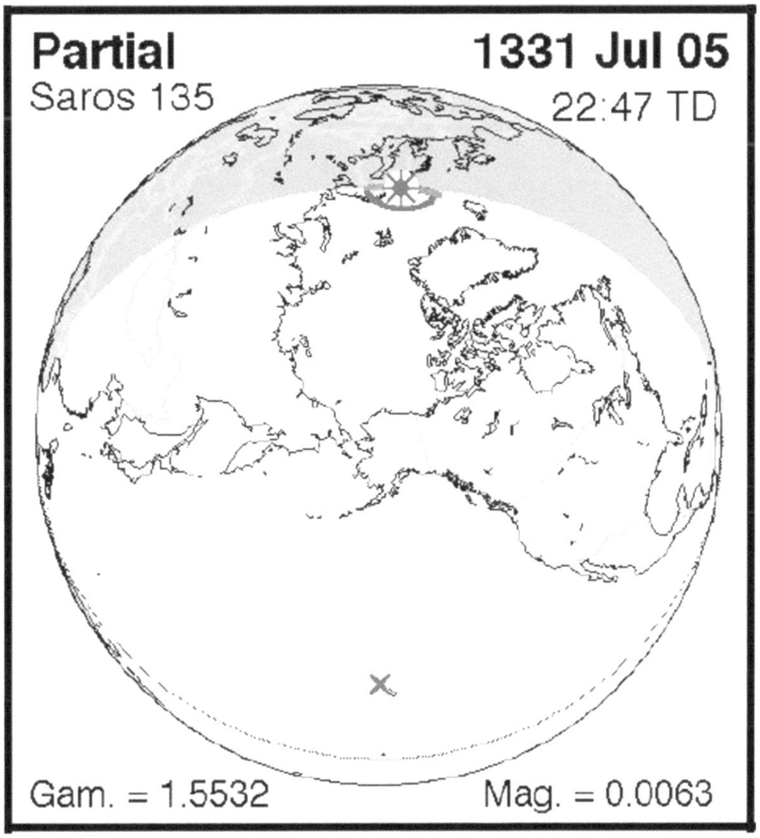

While the events associated with a previous eclipse will not, of course, be exactly duplicated in the months to come, they will at least give us a general idea of what we can expect as we confront the challenges and embrace the opportunities that lie ahead of us.

For example, in 1331 a civil war began in Japan as Emperor Godaigo tried to regain power from the Hojo regent. The death of Takatoki Hojo two years later ended the Kamakura period that began in 1185. Godaigo regained power from the shogunate, levied higher taxes, and began to rebuild the imperial palaces as he consolidated his rule.

This motif of the "beginning of the end" in long-standing power structures is characteristic in many of the periods around the solar eclipses I Saros series 135. It's definitely something that we'll need to keep in mind during the coming months. But since our primary concern is with the eclipse impact on the markets and on our financial opportunities, let's focus on the most recent examples of solar eclipses in Saros series 135.

There have been five solar eclipses in this series during the past hundred years. In each case, we'll take a look at the horoscope for the solar eclipse, along with a chart for the Dow Jones Industrial Average for the corresponding year, letting the charts speak for themselves.

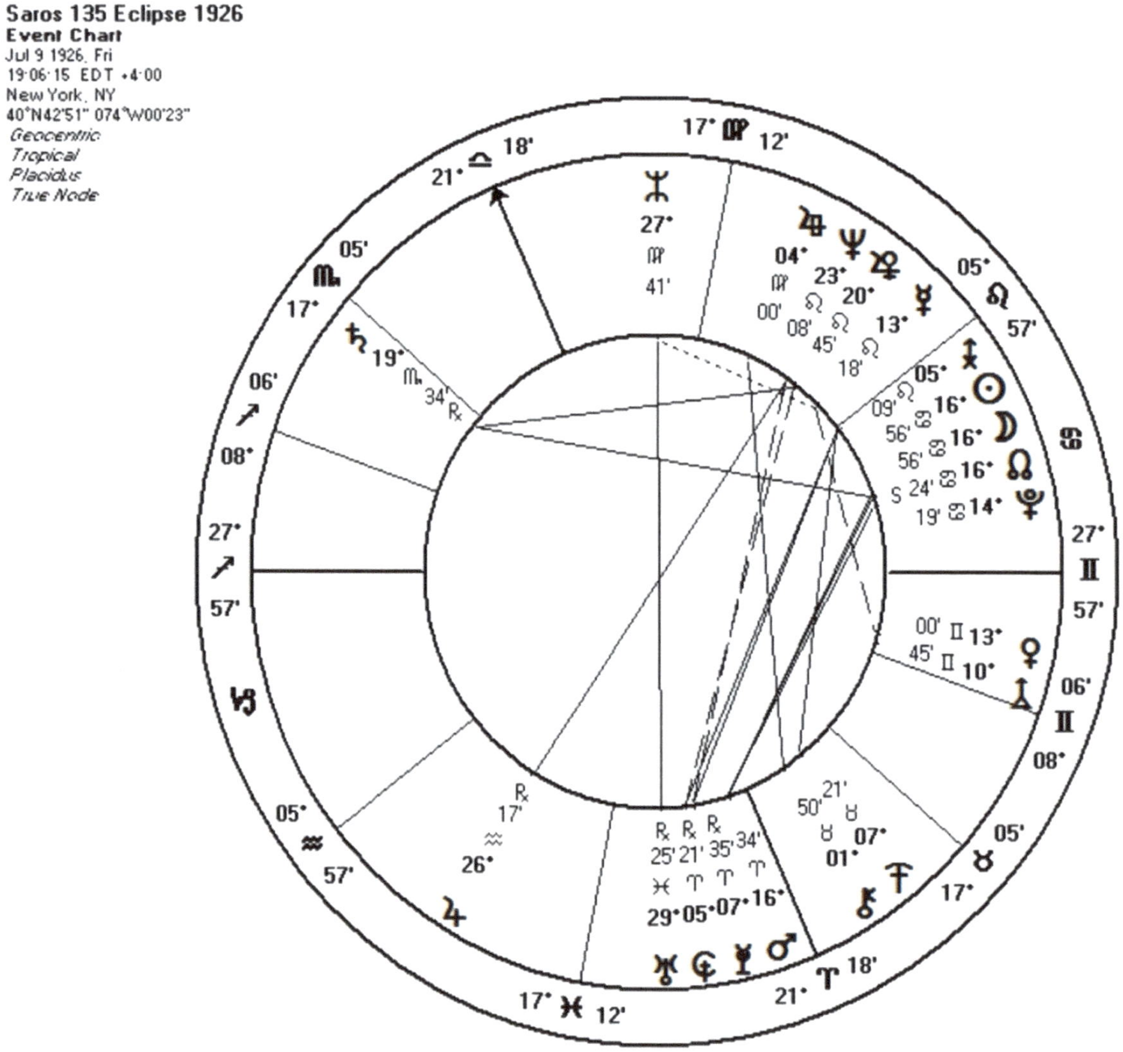

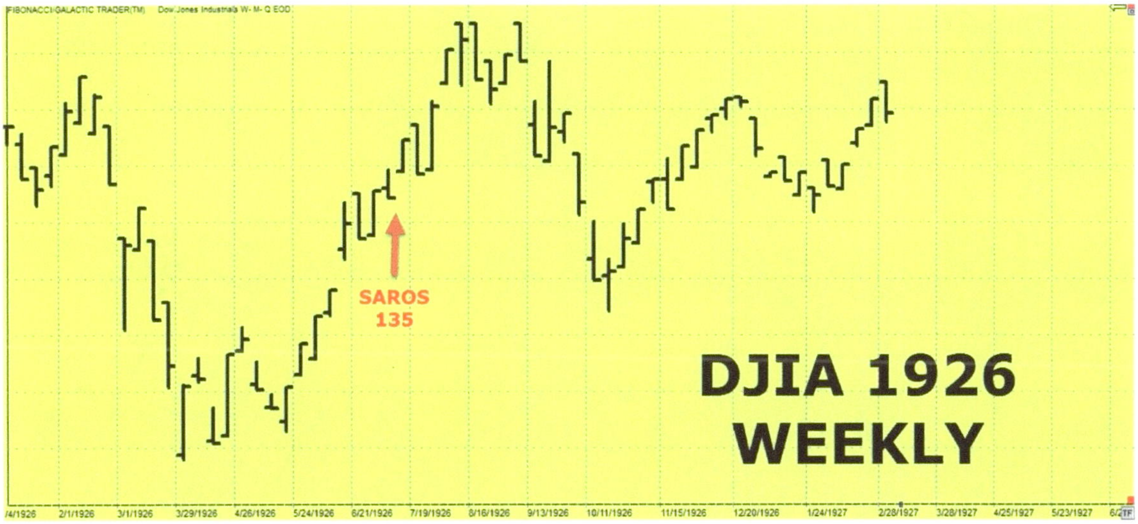

In 1926 the eclipse point was square Mars and trine Saturn, creating a dynamic pattern. Prices in the Dow rallied both before and after the eclipse, but the trading range at the time of the eclipse proved to be important at the end of the trading year.

Saros 135 Eclipse 1944
Event Chart
Jul 20 1944, Thu
01:42:24 EWT +4:00
New York, NY
40°N42'51" 074°W00'23"
Geocentric
Tropical
Placidus
True Node

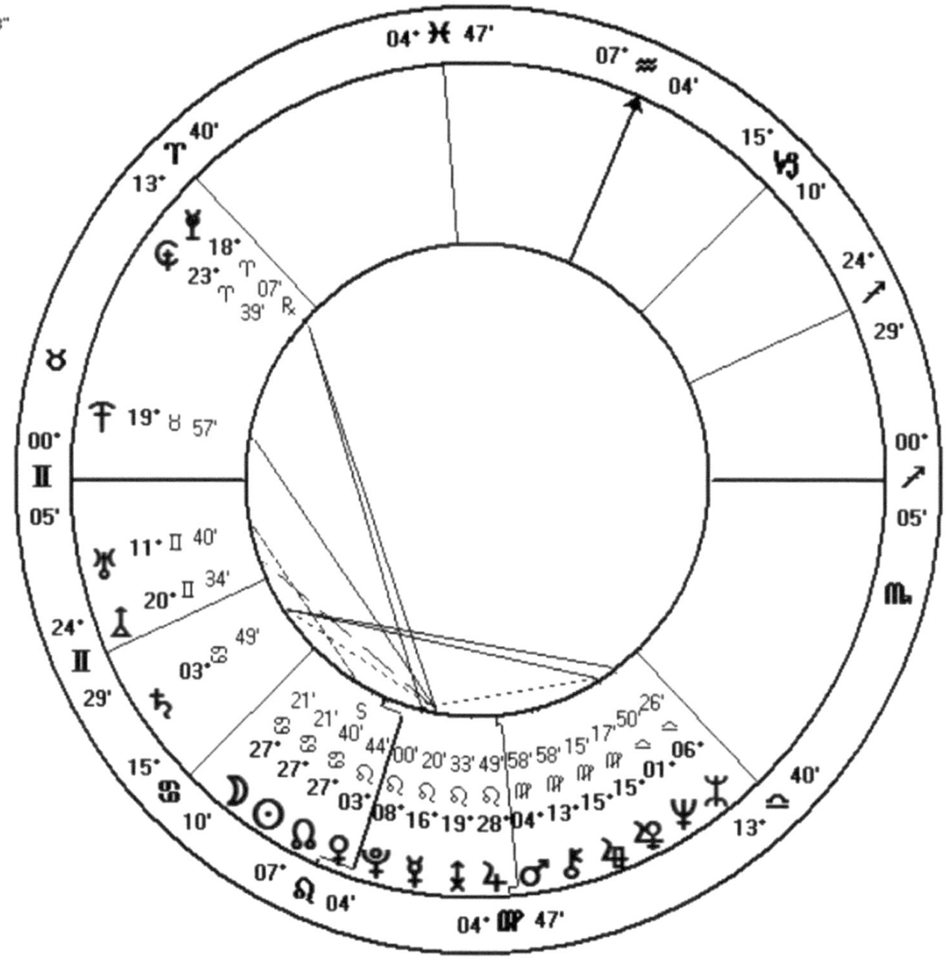

The solar eclipse in 1944 was semi-square Uranus. The trading action in the Dow saw some volatile price swings defining longer-term trading congestion.

Saros 135 Eclipse 1962
Event Chart
Jul 31 1962, Tue
08:23:39 EDT +4:00
New York, NY
40°N42'51" 074°W00'23"
Geocentric
Tropical
Placidus
True Node

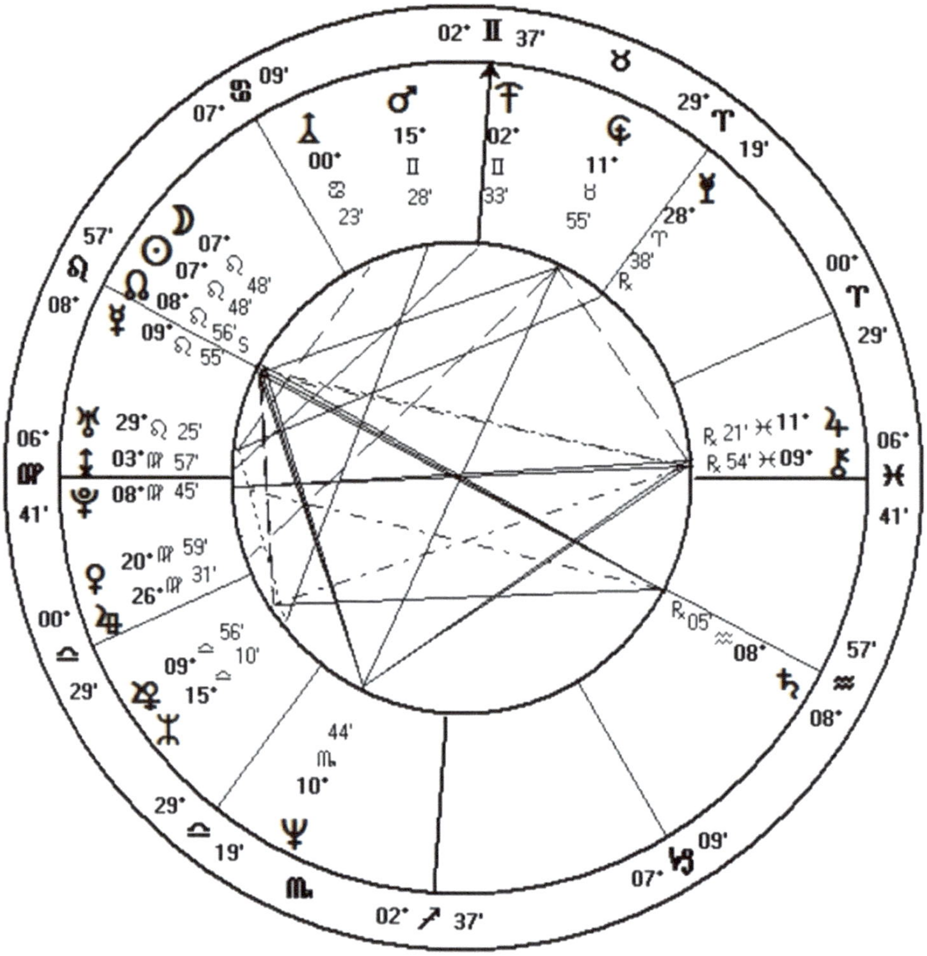

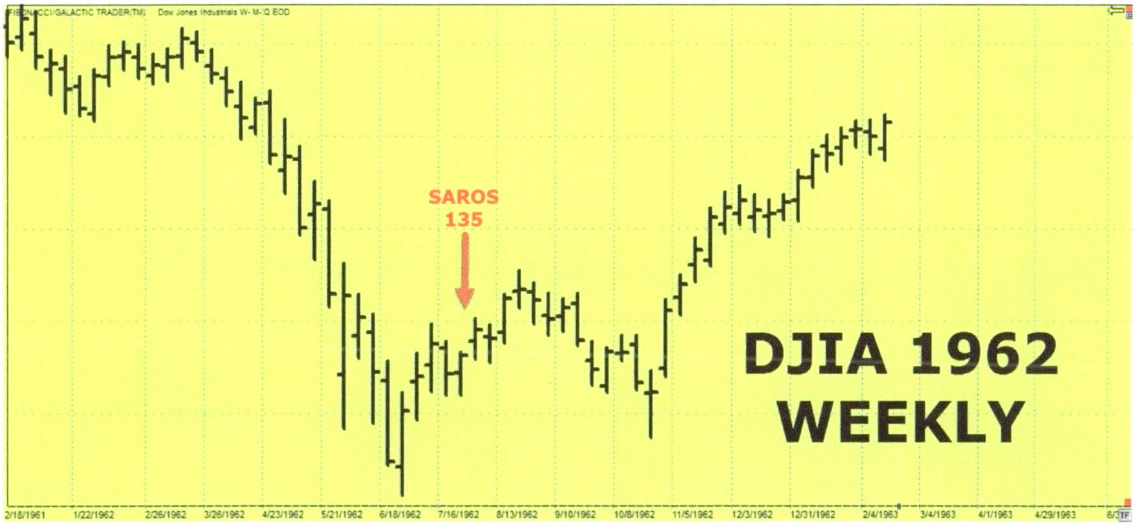

In 1962 the solar eclipse in Saros series 135 was in an opposition to Saturn, and was applying to the completion of a T-square pattern with Neptune and Hades. The Dow rallied for a few weeks following the eclipse, but then sold off sharply before rebounding into the end of the year.

Saros 135 Eclipse 1980
Event Chart
Aug 10 1980, Sun
15:09:17 EDT +4:00
New York, NY
40°N42'51" 074°W00'23"
Geocentric
Tropical
Placidus
True Node

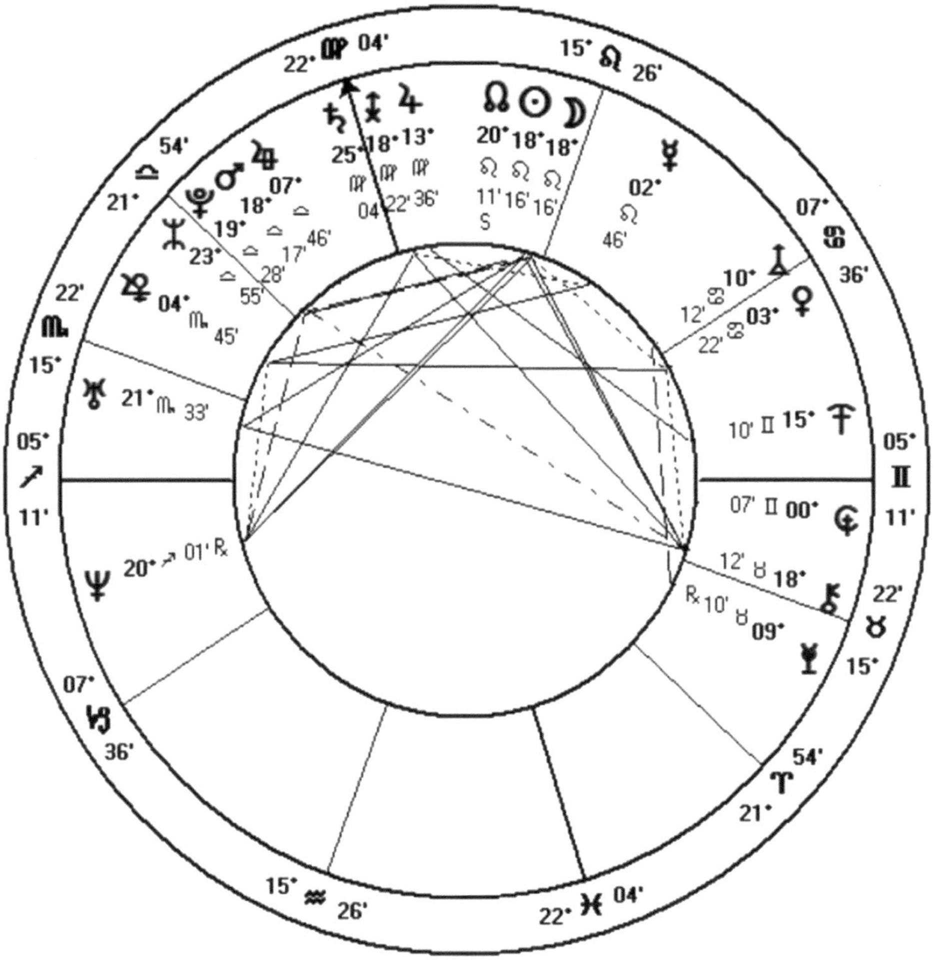

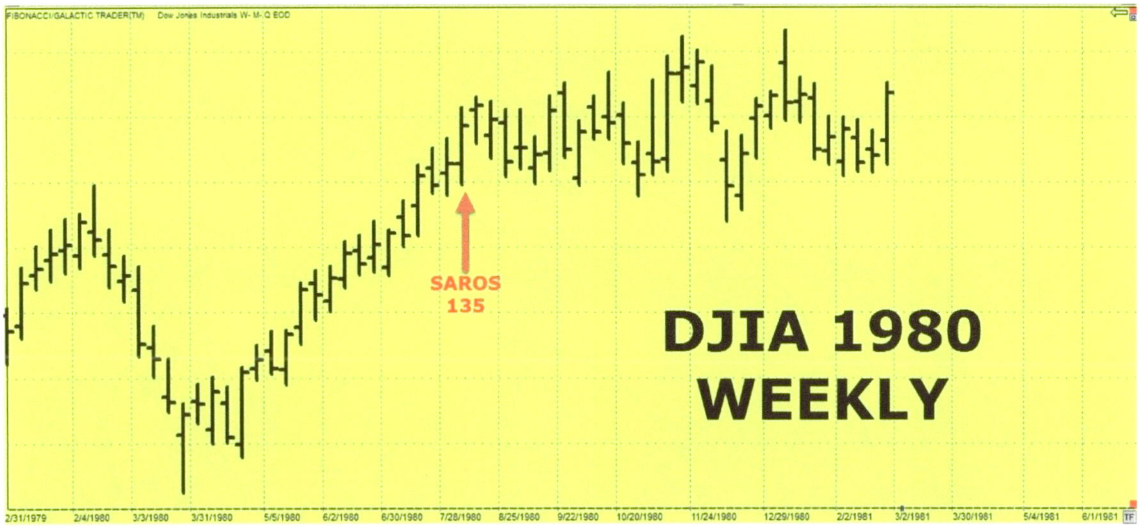

In 1980 the solar eclipse was sextile a Mars/Pluto conjunction; it also formed a T-square with Chiron and Uranus. The Dow went into an extended period of trading congestion immediately following the solar eclipse.

Saros 135 Eclipse 1998
Event Chart
Aug 21 1998, Fri
22:03:05 EDT +4:00
New York, NY
40°N42'51" 074°W00'23"
Geocentric
Tropical
Placidus
True Node

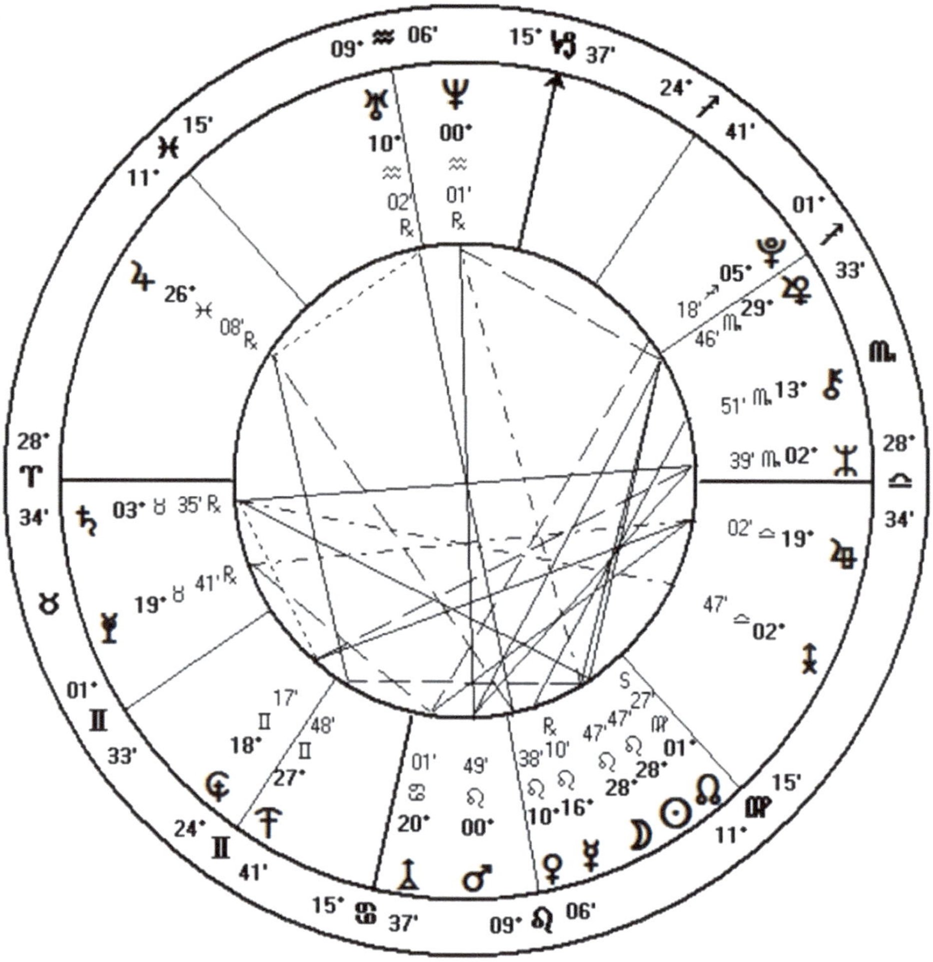

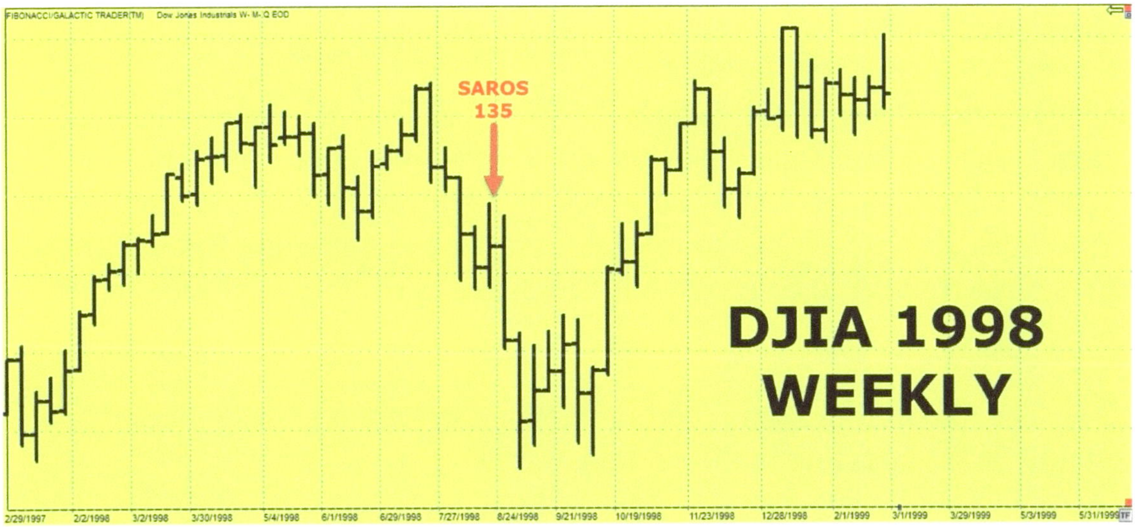

The solar eclipse in 1998 was sextile Kronos and square Cupido. The Dow had already been selling off for about a month prior to the eclipse; it accelerated its plunge afterwards, moving into a significant double bottom.

The Solar Eclipse and Key Financial Horoscopes

While an examination of the horoscope for the September 1 solar eclipse and its precursors in Saros series 135 is useful in itself, it's also revealing to look at the planets at the time of the eclipse in connection with other important horoscopes – not only those of nations, but also key financial charts.

More and more, however, the financial charts that have been the conventional domain of market astrology are becoming subordinated to national and multi-national charts, as the macroeconomic power of countries, NGO's, and corporations increasingly controls the vital issues that ultimately drive the markets. We also see the influence of unconventional organizations and economic influences that exist in the fringes – outside of the traditional social and economic structures, or in the ephemeral realm of cyberspace.

In recent years, for example, we have seen the emergence of the Islamic State, which maintains its most effective public presence on the internet, but which has issued currency in the form of gold and silver coins. It provides an interesting contrast to the crypto-currency Bitcoin, which offers an alternative to conventional currencies in the interconnected realm of cycberspace.

The possibilities and permutations here are virtually endless, and certainly mind-boggling in their implications.

Even so, by looking at a selection of key financial horoscopes, we can get a good feel for the economic and investment environment that lies ahead. In each case, we have chosen to show these charts on a 90-degree dial, with the pointer on the dial indicating the position of the September 2016 solar eclipse.

Instead of digging into an in-depth analysis of each financial entity, this approach allows us to spot the key midpoint structures that are being activated by the solar eclipse, revealing important dynamics that we might otherwise overlook.

In essence, we get a quick snapshot of the most salient energies likely to impact the economic and market activities which are most closely associated with each individual horoscope.

THE FEDERAL RESERVE

Federal Reserve Bank
Washington DC
Dec 23 1913
6:02:00 PM EST

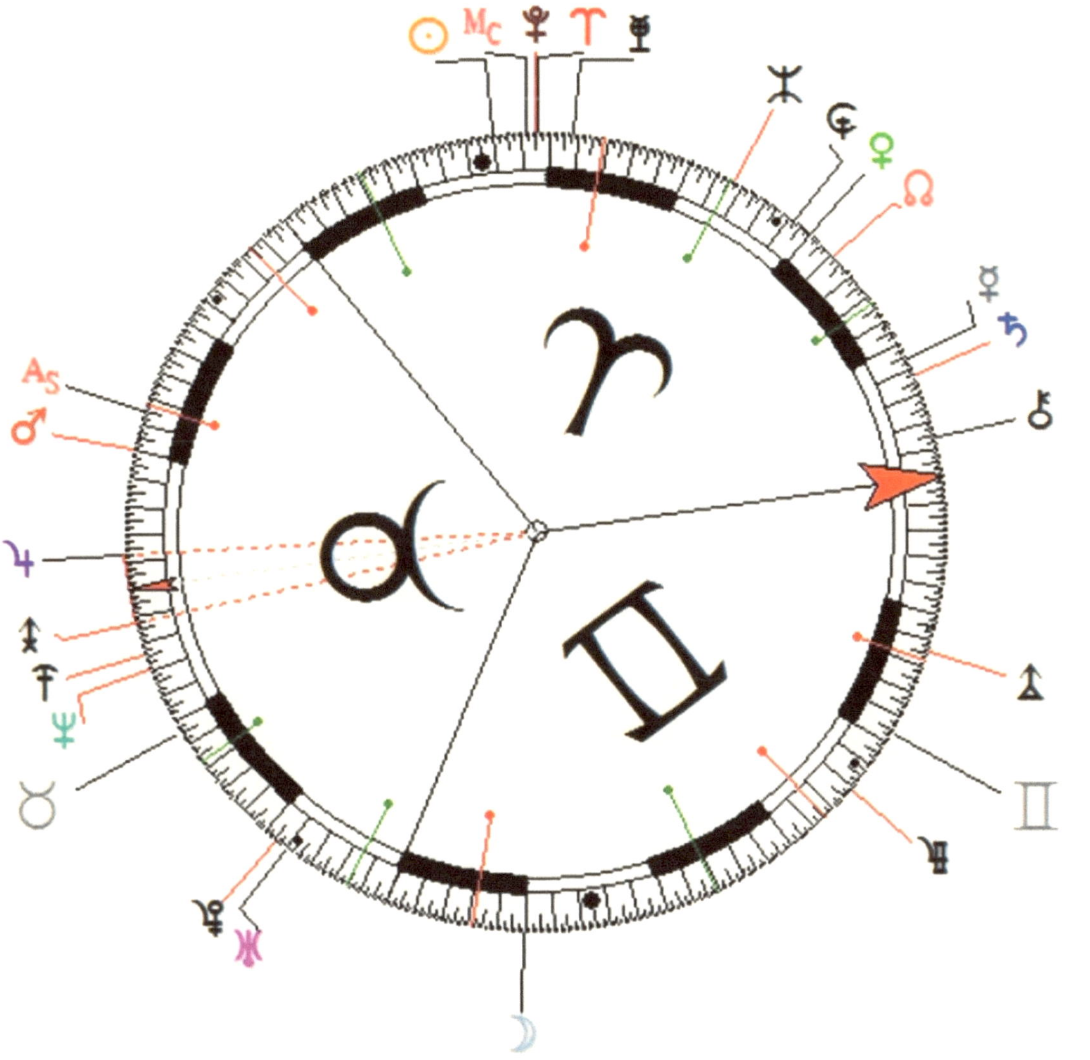

The September solar eclipse activates the Jupiter/Zeus midpoint in the horoscope for the Federal Reserve. In spite of the Fed's repeated promises of tighter interest rates to come, this configuration suggests an atmosphere of monetary easing rather than tightening during the months ahead. The Fed is likely to try to stimulate economic activity by doing nothing, but there's even a possibility here of active stimulus as well.

FEDERAL RESERVE OPERATIONS

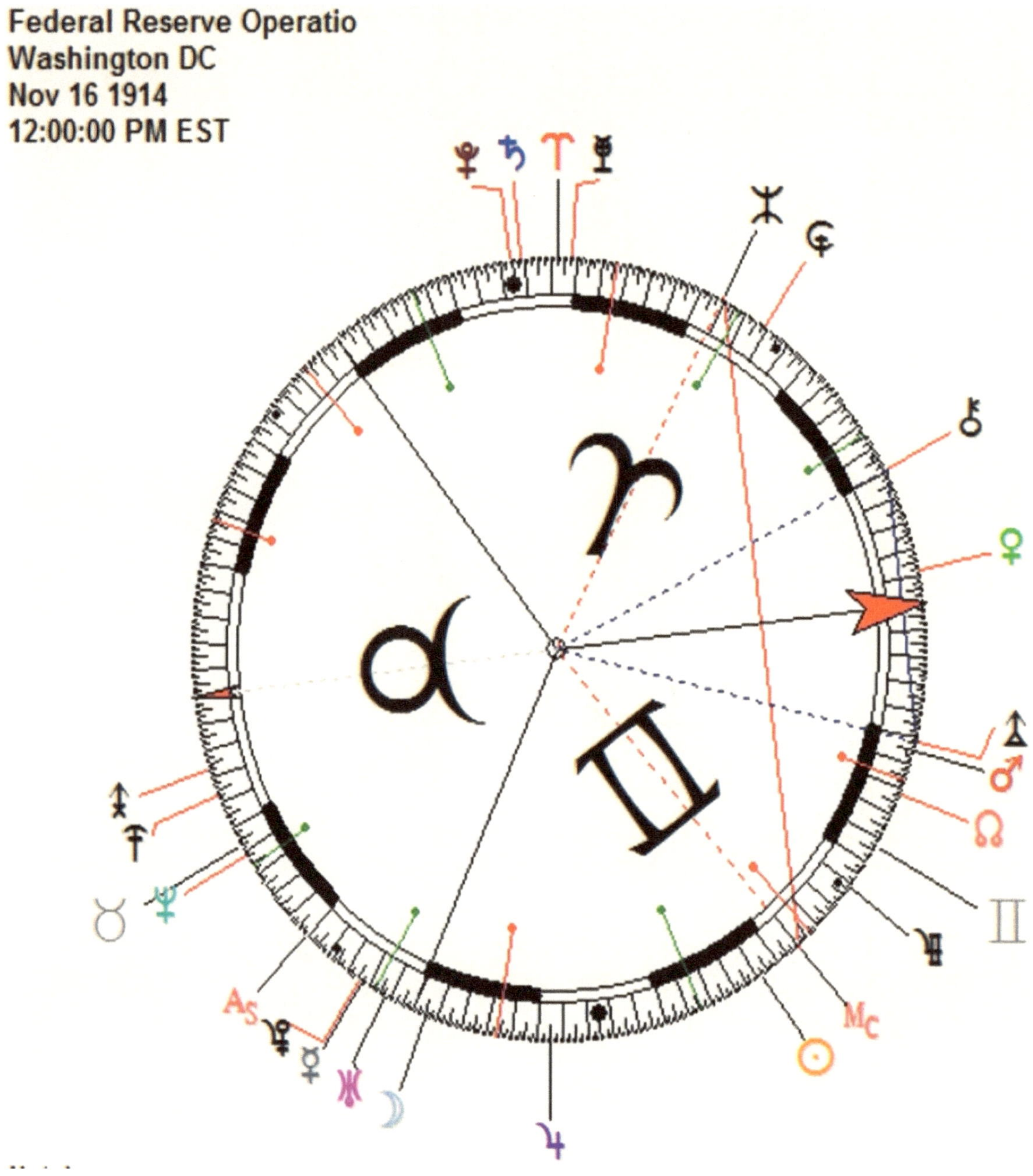

The horoscope for the commencement of operations at the Federal Reserve is often overlooked by financial astrologers, but it can often be quite useful in answering timing questions about the central bank. In this case, with the solar eclipse activating the Poseidon/Midheaven midpoint, there's an indication that the Fed may be rethinking its policies in fundamental ways. With the Chiron/Vulcanus midpoint also in play, there may be new plans or strategies from the central bank in the works, even though they may not produce the desired reactions from the markets.

NEW YORK STOCK EXCHANGE

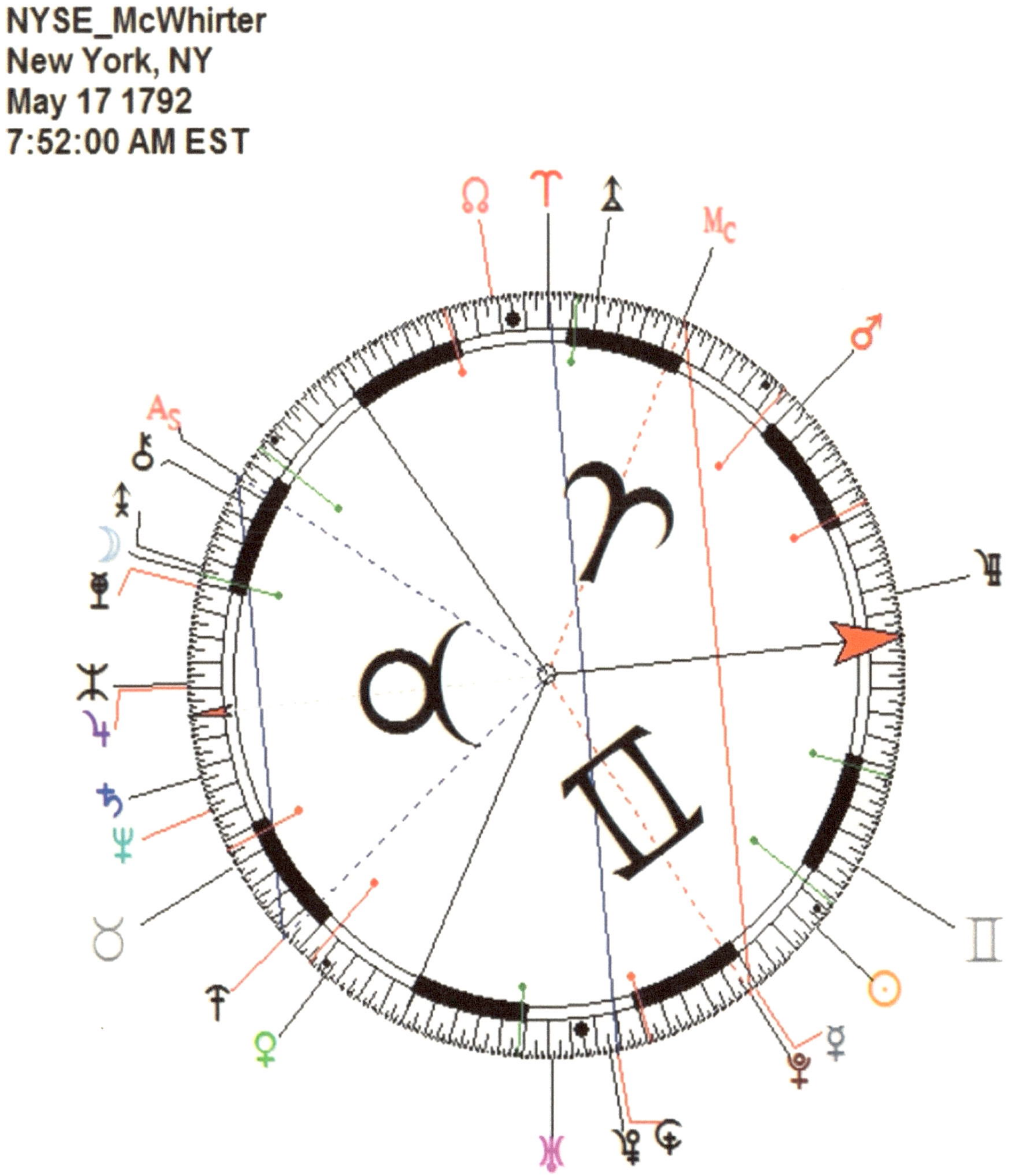

When we examine the potential eclipse effects on the horoscope of the New York Stock Exchange, we get a picture of enormous influence on the world stage during the months following the solar eclipse. The eclipse triggers the Kronos/Ascendant midpoint, putting the NYSE in a key leadership role. That power is underscored by the activation of the Pluto/Midheaven midpoint as well – but the Hades/Aries Point trigger hints that the net effect may be negative instead of positive.

NASDAQ

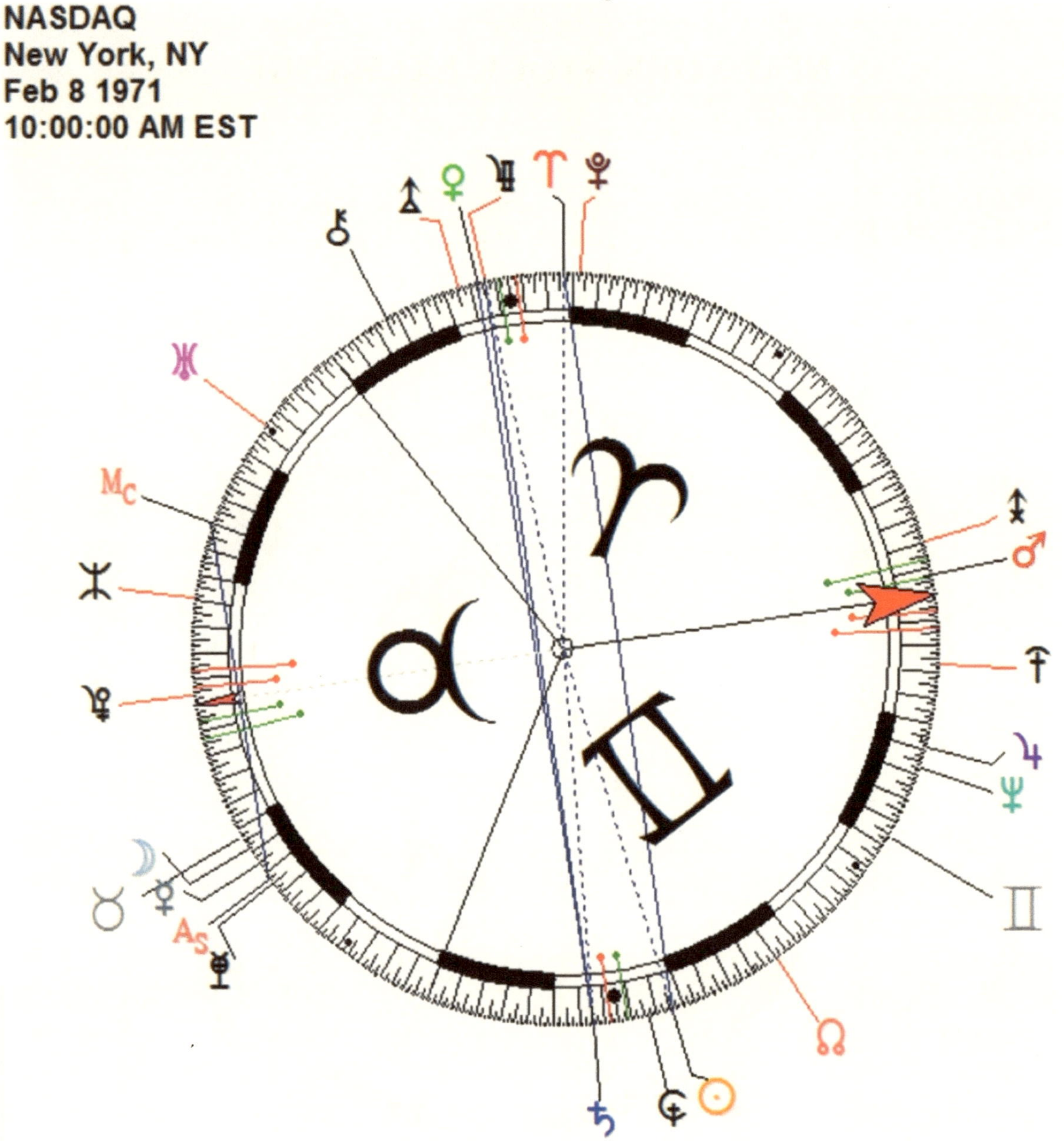

The eclipse interactions with the horoscope for the NASDAQ are quite dramatic, with a lot of planetary action going on. The September eclipse triggers the NASDAQ Ascendant/Midheaven midpoint, so it resonates very strongly with the essential nature of this trading venue. Cupido is directly activated here as well, so we get a strong social and cultural implication – there may be efforts underway to attract new retail investors, even if the market dynamics look risky to the man in the street. That risk is emphasized by the activations of the Venus/Saturn midpoint and the Saturn/Apollon midpoint – both of these configurations suggest sharp limits to expansive efforts, whether it's in trading volume or in the general price trends in the market. But the Sun/Aries Midpoint is also getting some powerful emphasis here, so the NASDAQ is likely to remain attractive in spite of market fluctuations, with its public reputation untarnished regardless of the potential for distressing news.

LONDON STOCK EXCHANGE

London Stock Exchange
London, England
May 18 1901
12:00:00 PM GMT

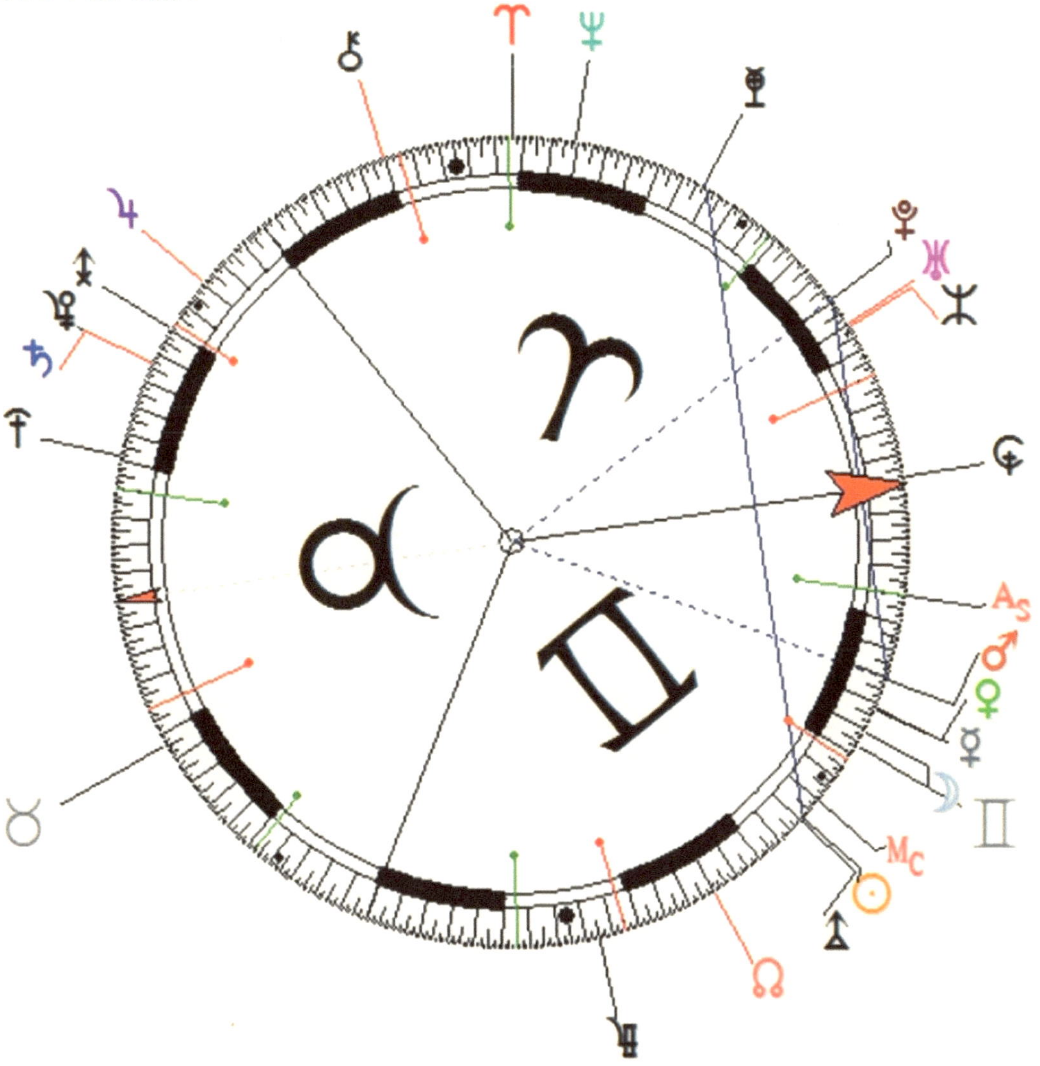

The situation during the coming months looks fairly serious for the London Stock Exchange. With both the Venus/Pluto and Mars/Pluto midpoints activated by the September eclipse, there should be plenty of trading action ahead, with large blocks of stocks trading hands as bigger and bigger players jump on board. But the Sun/Admetos and Vulcanus/Admetos midpoints are both also triggers by the solar eclipse. This suggest some rather severe set-backs in this arena, so it will be important to keep a close eye on the trading action here.

BOLSA DE VALORES DE SAO PAULO

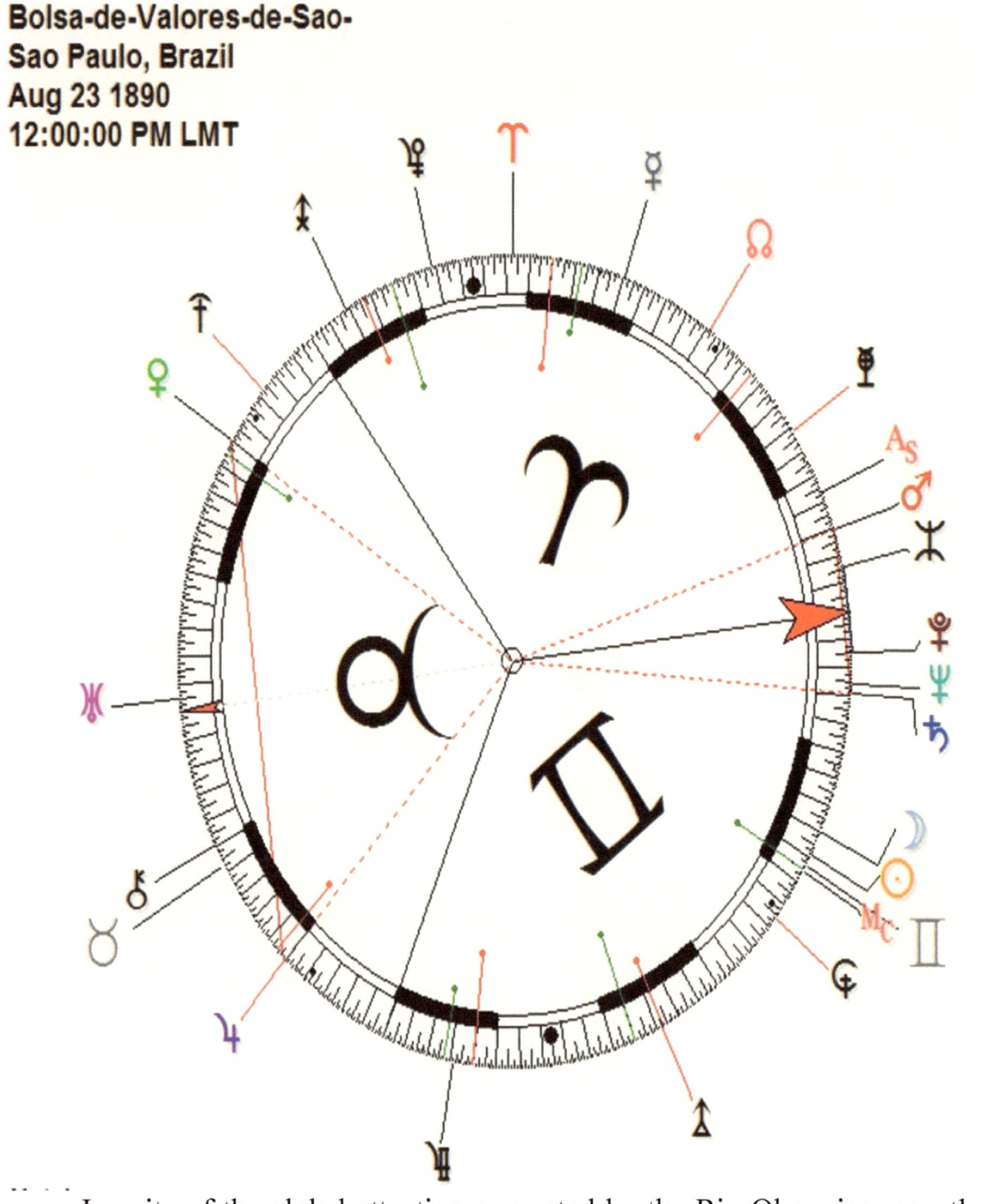

In spite of the global attention generated by the Rio Olympics recently, there have been plenty of tough times in Brazil, and many pundits are questioning the country's longer-term economic viability. This solar eclipse suggests that the future may be unexpectedly bright, however. With the September solar eclipse triggering the Venus/Jupiter midpoint in the BOLSA horoscope, the outlook could be positive, but the Mars/Saturn activation may prove restrictive nevertheless.

BOMBAY STOCK EXCHANGE

Bombay Stock Exchange
Bombay, India
Jul 9 1875
12:44:00 PM LMT

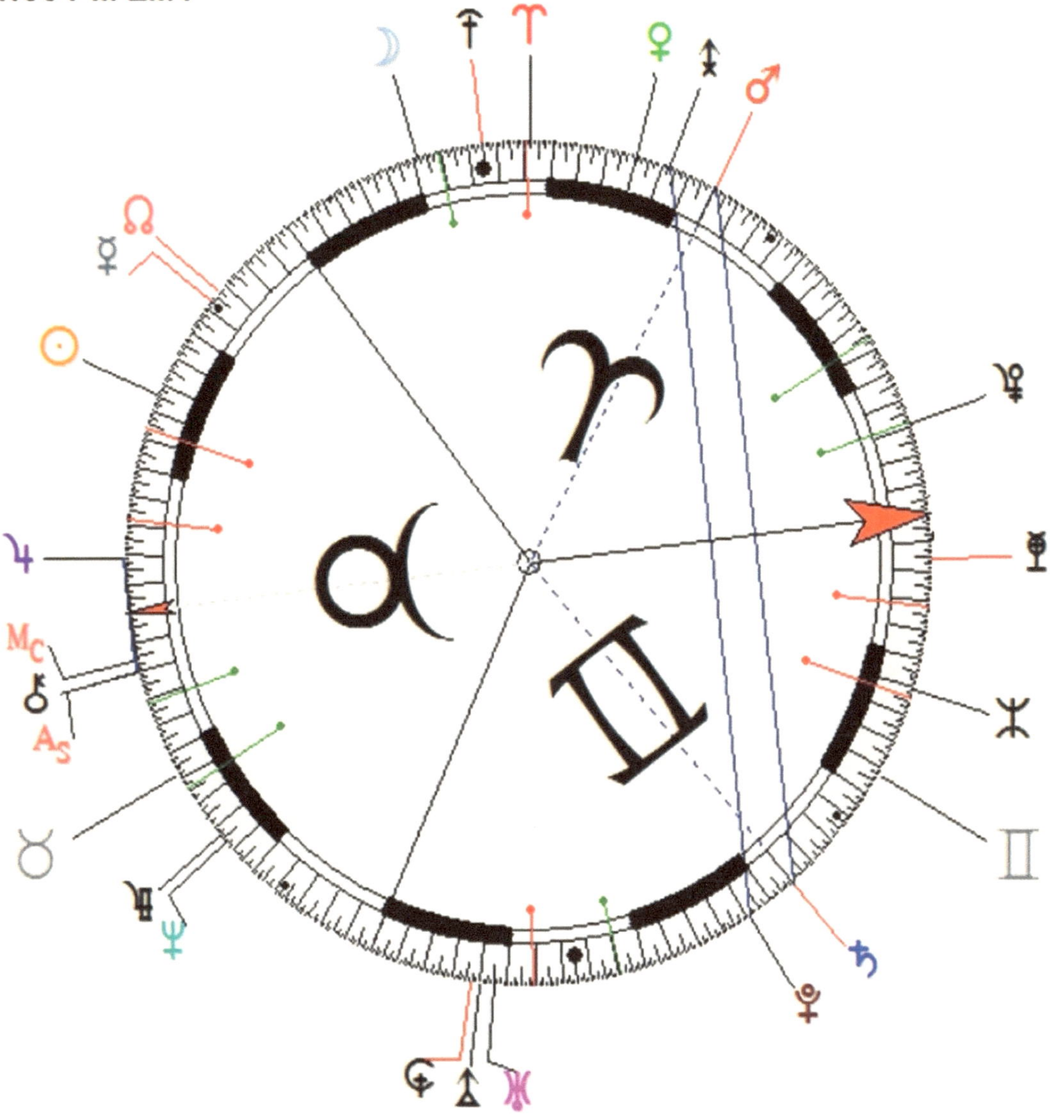

There could be some tough times ahead for the Indian markets, with the September eclipse activating the Jupiter/Chiron midpoint to create a generally stressful atmosphere. The triggering of the Pluto/Zeus midpoint indicates a potential for volatile trading and lots of capital changing hands during the coming months, but the Mars/Saturn activation is likely to put the brakes on if rallies get underway. This could be a very chaotic situation, so active traders here will need to exercise considerable caution.

THE BILDERBERG GROUP

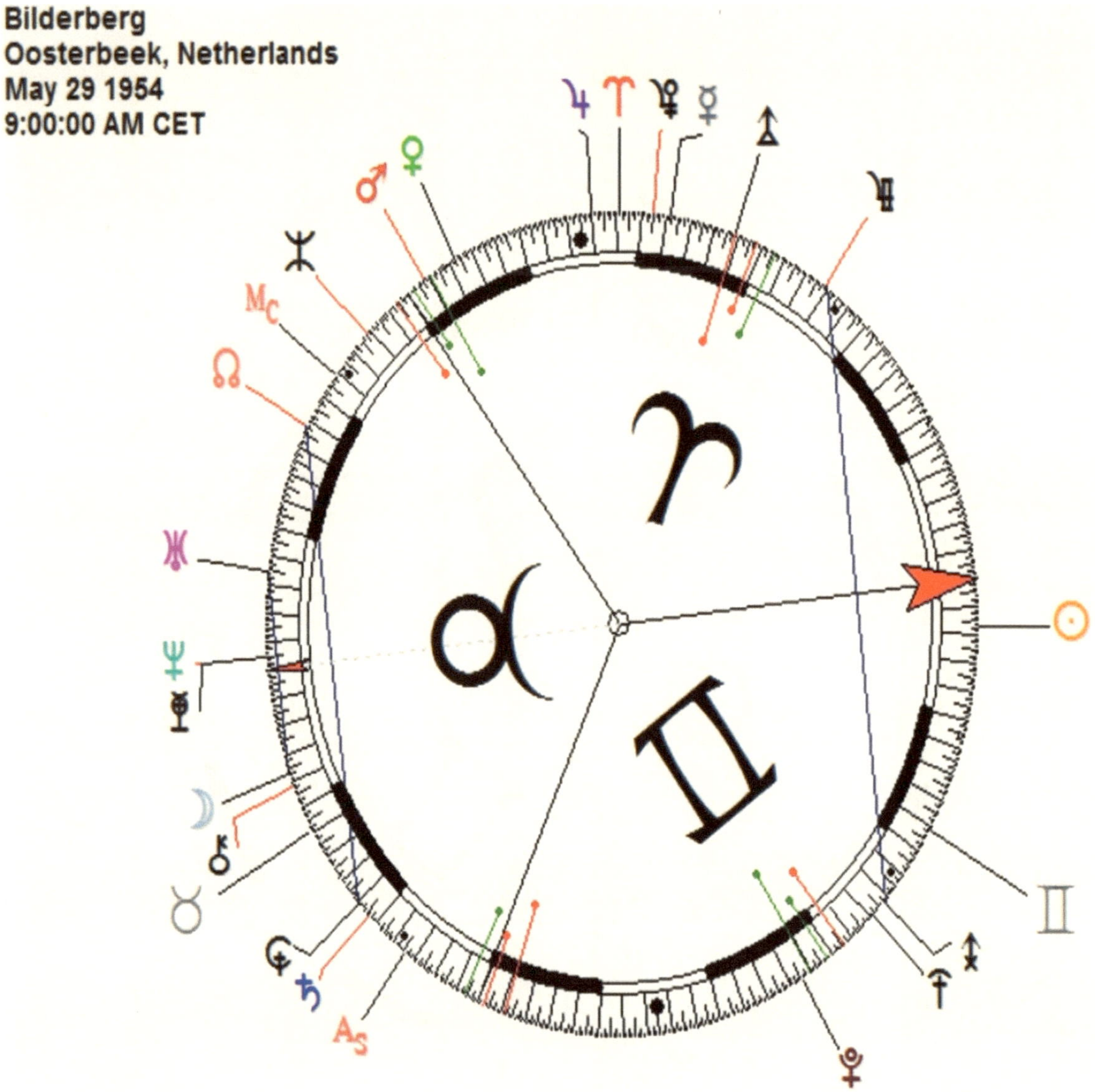

Whether or not you're a fan of conspiracy theories claiming that the Bilderberg Group is scheming behind the scenes to control the fate of the world, it's clear that this secretive organization has been faced with increasing challenges during recent years, both in terms of its public image and in terms of its control and influence as well. The September eclipse does little to help this group's reputation. The activation of the Hades/True Lunar Node midpoint indicates that public connections are decidedly negative in the months ahead, and with the Moon/Uranus midpoint in play as well, relationships with the world at large are volatile to say the least. But the Zeus/Apollon midpoint is also triggered here, so we can expect this group's power and influence to keep on growing – even if the mechanics are all hidden behind the scenes.

TREASURY BONDS

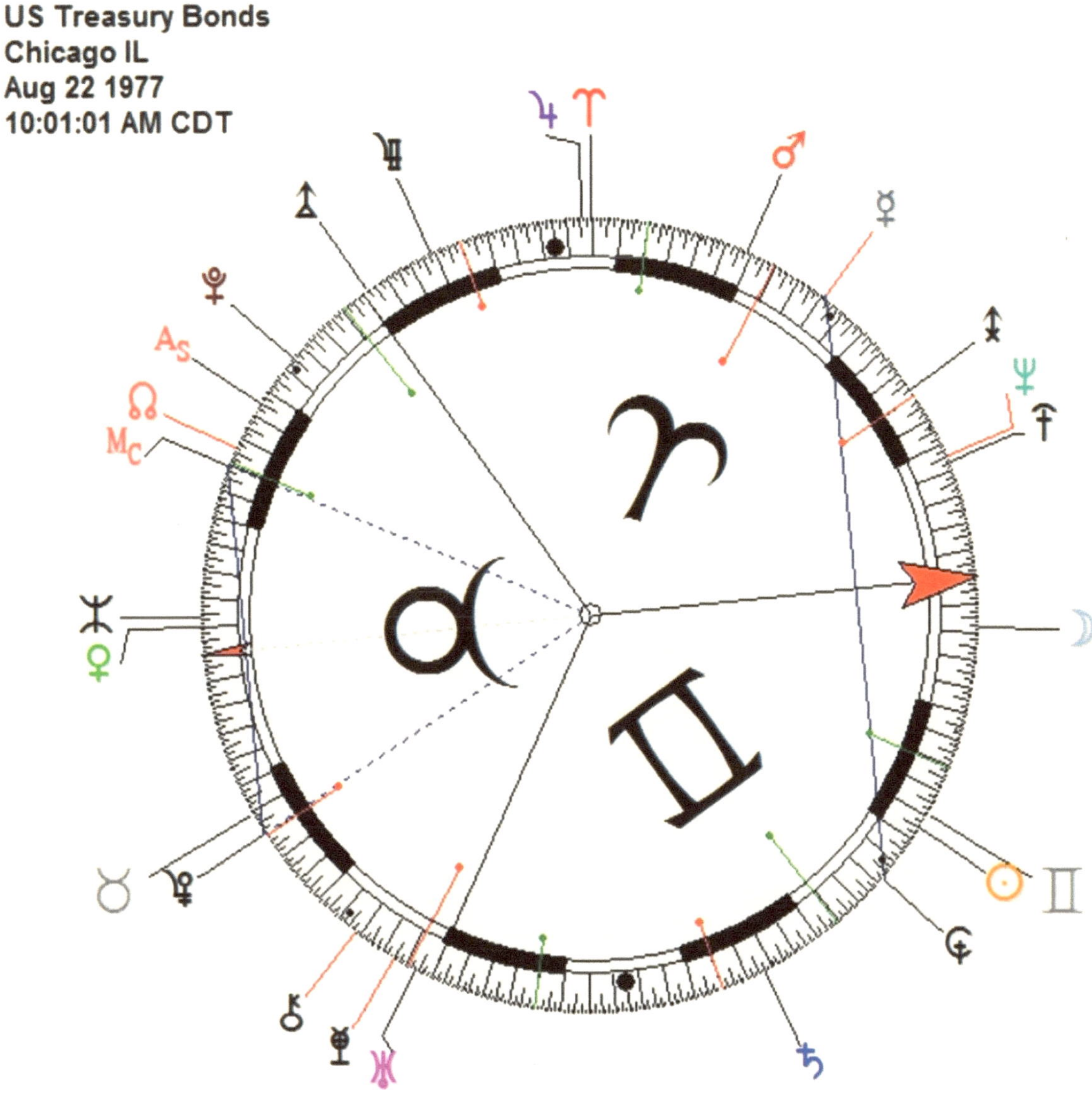

The solar eclipse doesn't offer much in the way of positive prospects for the T-Bond market. Even though the activation of the Cupido/Midheaven midpoint in the T-Bond horoscope suggests growing interest in bond trading, we can't overlook the influence of the Mercury/Hades activation as well. This message is pretty clear – bad news for bond speculators, and a big potential for disappointment.

THE U.S. DOLLAR

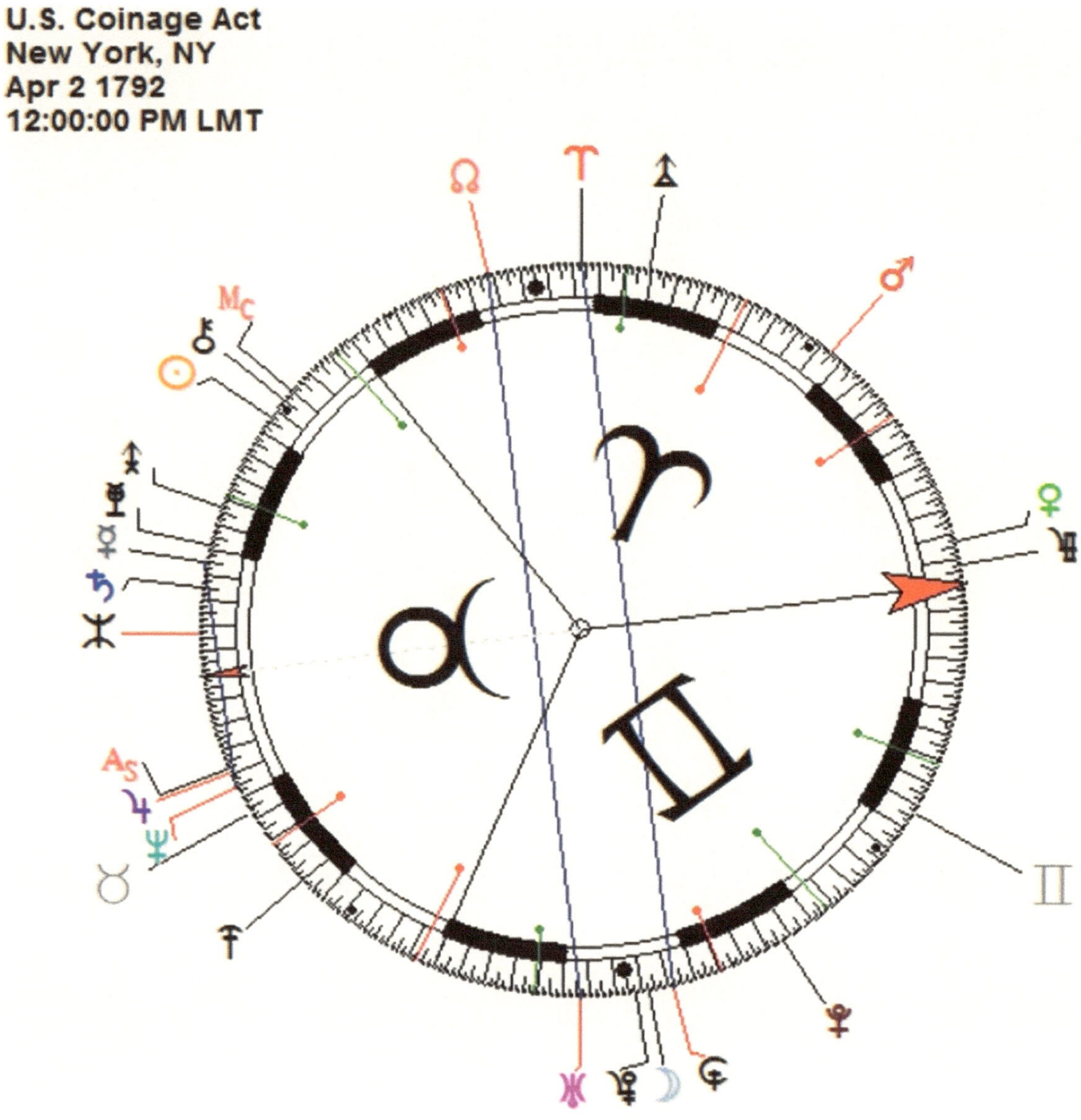

The months following the September eclipse have the potential for bringing some very confusing times for the U.S. Dollar. The Mercury/Jupiter midpoint in the dollar chart is triggered by the eclipse, so we can expect plenty of positive news for those who are looking for a stronger greenback. But the problem here is one of trust. How will positive news play out in the rest of the world, and will it even be believed at all? The activation of the Uranus/True Lunar Node midpoint suggests some very unstable connections with other players in the global currency arena, and the Hades/Aries Point trigger indicates a willingness to expect the worst. This could create a lot of turmoil, which could lead to some very interesting times for currency traders.

THE JAPANESE YEN

Japanese Yen
Tokyo, Japan
May 10 1871
12:00:00 PM LMT

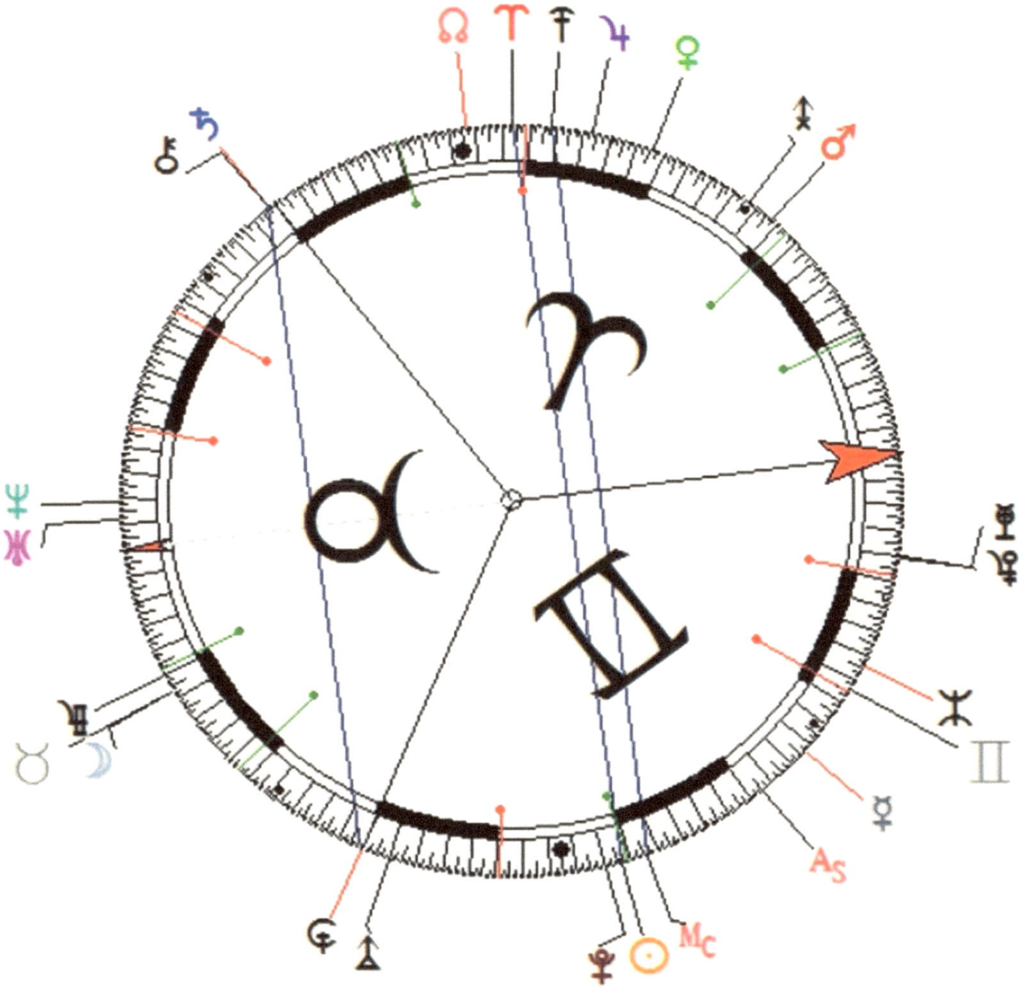

The yen is likely to push hard for greater dominance in the coming months, thanks to the activations of the Kronos/Midheaven and Sun/Aries Point midpoints in its horoscope. But those effort may prove to be an uphill struggle. The Saturn/Hades and Chiron/Hades midpoints are also in play here, so there a high potential for frustration in the months following the September solar eclipse.

BITCOIN

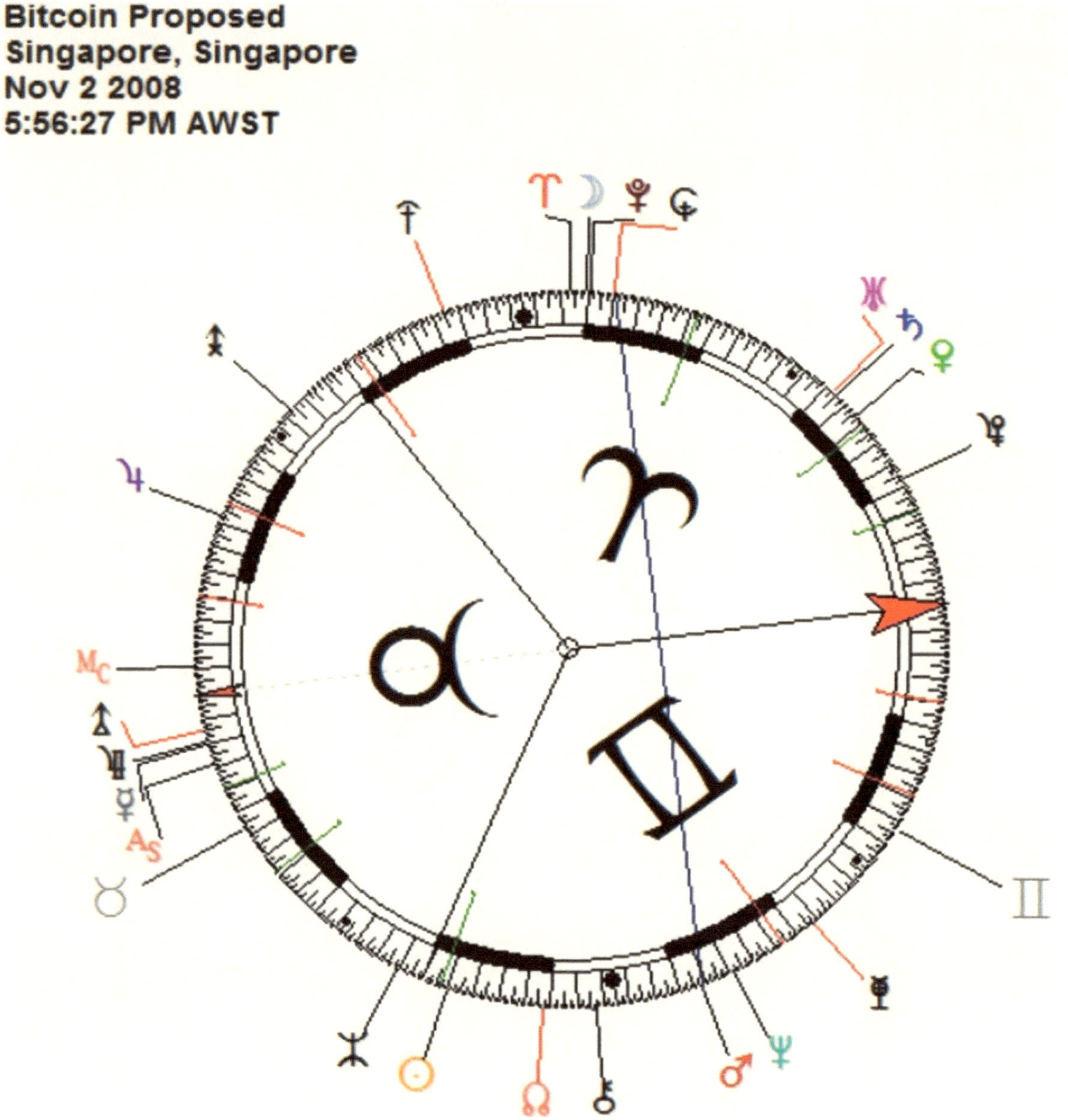

The BitCoin crypto-currency has been the subject of much debate since its inception, with true believers hanging on persistently in the face of relentless challenges. Those challenges are likely to continue after the September solar eclipse, since the eclipse triggers the Mars/Hades midpoint in the BitCoin horoscope. It could prove to be a very difficult situation, but it may lead to some buying opportunities for short-term players. The bottom line here is that BitCoin remains a market for speculators rather than for long-term investors.

RENMINBI

Chinese Renminbi
Shijiazhuang, China
Dec 1 1948
12:00:00 PM AWST

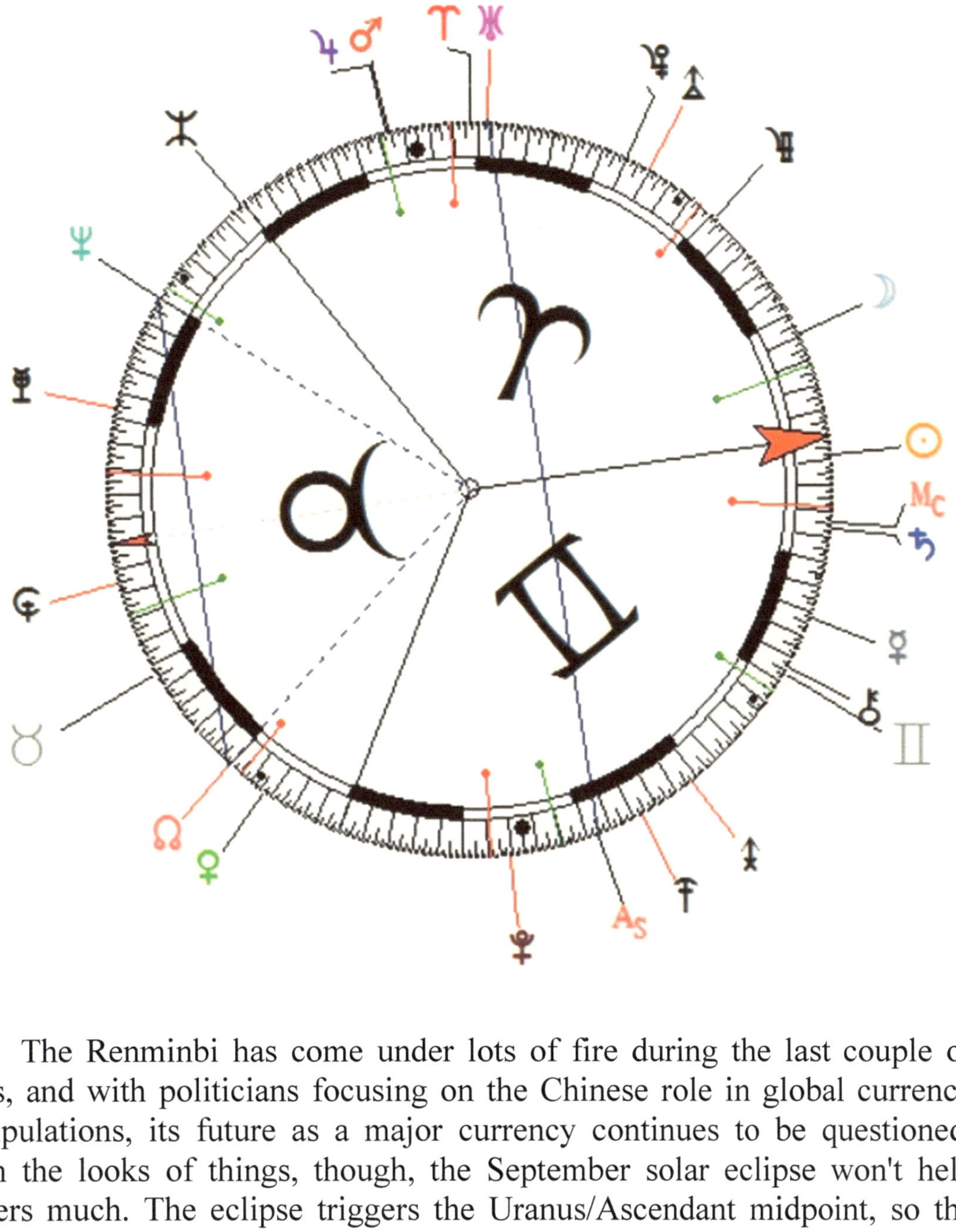

The Renminbi has come under lots of fire during the last couple of years, and with politicians focusing on the Chinese role in global currency manipulations, its future as a major currency continues to be questioned. From the looks of things, though, the September solar eclipse won't help matters much. The eclipse triggers the Uranus/Ascendant midpoint, so the public image of the currency is likely to be quite uncertain, especially if there are unanticipated moves from the Chinese central bank. And with the Neptune/True Lunar Node midpoint also in play, there's a distinct possibility of outright deception in the months ahead.

EURO

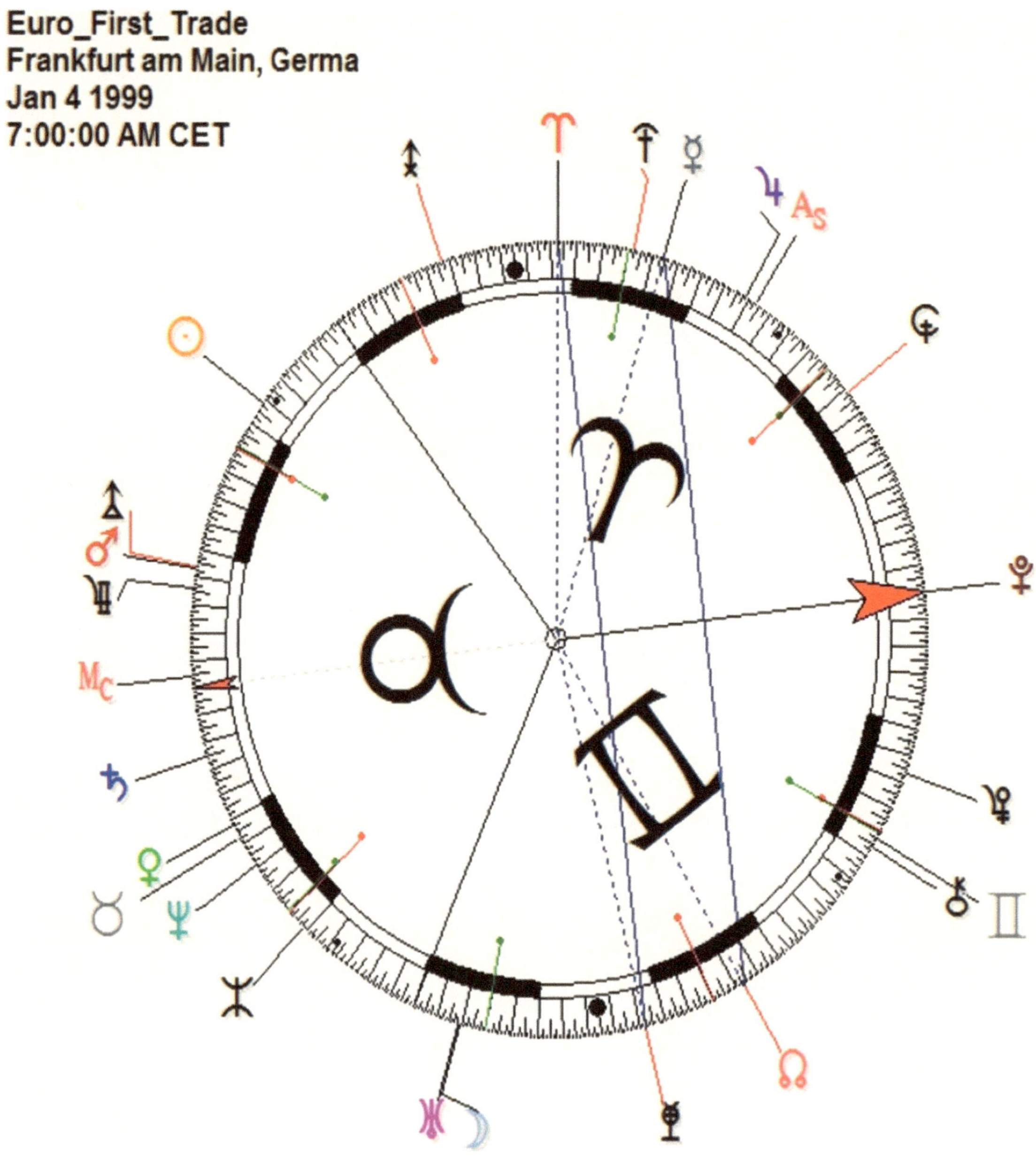

With the Brexit, questions about NATO, and the raging refugee crisis, the future of the European Union is anything but certain. Even so, the September solar eclipse may prove to be a positive influence for the euro. The eclipse does activate the Admetos/Aries Point midpoint, so there are definitely some major challenges on a global scale. But the eclipse also triggers Pluto, adding a lot of potential power, and the triggering of the Mercury/True Lunar Node midpoint can boost the currency's viability, too.

POUND STERLING

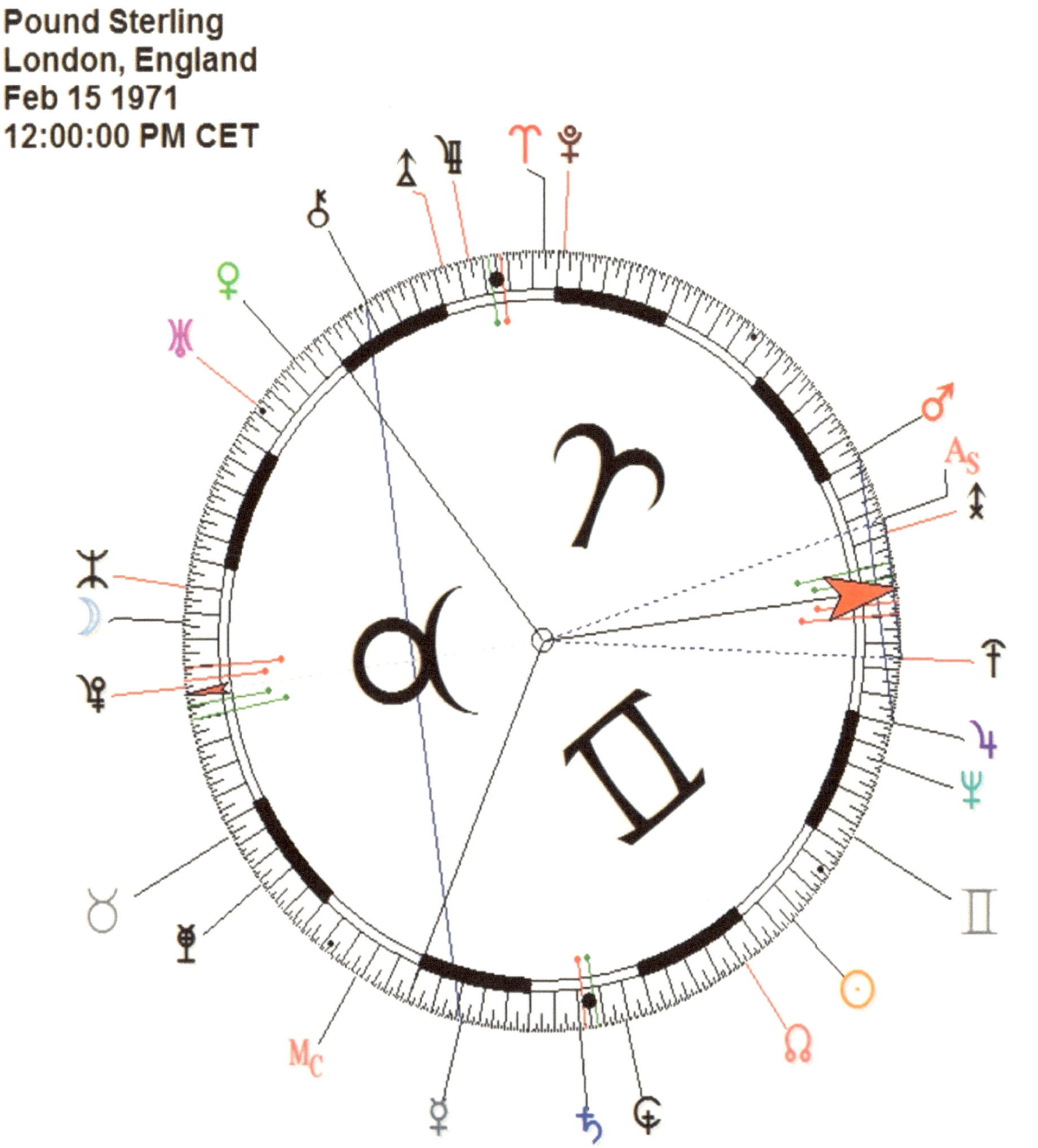

The British pound sterling is facing a lot of uncertainty following the September solar eclipse. On the one hand, the eclipse activation of the Mars/Jupiter midpoint suggests a very successful time ahead, with the currency gaining strength. But the Mercury/Chiron midpoint is also in play here, so there can be some very inconvenient problems that arise. They may create some potentially profitable trading opportunities, as long as traders can sort out the seeming inconsistencies.

ISIS GOLD DINAR

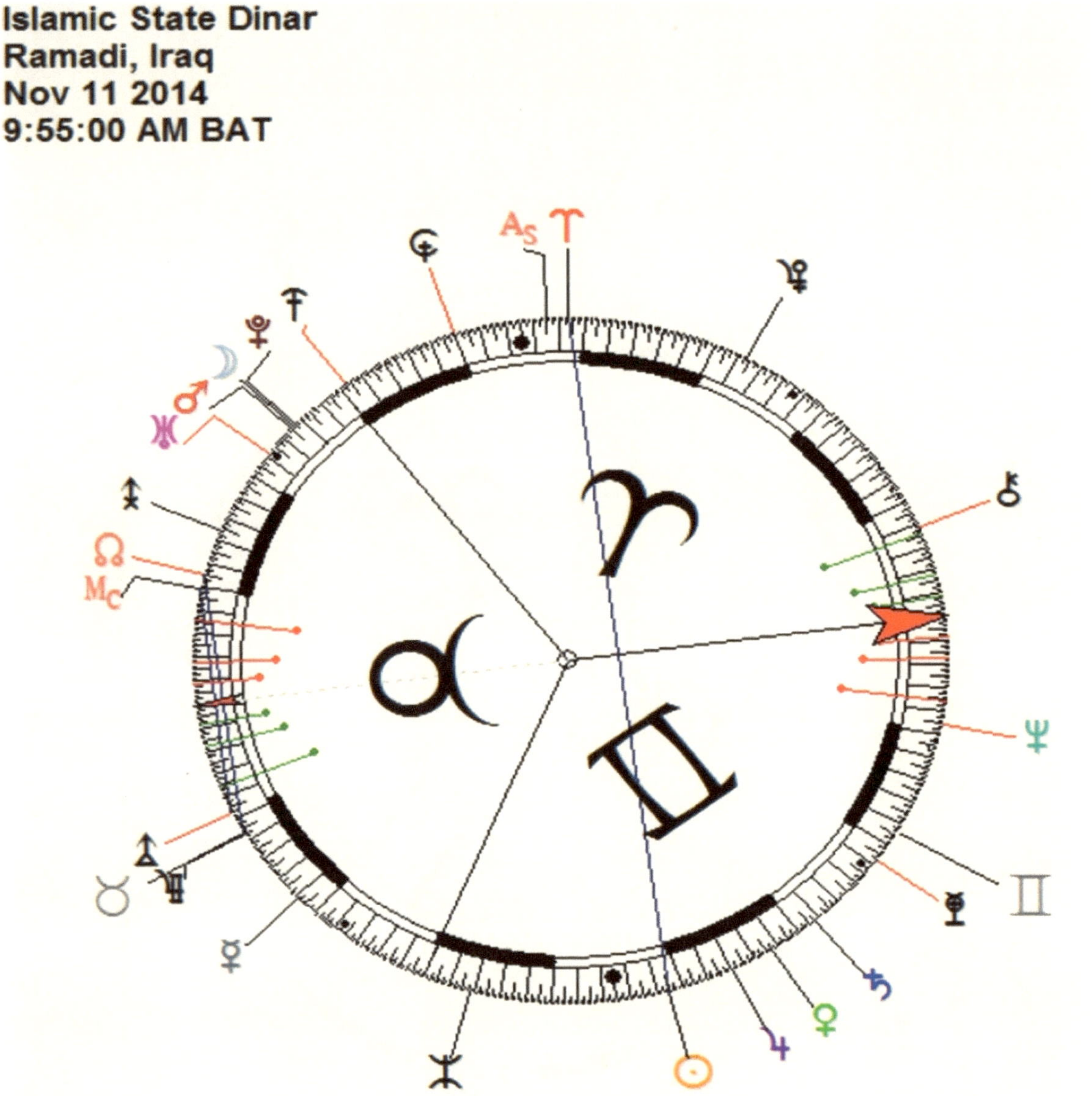

ISIS is still frequently in the news with heinous terrorist attacks and increasing efforts at online recruiting, and the efforts of the international community at combating its influence seem convoluted at best. Because it connects with the group's own perception of its core values, our chart for the Islamic State currency has proven to be a useful tool in assessing the situation, which makes the impact of the September solar eclipse particularly interesting. The Vulcanus/Midheaven midpoint is triggered here, which hints that the group may be ready for a major reorganization that would give it a fresh start. With the Sun/Aries Point midpoint activated as well, ISIS definitely continues to play a pivotal role on the global stage. And with the solar eclipse triggering the Apollon/True Lunar Node midpoint, its efforts at expansion and recruiting are likely to be successful, and least for the time being. It's not a pretty picture; it underscores the need for creative solutions.

CBOT

Chicago Board Of Trade
Chicago IL
Feb 18 1859
11:10:00 AM LMT

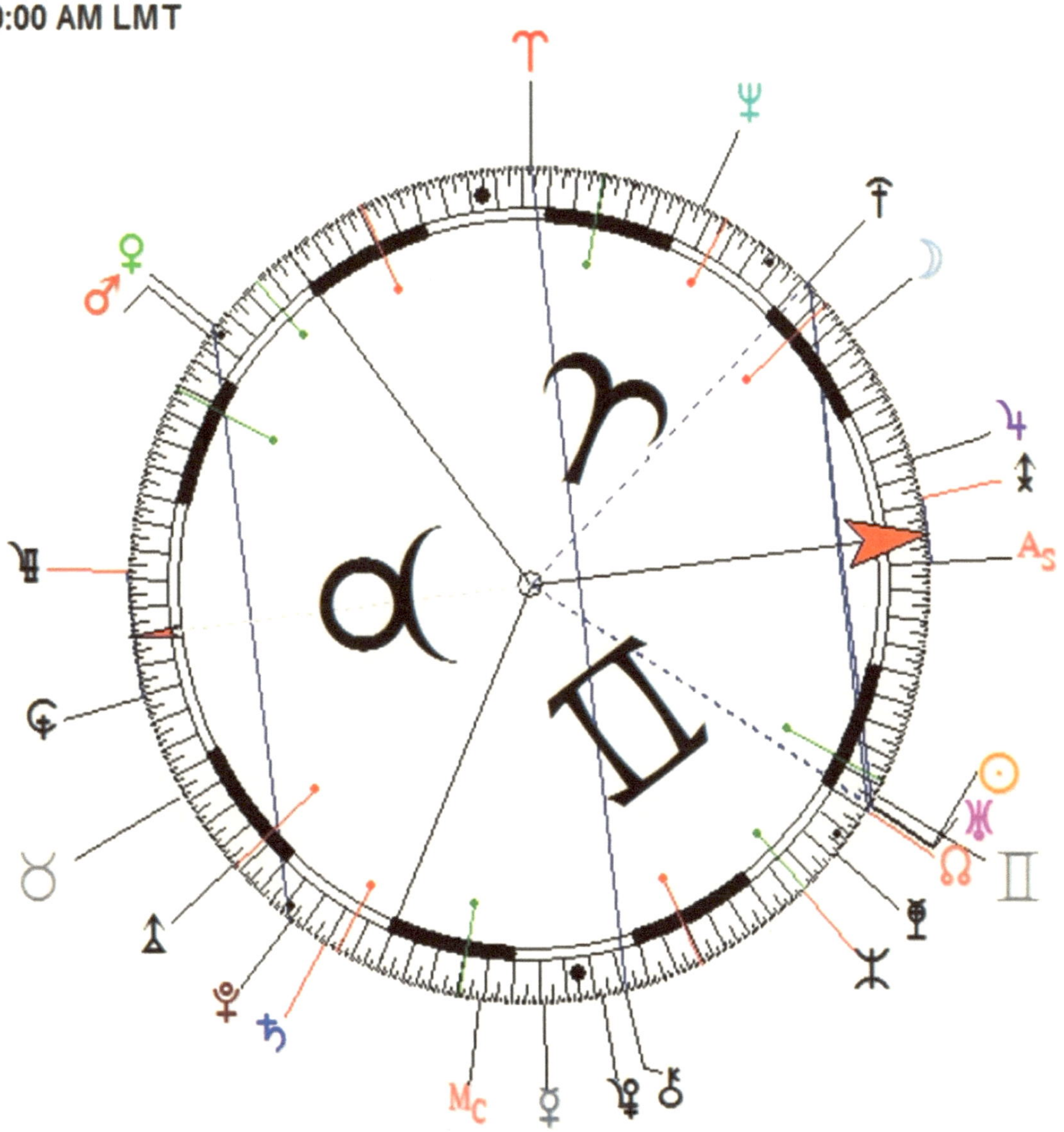

The impact of the September solar eclipse on the Chicago Board of Trade suggests that we could see things really booming in the commodities markets in the months following the eclipse. The Sun/Kronos and Uranus/Kronos midpoints are both activated by the eclipse, so we could see some surprising volatility and some major trading opportunities. The Chrion/Aries Point activation suggests the potential for challenges and confusion along the way, but the fact that the Venus/Pluto midpoint is also in play gives us a solid indication of the big potential for profits here.

NYMEX LIGHT CRUDE OIL

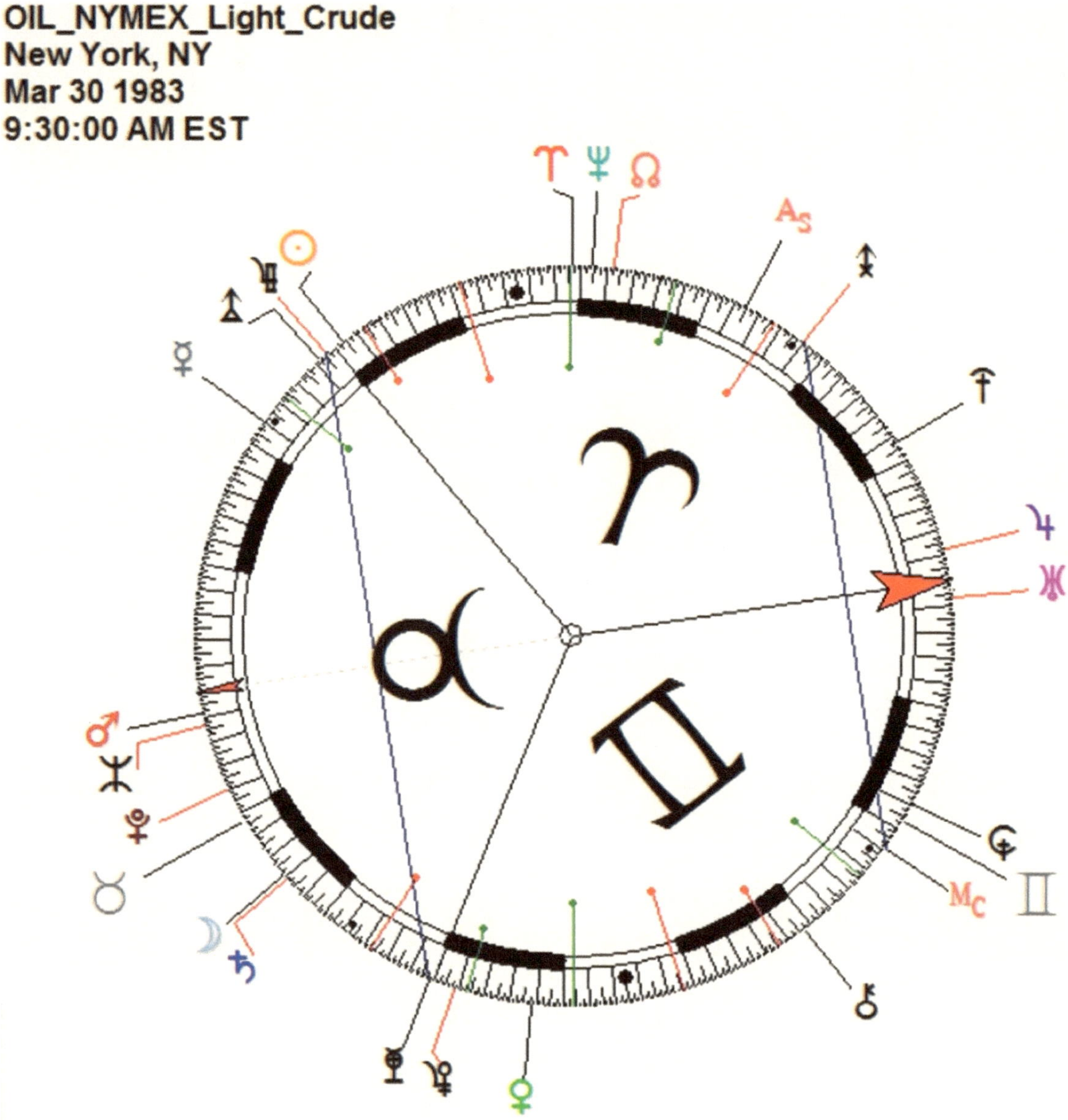

The solar eclipse suggests that we may see a big tug-of-war in the months ahead when it comes to oil prices. The eclipse trigger of the Jupiter/Uranus midpoint indicates big price swings and lots of surprises in the oil market, but those surprises could send prices in either direction at any given time. The Zeus/Midheaven activation adds to the potential for a high-energy market; whether oil traders react to external influences or are simply watching shifts in market trends, the results are likely to be quite dramatic. The biggest challenge, however, comes from the solar eclipse activation of the Apollon/Admetos midpoint, which pits the forces of market expansion against attitudes that impose severe limits. The best case scenario for oil bulls is that the limits are on supply, supporting a rapid price expansion.

SOUTH AFRICAN RAND

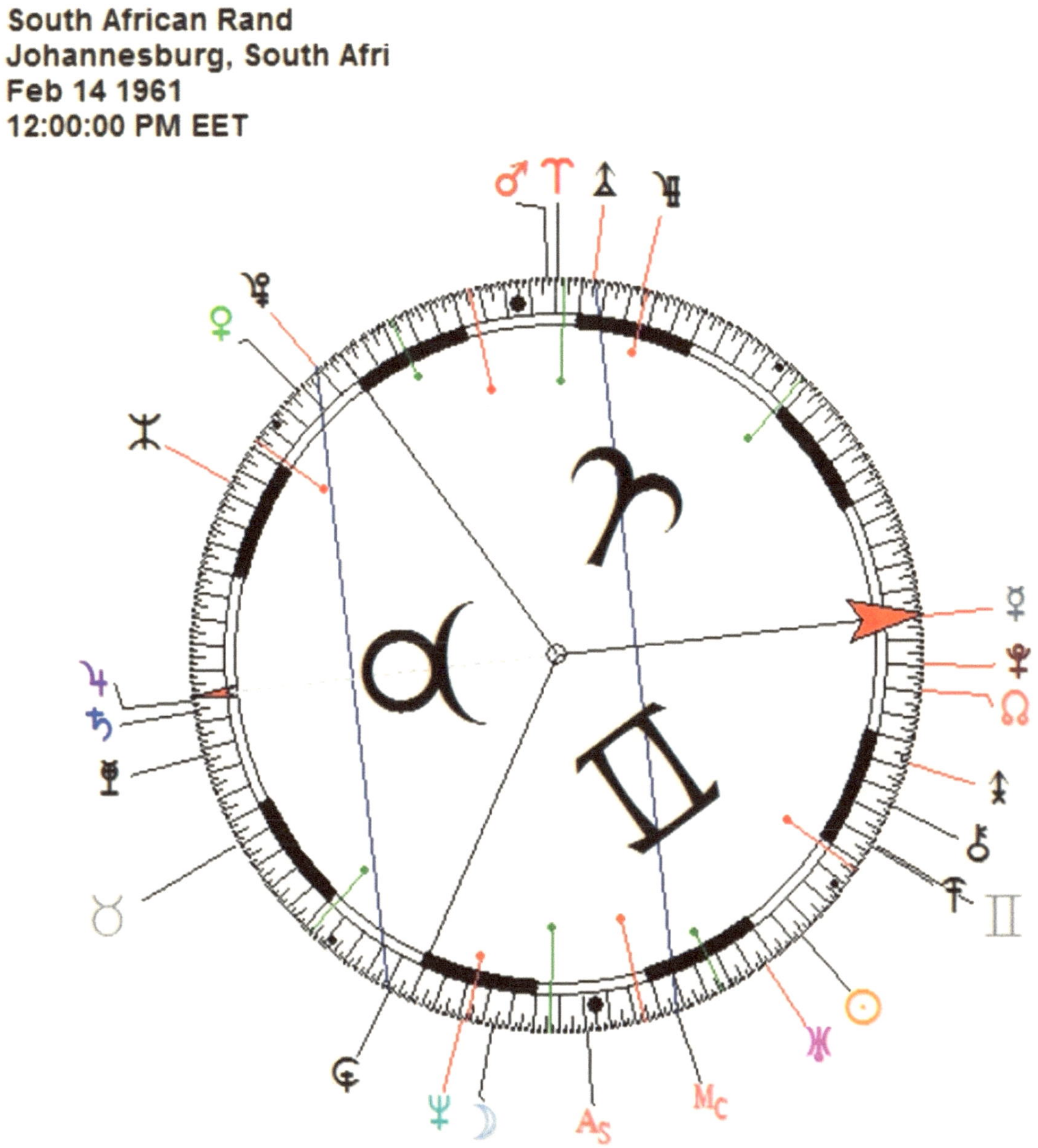

South Africa remains an area of particular interest in global economic considerations, and its currency continues to face real challenges. But the solar eclipse activation of Mercury in the chart for the Rand suggests increasing interest in the currency during the coming months, and with the Vulcanus/Midheaven midpoint in play it could be time to open up a new chapter in the South African economy. The biggest inhibiting factor is the solar eclipse trigger of the Cupido/Hades midpoint – it highlights one of the country's major challenges: the need to reconcile the needs of a united community with cultural diversity on the one hand, with the baser expressions of an oppressive history on the other.

INDIAN NIFTY INDEX

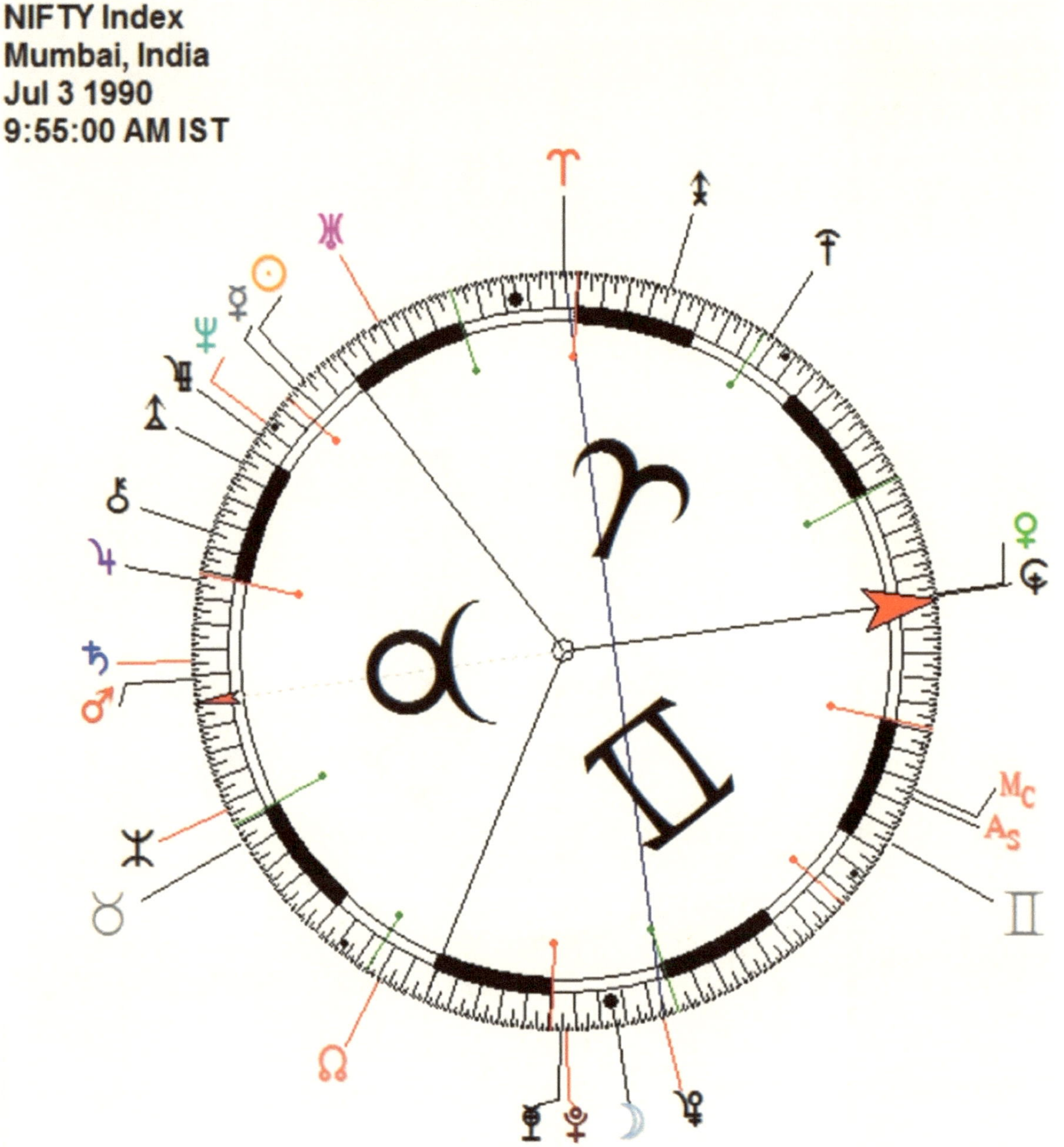

As we noted in our analysis of the chart of the Bombay Stock Exchange, there is a high potential of troubled times ahead for Indian equities, with a potential for occasional chaos in the markets. The impact of the September solar eclipse on the NIFTY index repeats that motif, at least in its activation of the Venus/Hades combination in the chart. There's clearly a battle going on between selfish interests and loftier ideals; with the Cupido/Aries Point midpoint in play as well the global reputation of India's financial markets may ultimately be at stake.

CORN

CBOT Corn
Chicago, IL
May 1 1884
10:34:00 AM CST

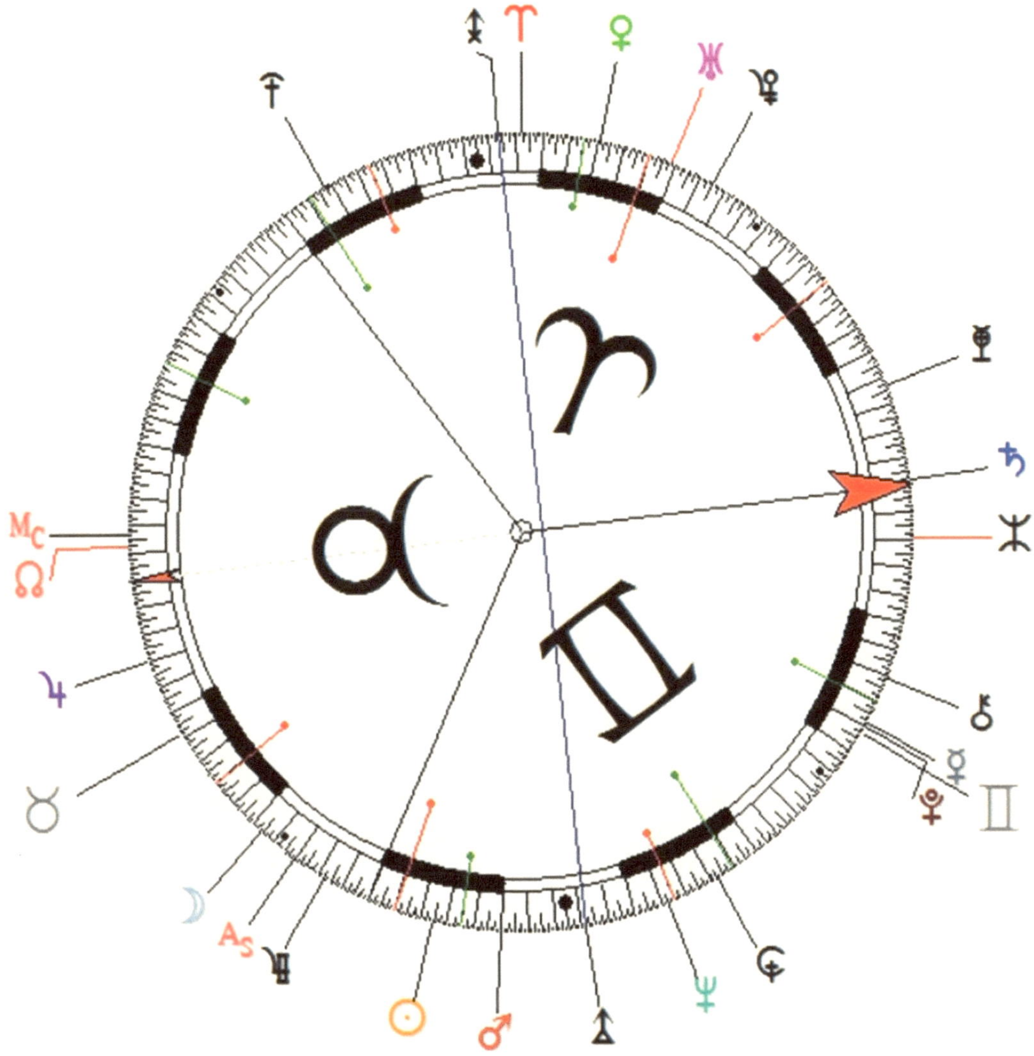

With the solar eclipse triggering both Saturn and the Zeus/Vulcanus midpoint in the horoscope for CBOT Corn, we can expect to see a trading environment that moves in fits and starts, with sudden interruptions in emerging trends as the effects of the eclipse play out. Whenever it looks like a clear market direction has been established, there are likely to be big shifts or what seem to be complete stand-stills. It could be a very challenging situation for traders in this market.

SOYBEANS

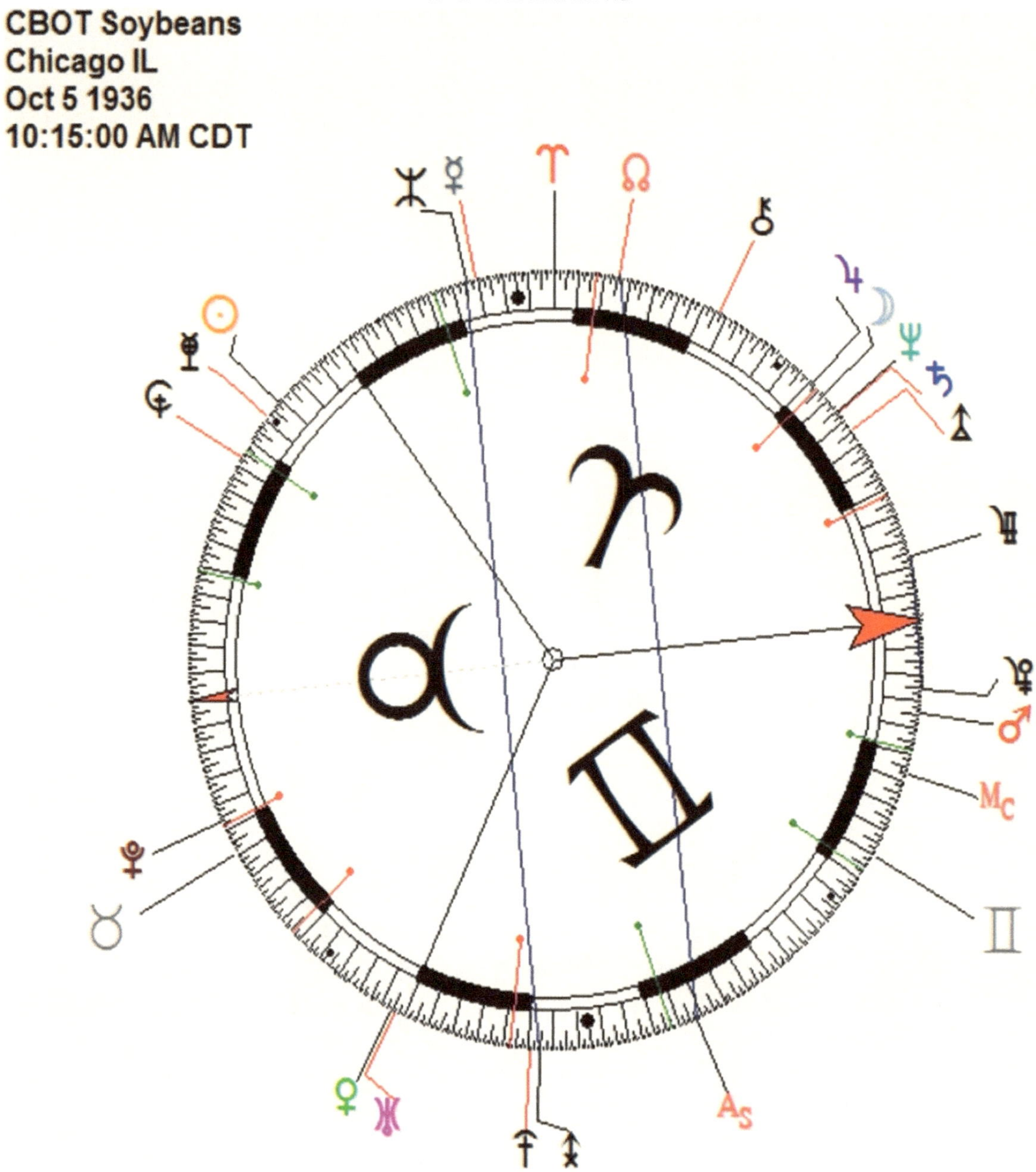

The prospects for soybeans look very positive in the weeks and months following the September solar eclipse. The activation of the Ascendant/True Lunar Node midpoint makes this market very attractive, and the eclipse trigger of the Zeus/Poseidon midpoint offers traders an opportunity to get engaged in this market with unusual clarity and conviction. It's also likely that bullish expectations for soybeans could be generously rewarded, thanks to the impact of the eclipse-activated midpoint of Cupido and Apollon in this horoscope.

SOYBEAN OIL

CBOT Soybean_Oil
Chicago, IL
Jul 17 1950
9:15:00 AM CDT

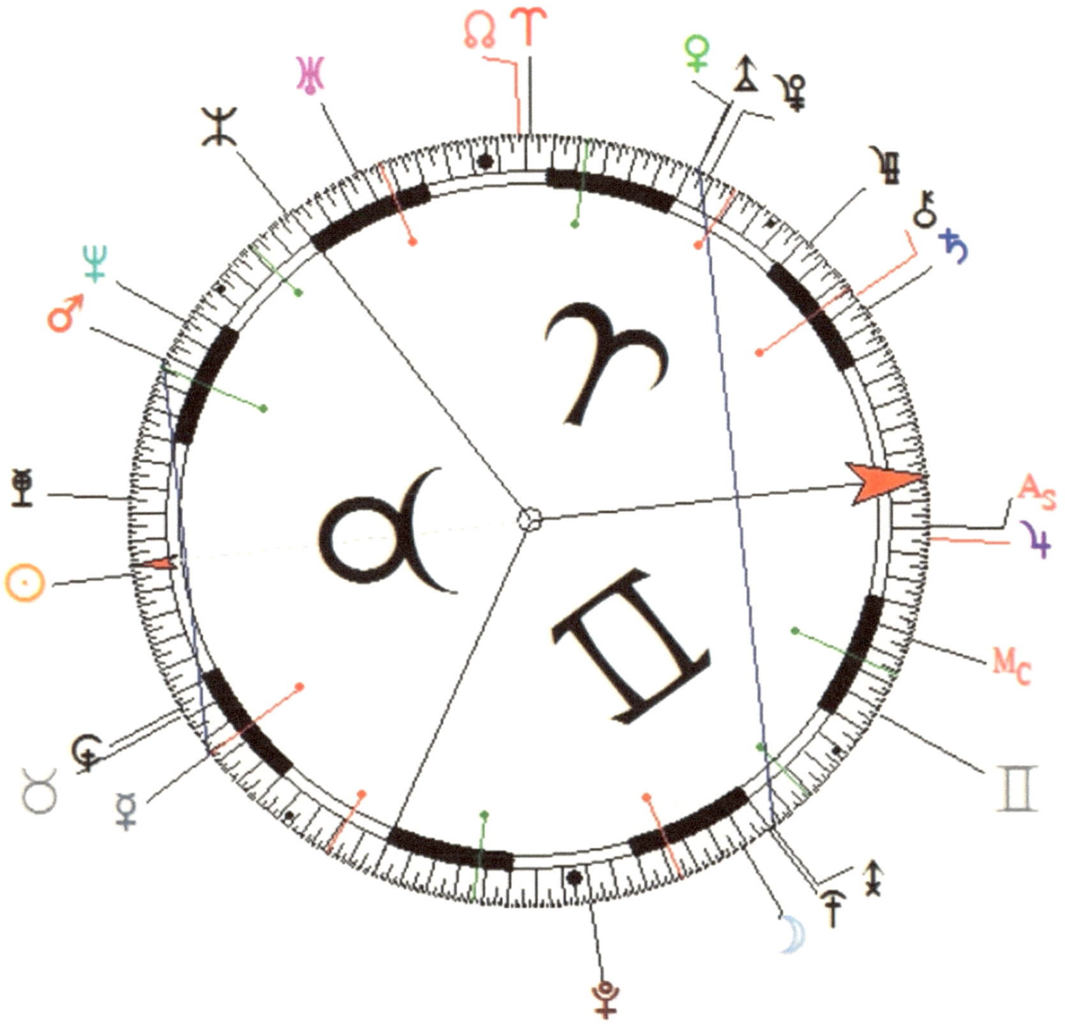

If you like the beans, what about the oil? The chart for soybean oil adds further confirmation for bullish expectations in this agricultural sector. The eclipse activates the Bean Oil Mercury/Mars midpoint, driving market activity in a positive direction. Thanks to the Zeus/Vulcanus activation, we can expect an extremely powerful trading dynamic in the coming months, and the triggering of the midpoint of Zeus and Venus (the natural ruler of soybeans) the outlook seems even more positive.

SUGAR

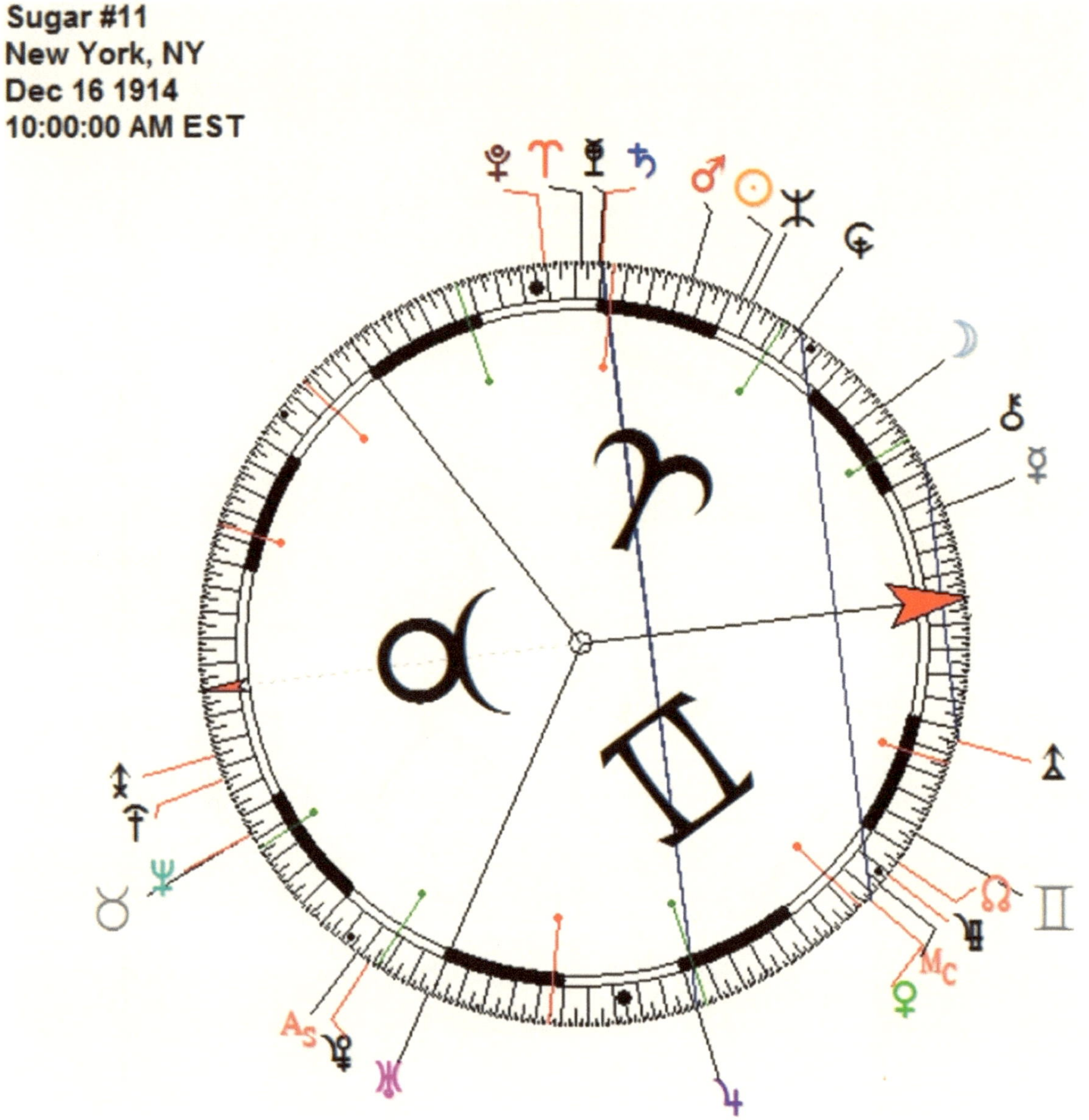

Oops! What's shutting the door on sugar? The September solar eclipse seems to be conspiring to inhibit bullish action here. The triggering of the Chiron/Vulcanus midpoint suggests that aggressive market action will inevitably run into problems and blockages. A potentially positive Venus sweet tooth is getting slammed by rotten Hades. And both the Jupiter/Saturn and Jupiter/Admetos midpoints are getting activated, too, giving us yet another reminder that sugar traders need to looking at the short side of the market, or possibly avoiding it altogether.

COCOA

CSCE Cocoa
New York NY
Oct 1 1925
9:30:00 AM EST

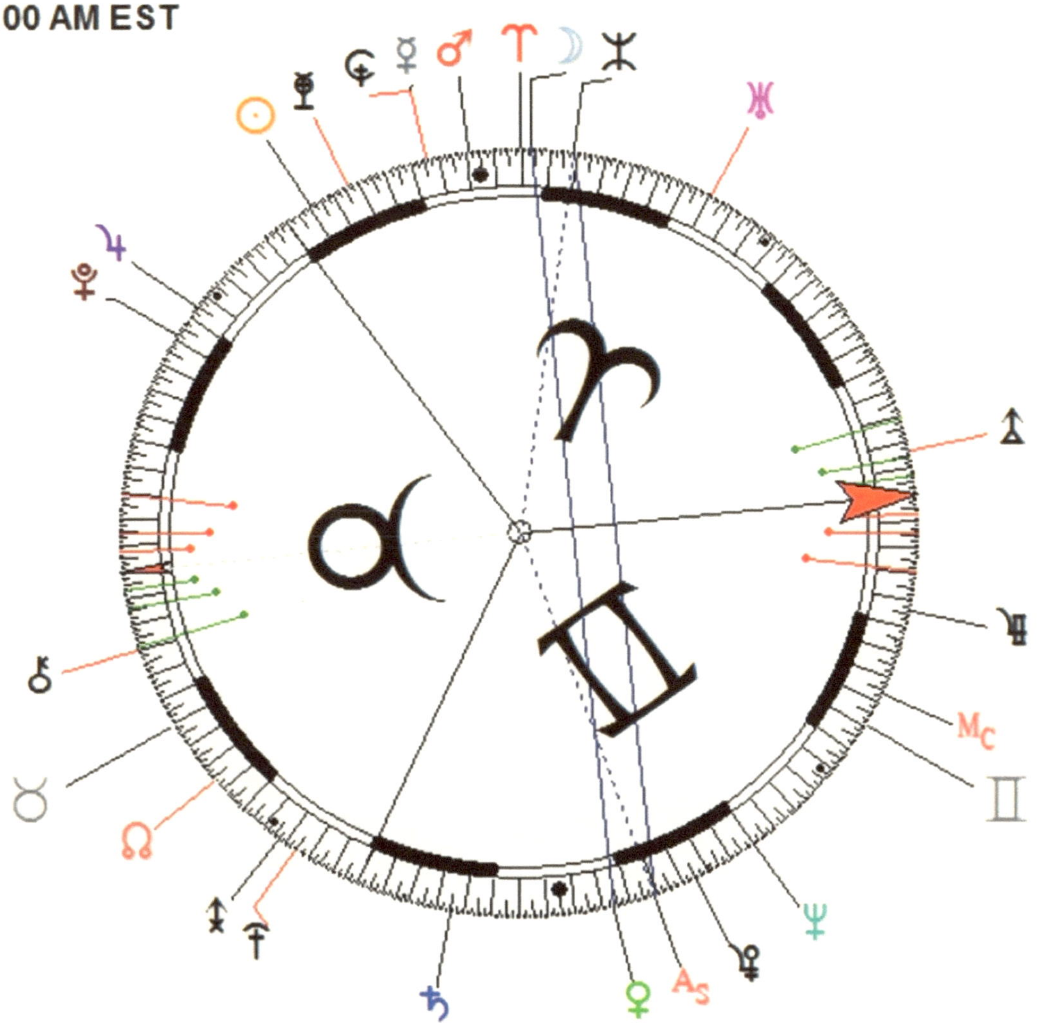

Compared to sugar, the prospects for Cocoa look very tasty indeed! The September solar eclipse triggers the Poseidon/Ascendant midpoint, offering traders a fresh opportunity to see things in a positive perspective. And with the Moon/Venus midpoint also in play to influence this market in the months after the solar eclipse, what's not to like?

COFFEE

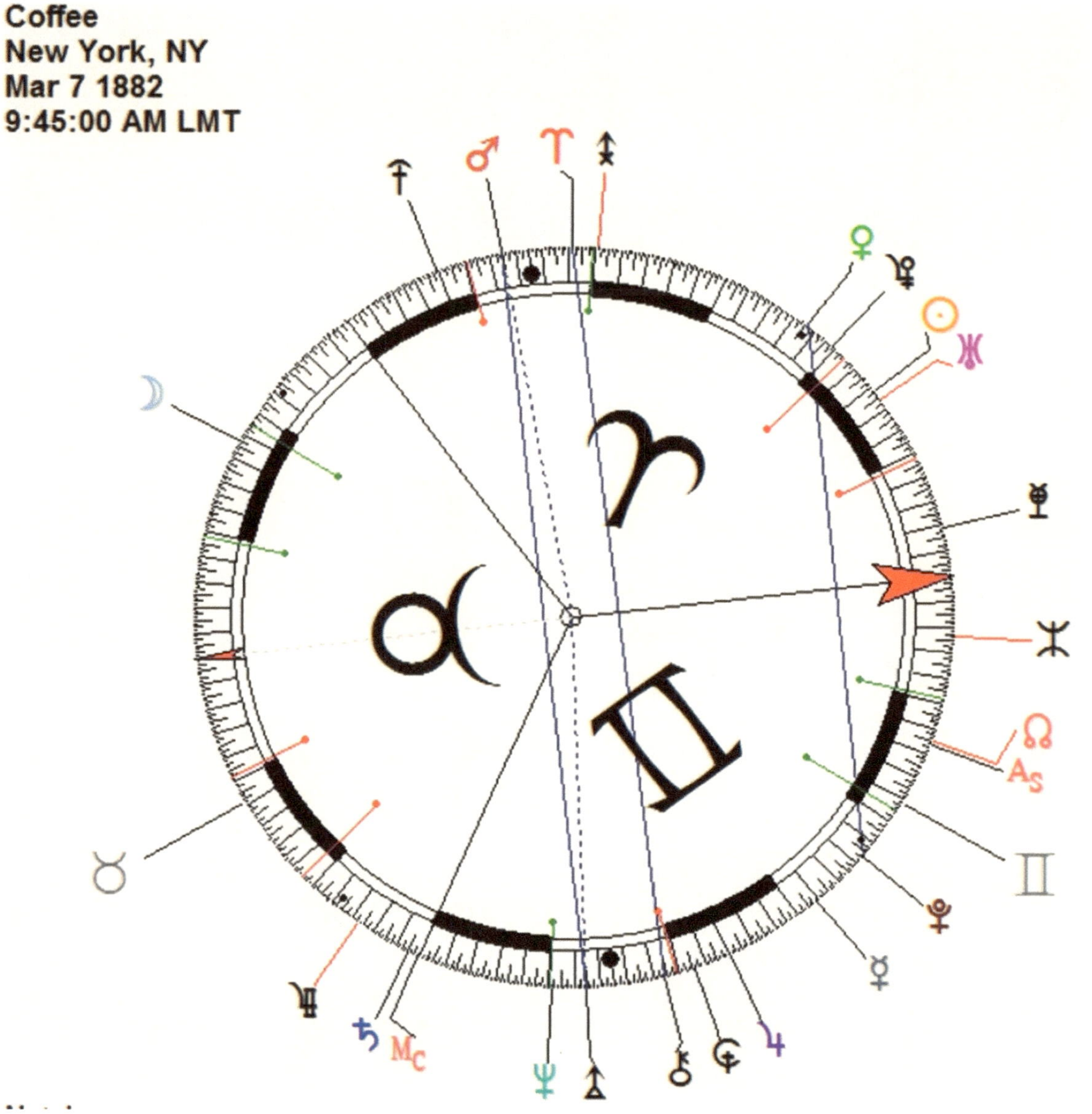

Coffee traders may get quite a kick from the market in the months following the September solar eclipse. The activation of the Admetos/Poseidon midpoint suggests some inhibited thinking when it comes to this market, and the Chiron/Aries Point trigger hints that this commodity may be seen as problematical on a global basis. But the eclipse activations of both the Venus/Pluto and Mars/Vulcanus midpoints add tremendous power and potential here. Unless you prefer decaf, this is one market you may want to indulge in!

COPPER

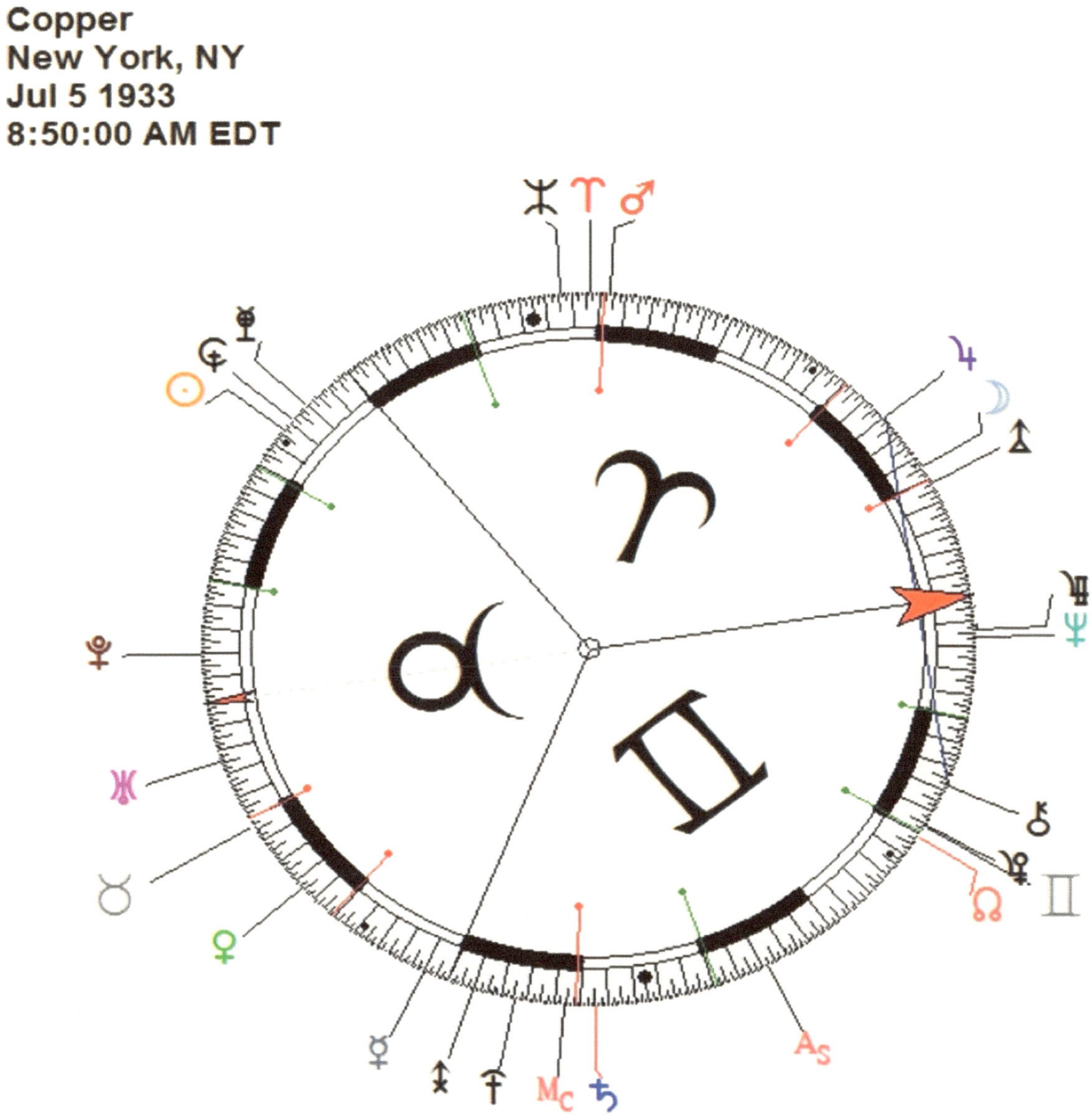

There's really not much to say about the Copper market in the months following the September solar eclipse. The only midpoint activation here is with Jupiter and Chiron. That combination suggests that there will be some bullish energy in the Copper market, but that it's likely to be met with some surprising challenges. Savvy traders who are experienced in this market will probably be able to see past the inconvenience and confusion to discover potentially profitable trading opportunities, but novices may find it better to step aside for the time being.

PALLADIUM

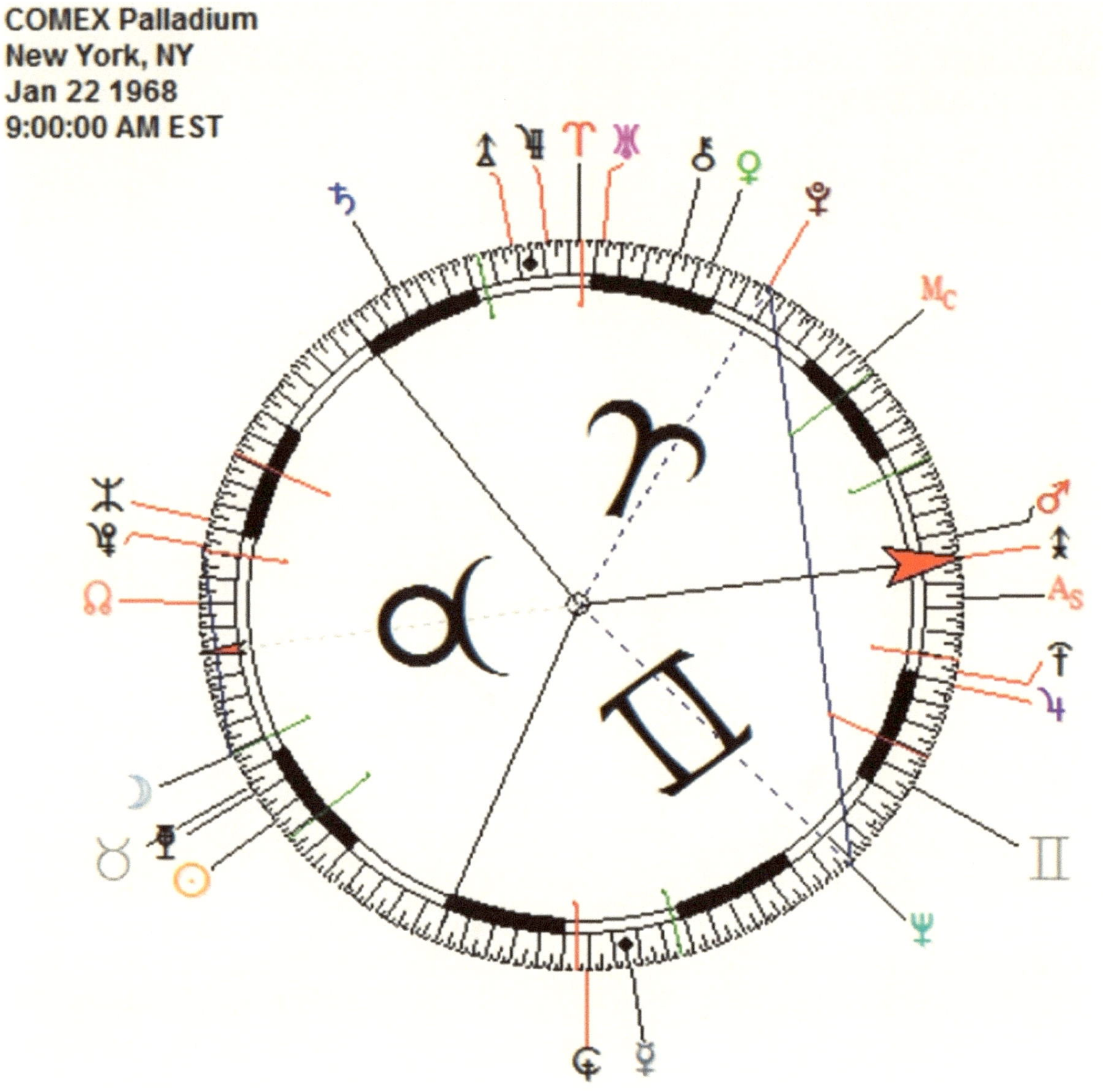

We haven't been tracking the Palladium market very long, but once again a solar eclipse brings into focus for us. The September eclipse directly activates Zeus in the Palladium horoscope, so we can expect to see a surprising amount of trading energy in play. The Mars/Ascendant midpoint is also getting triggered, adding to the general energy level, and with the Moon/Cupido midpoint coming into focus as well, we could see a marked increase in the attention that's being paid to this market. The big kicker here, however, is the activation of the Palladium Neptune/Pluto midpoint by the September solar eclipse. That signals plenty of high-volume, high-stakes speculation during the coming months, so if you're interested in this market, it's time to fasten your seat belt!

COMEX GOLD

COMEX Gold
New York NY
Dec 31 1974
9:30:00 AM EST

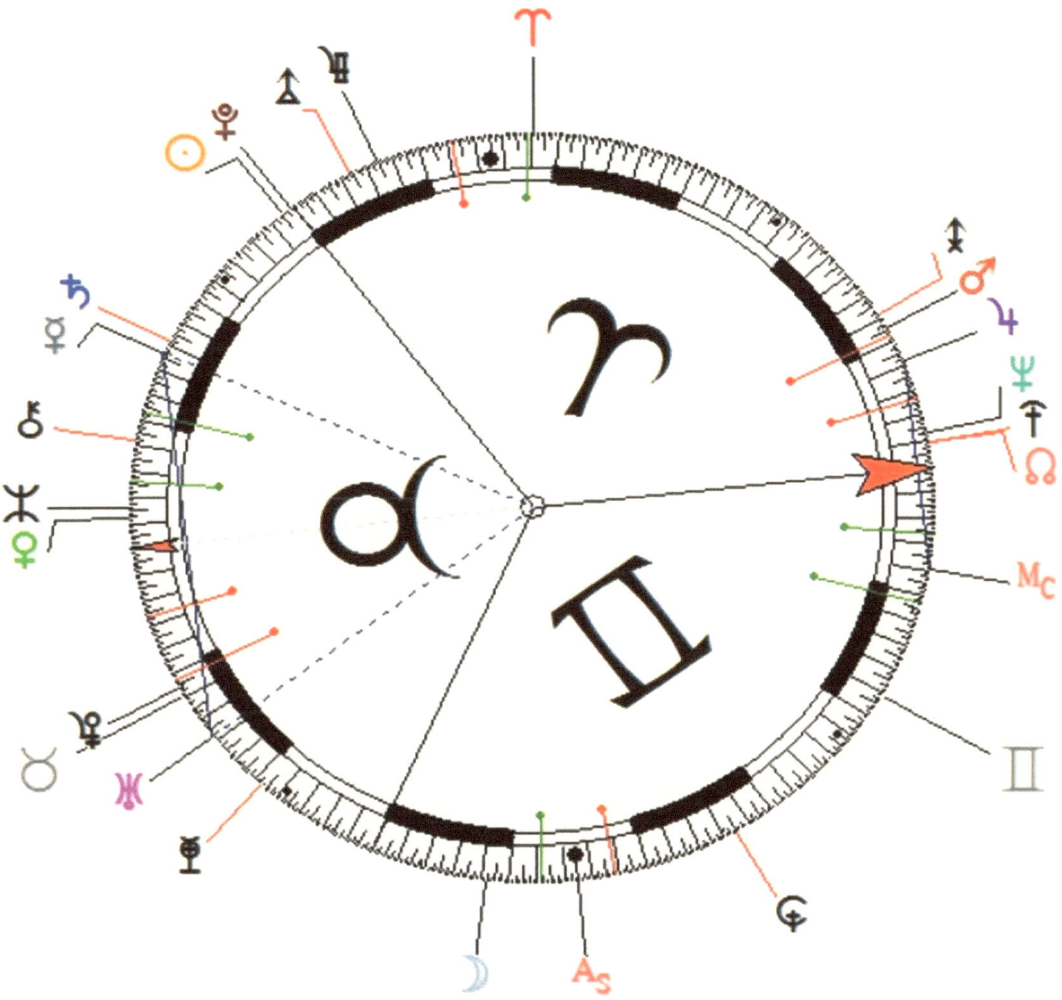

While the long-term fundamental outlook for Gold remains quite solid, shorter-term traders in the yellow metal have frequently found themselves facing disappointment in recent years. That outlook may be changing with the September solar eclipse, however. The eclipse creates a decidedly bullish context for the Gold market, most notably by triggering the Jupiter/Midheaven midpoint in the horoscope for COMEX Gold. The Mercury/Uranus midpoint is also activated by the solar eclipse, so we can not only expect some good news for the Gold Bugs, but some underlying volatility and surprisingly dramatic price surges as well.

CBOT SILVER

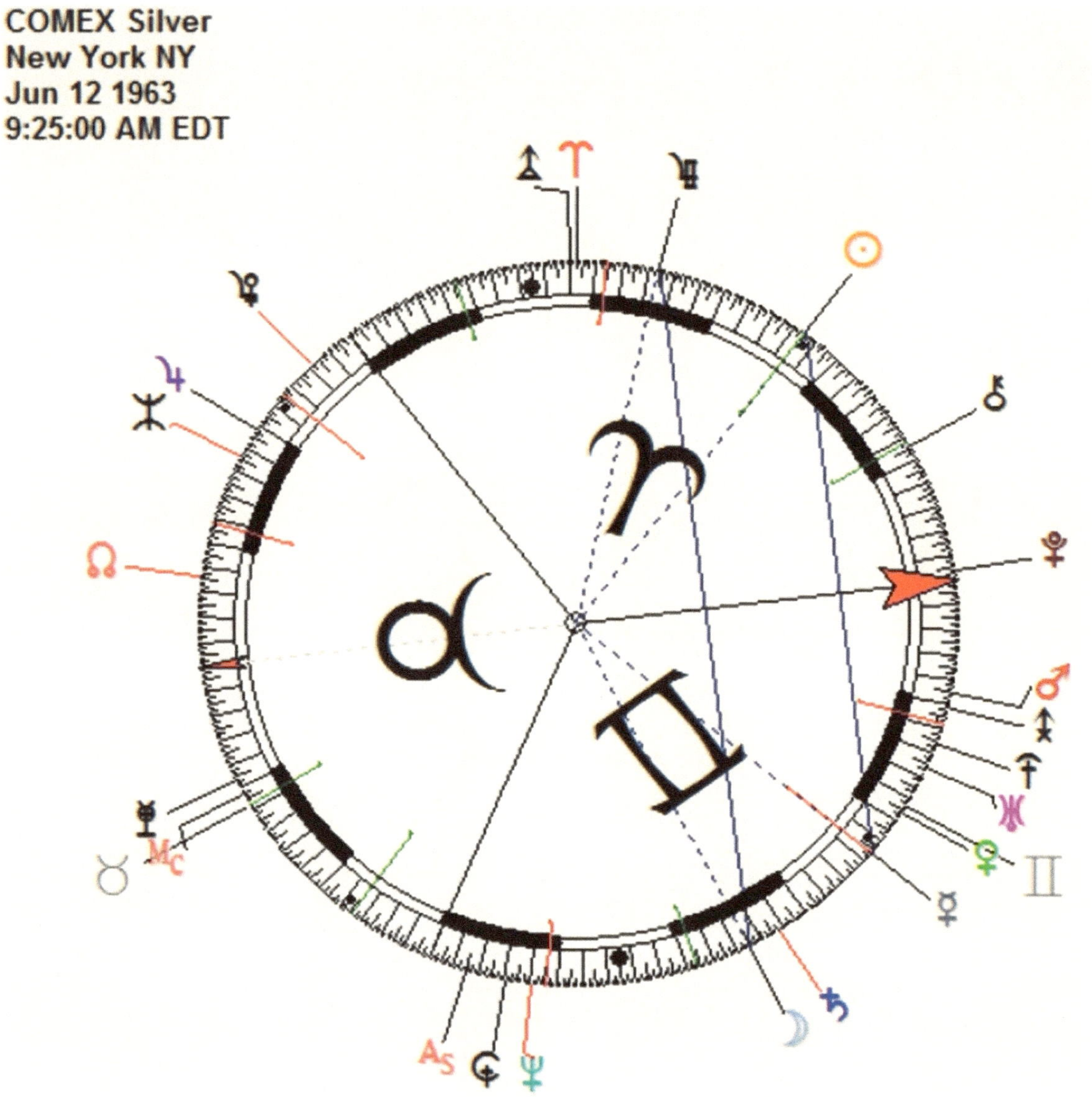

The outlook ahead for Silver completes our generally bullish take on precious metals during the months following the September solar eclipse. The eclipse directly triggers Pluto in the COMEX Silver horoscope, so we can look to a lot of money moving in this market. The activation of the Sun/Mercury midpoint lets us know that we can expect a lot of good news and a positive mood overall. And to top it all off, the solar eclipse triggers the midpoint of the Moon (the natural ruler of Silver) and Apollon, the transneptunian factor most associated with expanding markets. Need we say more?

MADAGASCAR

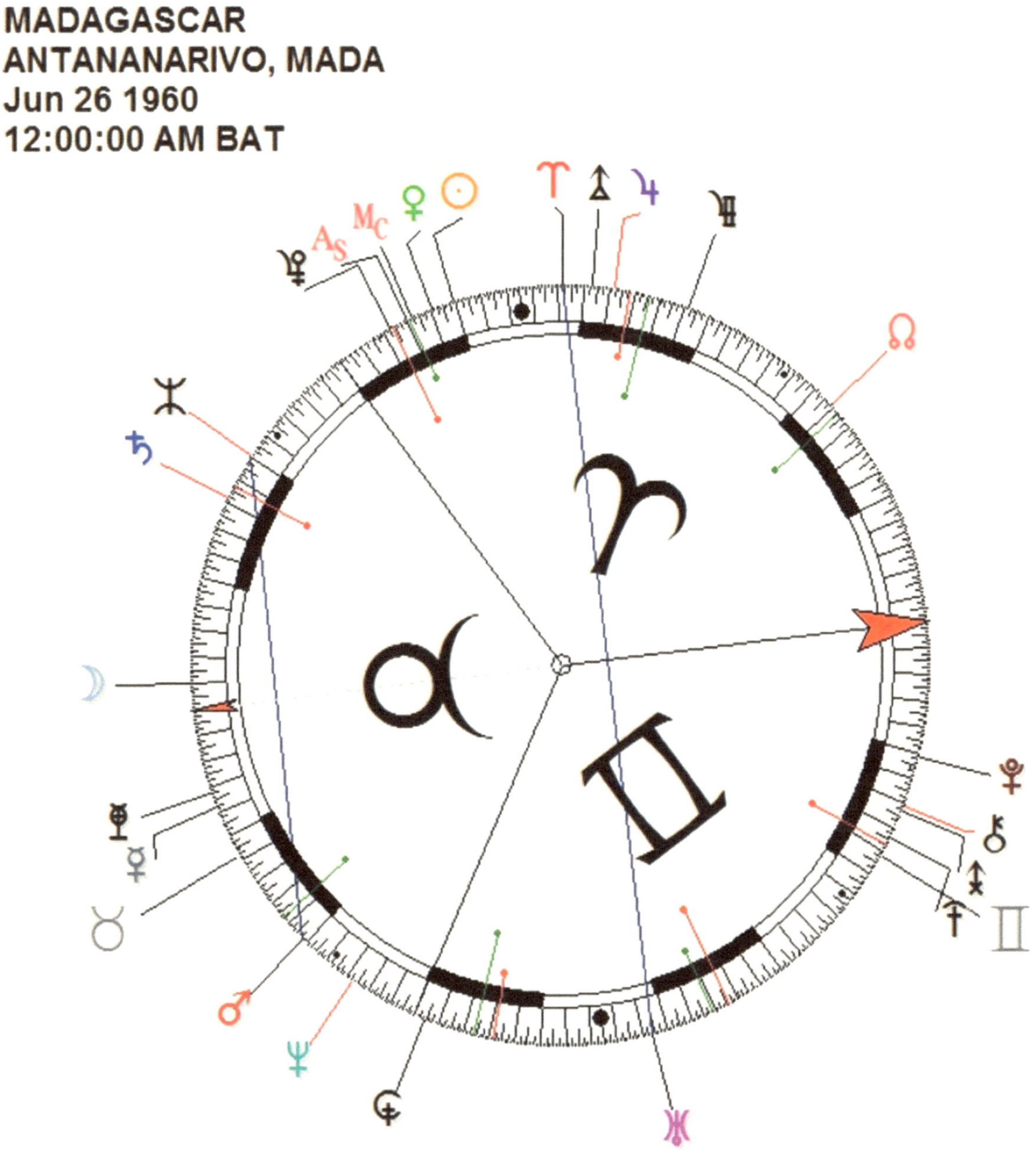

Because the path of the September 1 solar eclipse cuts right through the island nation of Madagascar, it's important to observe its horoscope as well. The eclipse point activates the Uranus/Aries Point midpoint in the national chart, so Madagascar may find itself thrust into the global spotlight in some surprising ways during the coming months. With the Mars/Poseidon midpoint also in play, we can also expect to see some radical new ideas associated with the country, perhaps providing a dramatic shift in its role on the world stage. We'll be keeping an eye on Madagascar, not only at the time of the solar eclipse, but during the following months as well.

Lunar Returns to the Solar Eclipse

The impact of the September 1 solar eclipse is not limited solely to the date when it takes place. From an astrological perspective, the eclipse event creates a powerful resonant field that continues to provide noteworthy opportunities for the eclipse energy to be activated well into the future—extending even beyond the time of the next solar eclipse, which in this case comes on February 26, 2017.

This resonant field operates through the zodiacal points at which the eclipse occurs and also through the antiscion (also known as the solstice point) of the eclipse. With the September 1 solar eclipse coming at 09° 21' Virgo, the eclipse antiscion falls at 20° 39' Aries.

One of the ways that we can best see the resonant field at work during the months following the eclipse is by tracking the series of Lunar Returns to the September solar eclipse. Each Lunar Return is set for the exact time that the Moon returns to the position it held at the time of the solar eclipse.

In general, Lunar Returns to solar eclipses often mark significant points in the markets, so they are worth watching as potential triggers for trend reversals and shifts in market momentum. While solar eclipse Lunar Returns don't impact all markets in an identical manner, they are nevertheless an extremely valuable key to unlocking the hidden dynamics that can move the markets in powerful ways.

Each Lunar Return relates to the solar eclipse as a resonating factor, which is what helps to provoke the kinds of trend reversals that we see so often in association with these events, but each one can also be considered by itself as a separate and significant moment in time.

Considering each solar eclipse Lunar Return as a separate event has the advantage of providing us with an emotional index of the month ahead, so we can get some insight into what is most likely to impact market trends during the four-week period following each lunar return.

As we do so, we are getting an overview of general market tendencies rather than a specific forecast of particular trends or turning points. Even so, this can provide valuable background information as we fine tune our market forecasts each month and as we look for specific trading opportunities during the course of each trading week throughout the nine-month period following the solar eclipse.

September 28, 2016

The first Lunar Return to the September solar eclipse comes on September 28. Mercury, which was in retrograde motion at the time of the solar eclipse itself, has now resumed direct motion and conjoins the Midheaven in the Lunar Return chart set for New York City.

This angularity gives Mercury strong emphasis in this horoscope, but it is not the only planet that takes on such prominence. The transneptunian factor Admetos is also angular, in a conjunction with the Descendant in the Lunar Return horoscope. The Mercury/Admetos combination is about restrictions in communication and the potential for major shutdowns in commercial activities, so it indicates the likelihood of bearish sentiment in the markets as September ends and October gets underway.

That bearish bias is also reflected in the T-square pattern between the Moon, Neptune, and Saturn. Neptune is in opposition to the Moon, suggesting delusional or emotionally-driven reactions to shifting circumstances in the markets. With Saturn completing the pattern as it forms a square to the Moon as well as a square to Neptune, speculative fantasies are likely to come to an abrupt termination in the weeks following the Lunar Return. Mars is the ruler of the fifth house of speculation in this chart, however, so we are likely to see active markets at this time.

Since Mars in this chart activates the midpoint of Vulcanus and the Ascendant, we can expect some extremes of trading volatility during this time frame. But with Mars also activating the Cupido/Hades midpoint in the chart, a sense of disillusionment and discouraging sentiment are likely to prevail, driving prices lower as a net result.

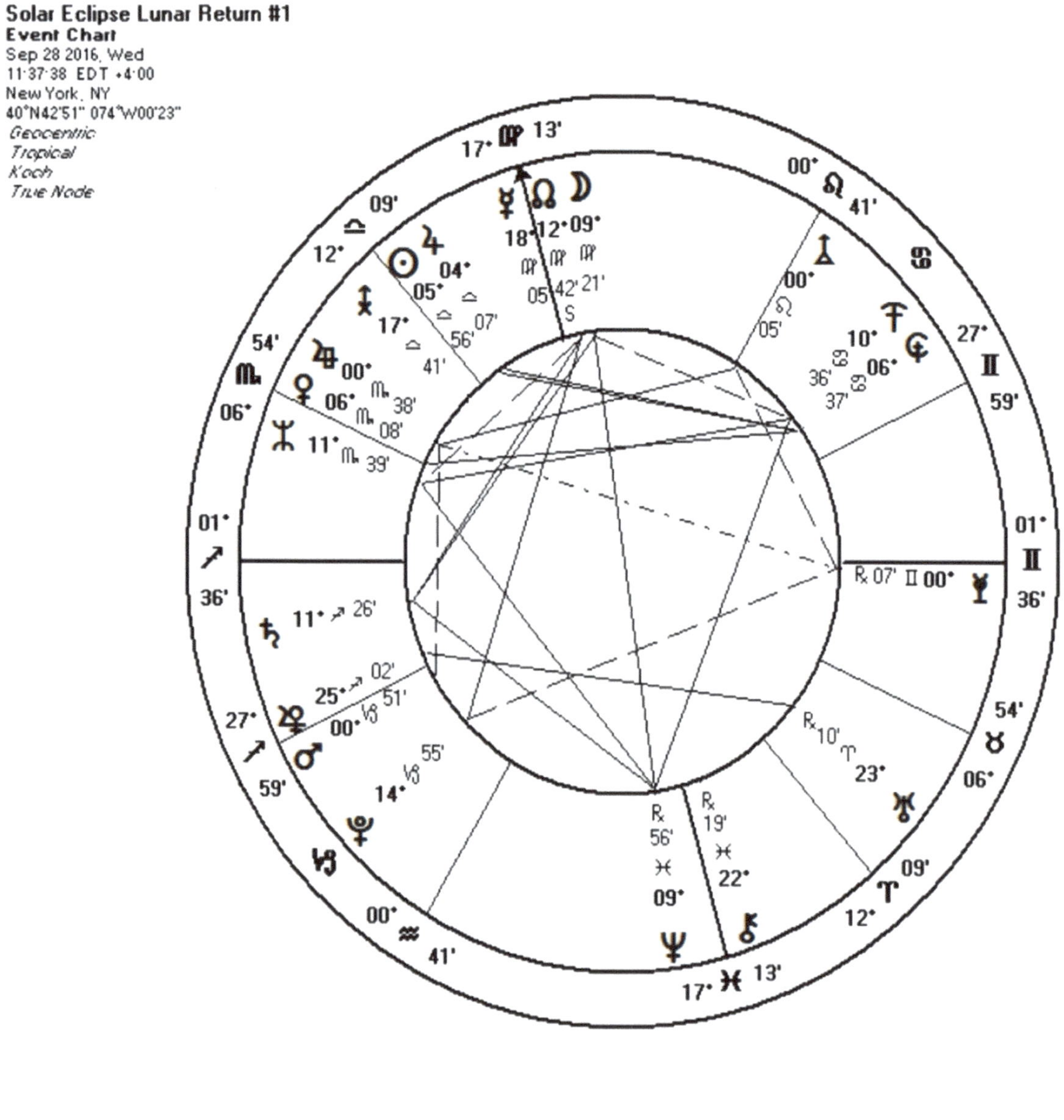

October 25, 2016

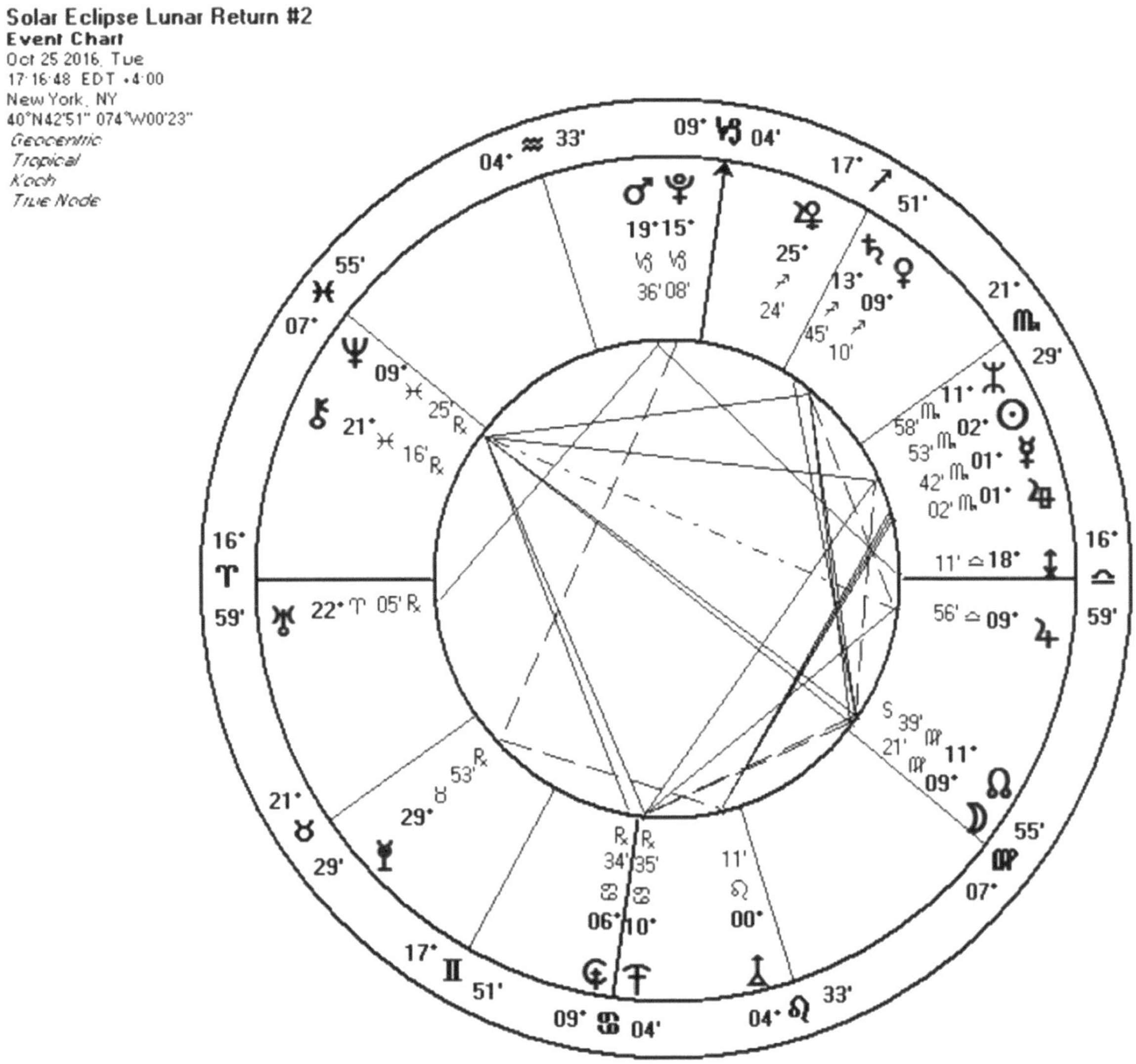

The Lunar Return chart for October 25, 2016 presents an interesting contrast to the previous Lunar Return near the end of September. While the September 28 Lunar Return horoscope featured a Moon/Neptune/Saturn T-square, by October 25 the heavenly picture has changed.

Saturn has moved out of the orb of the stressful alignment pattern that was in play at the end of September. Even so, however, the Lunar Return chart for October 25 also features a T-square configuration. That's because Venus has moved in to take the place of Saturn occupied on September 28, forming the midpoint alignment with the Moon and Neptune.

While any T-square is likely to present a dynamic state and an energetic expression that influences attitudes and activities, each T-square is also a unique projection of the specific planetary energies that are involved in the aspect pattern. With Venus taking the place of Saturn, we are quite likely to see a dramatic shift from inhibition to refinement, from an emphasis on rules and limits to a much more pleasant, easy-going focus on wealth, abundance, and enhanced value.

With the Moon activating the Venus/Neptune midpoint as well as the midpoint of Mercury and the New York City Ascendant, we can expect a definite drive toward more market optimism and bullish expression in the trading environment at the end of October and through much of November.

There are, however, some contrary indications here that need to be taken into account. The Moon also activates the Hades/Poseidon midpoint in this Lunar Return horoscope, so even though there is likely to be a strong push toward more a optimistic outlook in the markets we may see baser instincts and malicious manifestations prevail, at least in some circumstances. This is especially true since the Sun, the ruler of the fifth house of trading in this chart, activates the Hades/Admetos midpoint as well.

The Hades/Admetos combination is particularly potent. It was the astrological signature of the Great Depression in the 1930s, when the two transneptunian factors met for an extended conjunction in Aries.

Its emphasis in this Lunar Return horoscope gives us a clear indication that no matter how optimistic the bullish forces in the markets may be at this time, there are still likely to be deeply rooted strains of moral decay and economic deprivation weakening the fundamental outlook from behind the scenes. While that may be of little concern to short-term traders, it may prove to be significant for investors who have longer time horizons.

November 21, 2016

By the time we reach the solar eclipse Lunar Return on November 21, the energy of the T-square patterns we have seen during the previous months has dissipated completely. The Moon/Neptune opposition is still in effect, but instead of its being a part of a T-square pattern, it is aligned in what some astrologers call an "Easy Opposition," with Kronos forming a trine to Neptune and a sextile to the Moon.

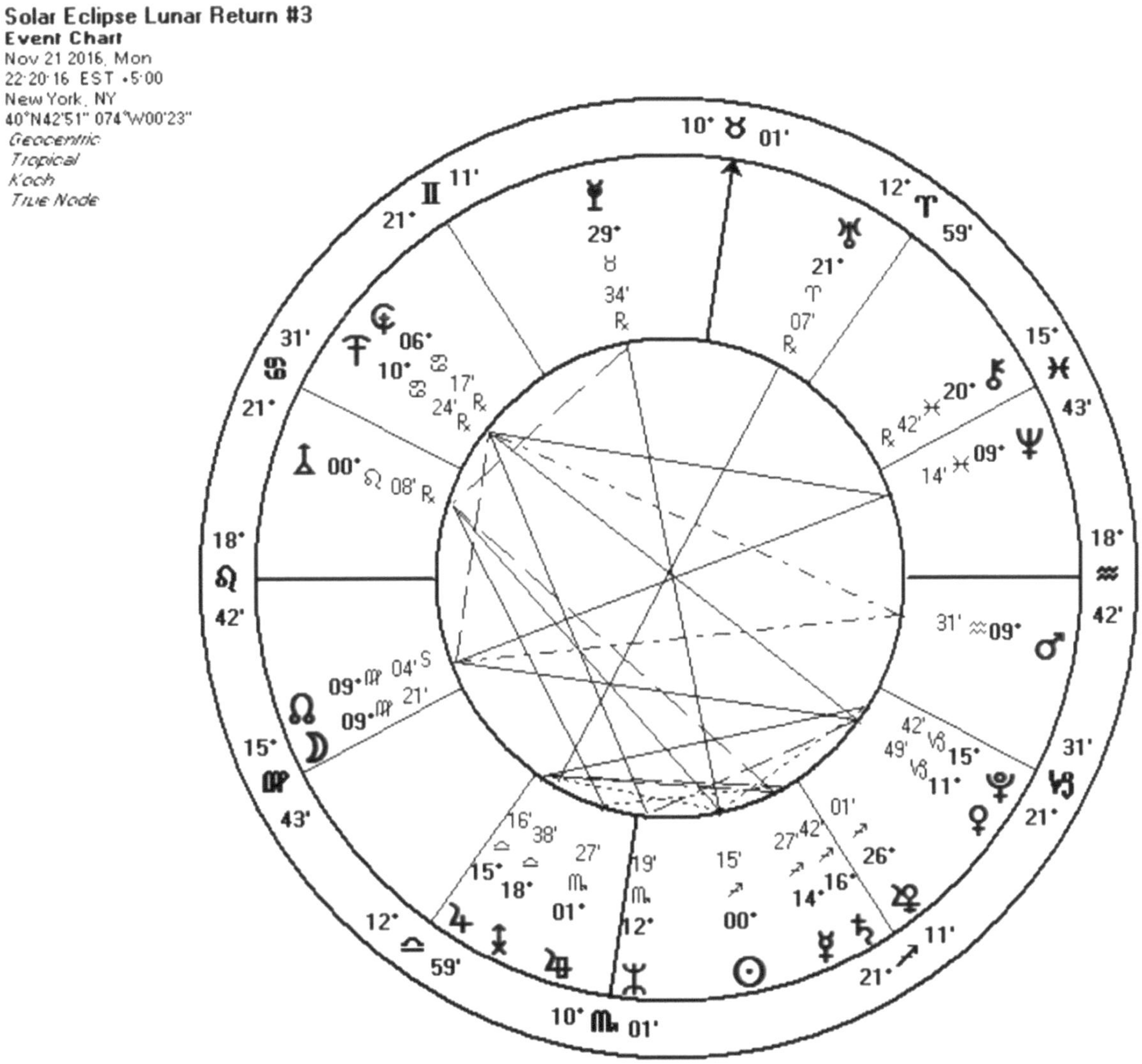

With the Moon as the ruler of the twelfth house of the chart and Neptune as co-ruler of the eighth house, this configuration suggests that financial authorities may be expressing some confusion or uncertainty about debt structures, taxation, and interest rates.

Although the markets are generally not particularly fond of uncertainty, in this case a little bit of vacillation by the Powers That Be is likely to be seen as a positive signal by the markets, especially if interest rate policies favor easier access to money.

Jupiter is the ruler of the fifth house of market activity in this horoscope, so it's not unreasonable to expect some bullish sentiment and rising prices. But Jupiter also activates the Midheaven/Chiron midpoint, so it would be wise to watch for potential problems in the trading environment. Those problems could indicate key divergences which offer profitable opportunities to savvy traders.

Note as well that Jupiter also activates the Sun/Admetos midpoint in this chart, so it will be important for any active trader to pay close attention to pragmatic limits and to the importance of essential raw materials in any estimation of market value.

Even so, our overall assessment of this particular Lunar Return remains decidedly bullish. As we conclude November and move into the final month of the calendar year, the Moon's influence in triggering the midpoint of Neptune and the True North Lunar Node should be strong enough to keep the spirit of speculative optimism alive.

December 19, 2016

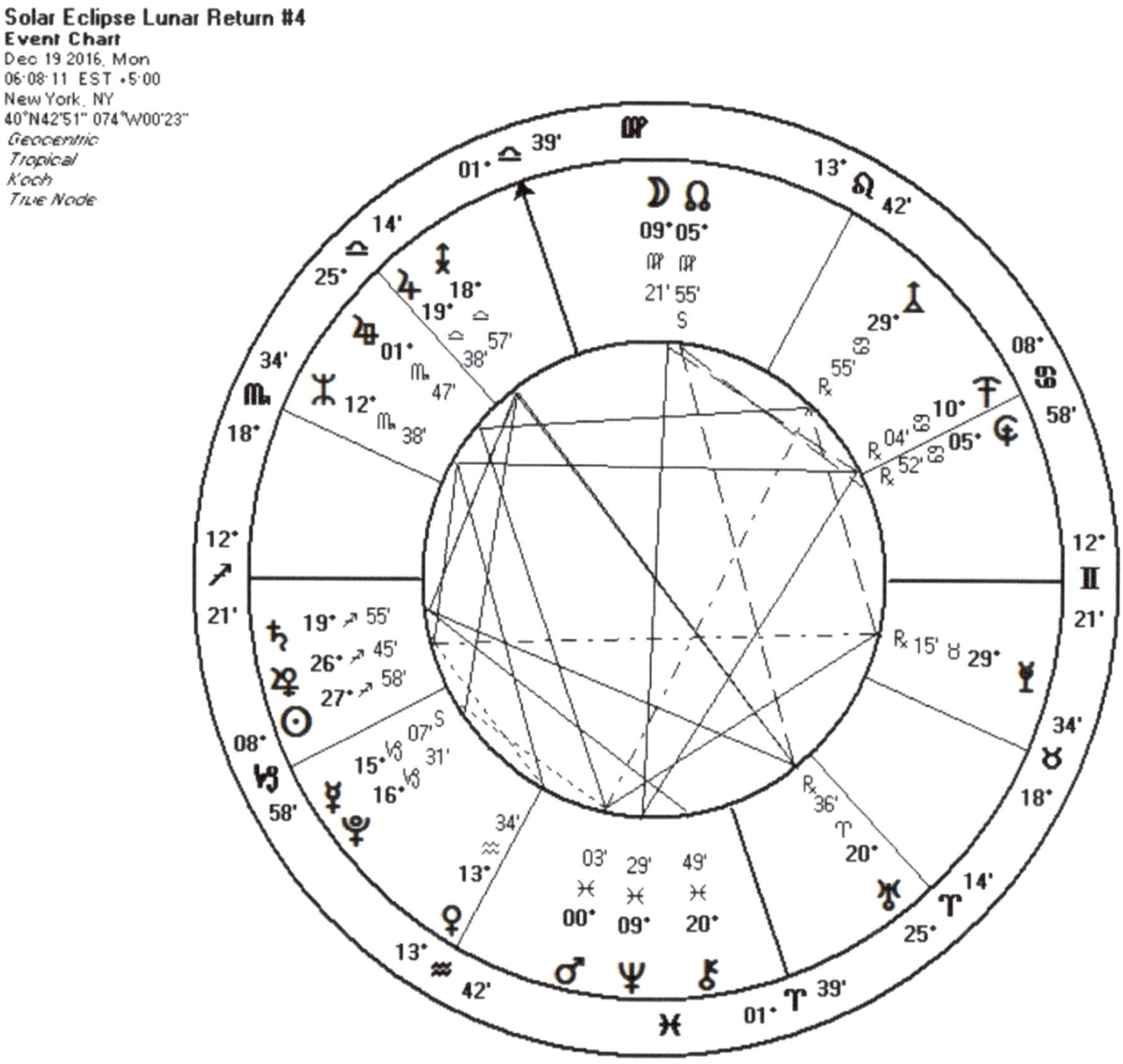

The final solar eclipse Lunar Return for 2016 comes on December 19, and the astrology here suggests that we are likely to see a fairly dramatic close to the trading year.

The Moon remains locked into its opposition to Neptune, so there is no shortage of hopeful interest in the potential for making money in the markets. But Jupiter, in conjunction with Zeus and in opposition to Uranus, adds the potential for surprise and upheaval to the market environment. Jupiter is in a sextile to Saturn, though, so there may be some efforts here to put the brakes on excessive speculation.

Mars is the ruler of the fifth house in this horoscope, and it takes on enormous strength because it triggers the midpoint of Vulcanus and the Aries Point in the horoscope. This suggests that market activity in the U.S. is likely to have dramatic global impacts as 2016 draws to a close and 2017 gets underway.

The net outcome is a bit uncertain, however, since Mars is aligned both to Apollon, suggesting dramatic growth in the markets, and at the same time is also separating from a square to Admetos, emphasizing strong inhibitions and the potential for a market standstill.

In short, the weeks immediately following the Lunar Return on December 19 may prove to be especially memorable for active traders. The likely scenario would be to see some nervousness and price consolidation at the time of the solstice, followed by a brief year end rally and then surprisingly strong bearishness after January 1.

January 15, 2017

If 2017 indeed gets off to a bearish start, that pessimistic bias is likely to dissipate after January 15, the date of the next solar eclipse Lunar Return. The Moon rules the Ascendant in this horoscope, so there may be some shifting sentiments and fairly surprising volatility during the final weeks of January and the start of February.

That potential is underscored by Mars, which is angular in a conjunction with Chiron at the Midheaven of the horoscope. With Mars also ruling the fifth house of trading activity, we are quite likely to see plenty of excitement in the trading environment during the weeks immediately following this Lunar Return.

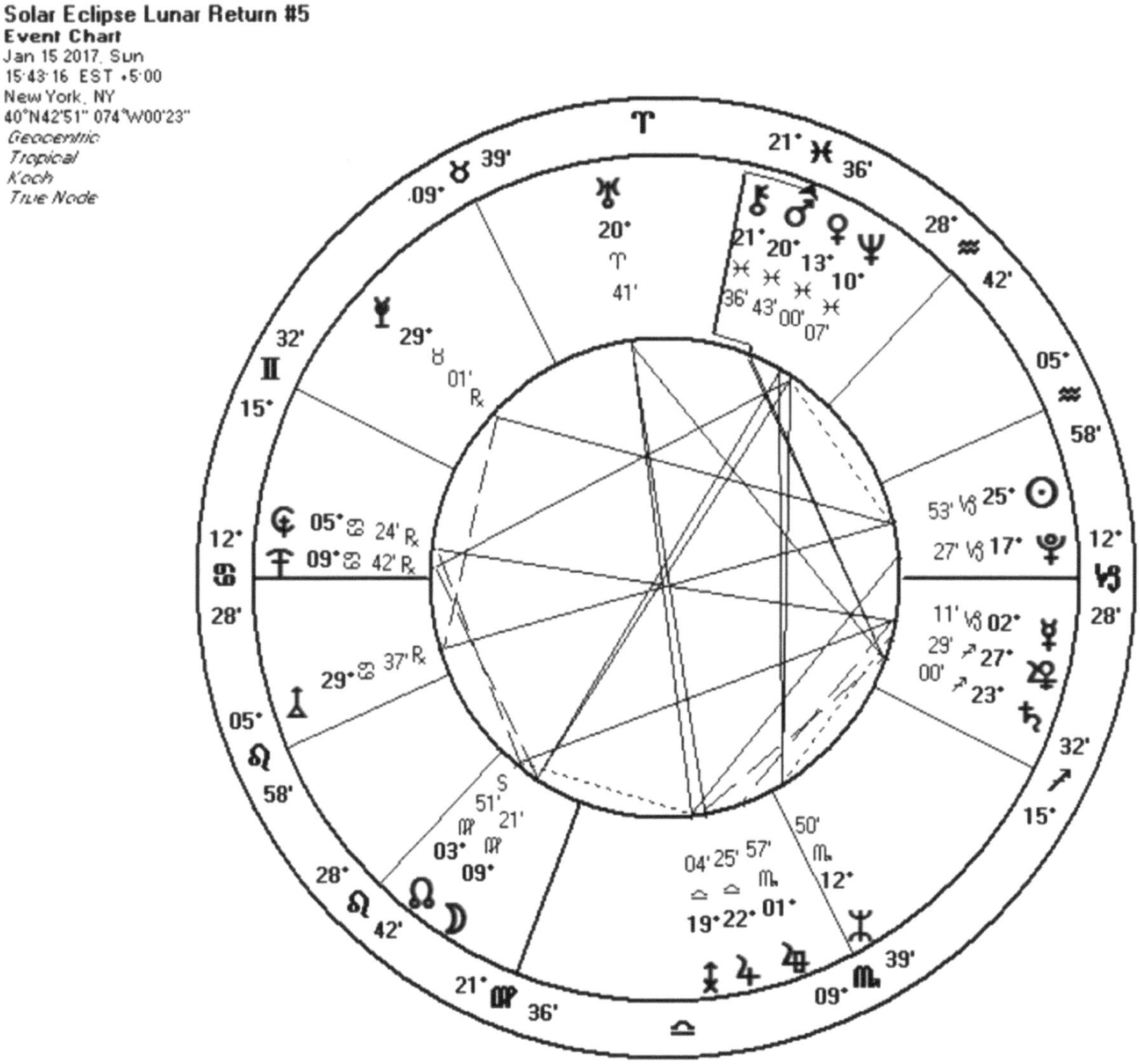

Mars is square Saturn, however, so the driving action in the markets may not be entirely bullish. In fact, with Mars also forming a square to the Ascendant/Admetos midpoint, there is a likelihood that rallies may be particularly short-lived during this time frame, with the bulls slamming into brick walls not long after they begin to stampede.

The bottom line here is that we're looking at a market with plenty of bullish potential, but it is a market that is emotionally-driven nevertheless. Mars triggers the Moon/Mercury midpoint, so most communications and market assessments tend to have a decidedly emotional edge at this time. And don't overlook the fact that the Moon is triggering the midpoint of Zeus and

Vulcanus as well. This means plenty of intensity, excitement, and explosive potential for this period of time.

February 12, 2017

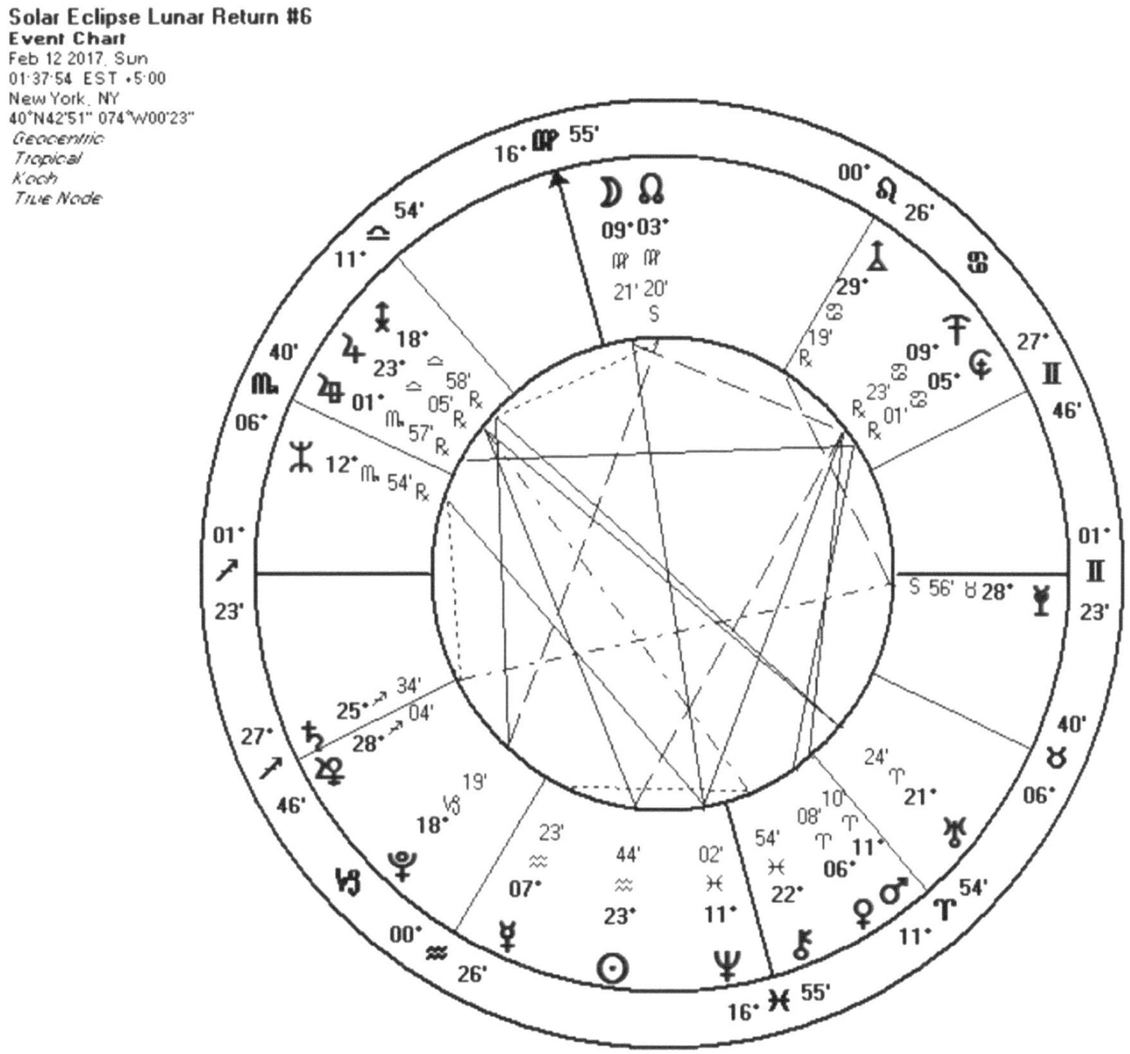

At first glance the chart for the February 12 Lunar Return seems to suggest a moderate amount of bullishness in the markets during the weeks following this event. Mars is the ruler of the fifth house in the chart, signaling active trading and an aggressive attitude toward speculation at this time.

Mars is situated on the cusp of the fifth house as well, a position which gives it additional strength, especially since it picks up the voice of authority through its square to Kronos in the eighth house.

Mars captures the energy of the Moon and Poseidon as it triggers their midpoint structure at the time of the Lunar Return. It also activates the Chiron/Vulcanus midpoint, so there are powerful decisions for traders to make, whether or not they happen to be convenient. And, with the Moon activating the Mercury/Mars midpoint as well, there should be plenty of emotional energy to drive traders into effective action during most of February and the early part of March.

There are, however, some concerns here. Even though Mars is in a powerful position and is also the final dispositor of the horoscope, the risk-taking that it promotes may not prove to be as rewarding as some traders would like.

The 11th house in this horoscope, which is concerned with the returns and rewards that come from risk-taking, is filled with potentially positive dynamics. Jupiter, Zeus, and Apollon are all posited there, so we should reasonably expect to see growing returns from the chances we are willing to take in the market environment at this time.

However, Venus, which is the ruler of the 11th house, seems somewhat stifled as it sits in the fourth house of this horoscope. By itself that is not a bad thing, but Venus is also square Hades, so the negative potential here should not bee ignored, even if this particular period turns out to be profitable in the short run.

March 11, 2017

The Lunar Return for March 11, 2017 marks a key inflection point in the cycle of Lunar Returns to the September 2016 solar eclipse. That's because it is the first Lunar Return in this cycle which occurs after the next solar eclipse, on February 26, 2017. That resonance is particularly strong because the Moon in this Lunar Return chart, like the Moon in all of the other Lunar Returns in this series, is in opposition to the February eclipse point.

In any financial horoscope, especially those associated with trading, with personal wealth, or with the speculation, we are always concerned to identify the dominant dynamics of the fifth and 11th houses in the chart. The fifth house, of course, represents the willingness to take risks, to put money into the markets, or to gamble with assets in one way or another. The 11th house, on the other hand, gives us a picture of the potential rewards involved. It represents the return on investment, the money that is received in any transaction, and the potential financial payoff of any speculative venture.

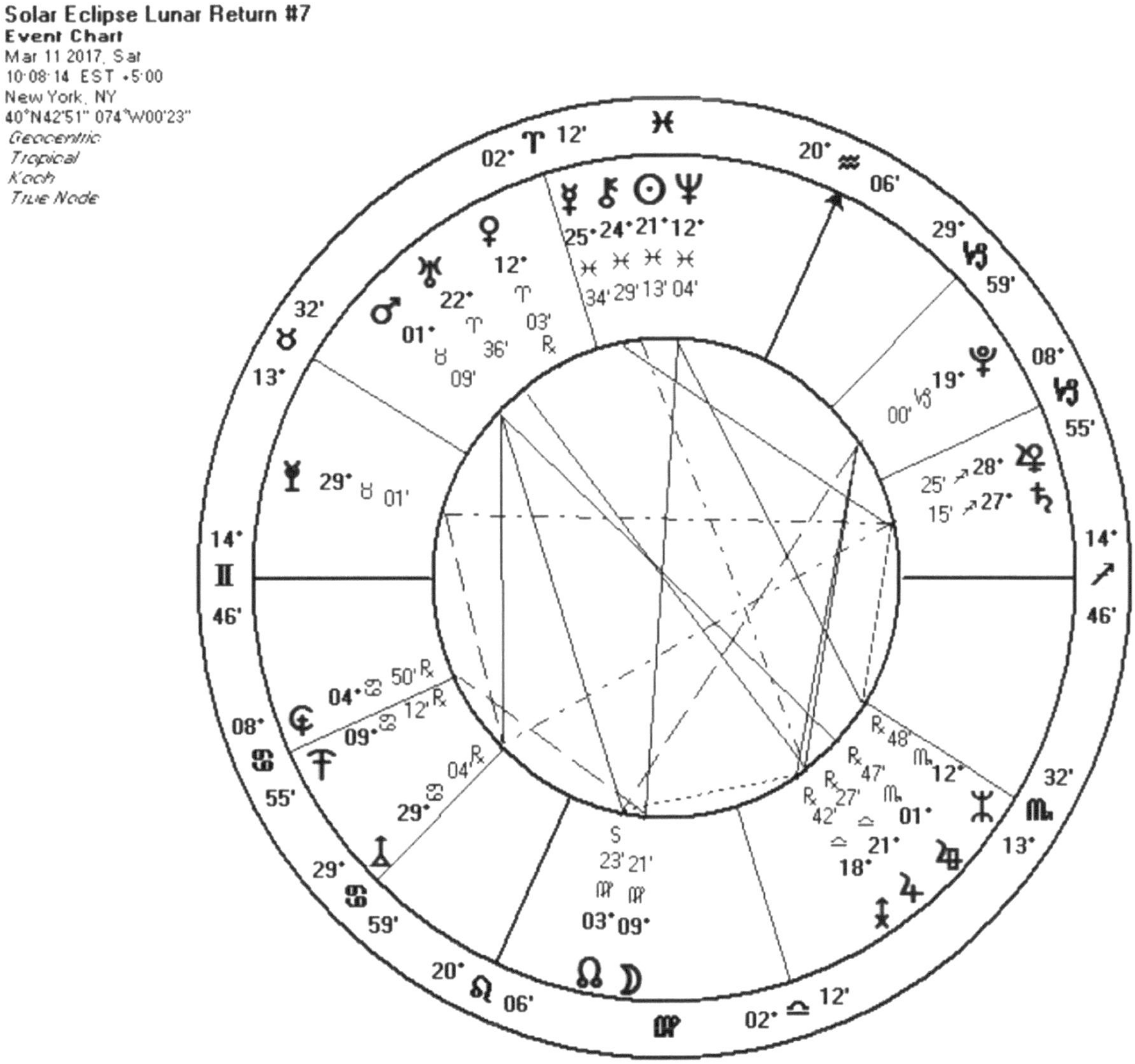

In the horoscope for the March 11 Lunar Return, Venus rules the fifth house and Mars rules the 11th house. What's noteworthy here, however, is that Venus, the ruler of the fifth, is posited in the 11th house. This creates a strong degree of connection between those two houses in the chart, signifying the high potential for positive returns from speculation at this time.

It's also worth noting that there is no single final dispositor to this horoscope. Instead, the chain of planetary energies in the chart resolves itself in a mutual reception between Venus and Mars. Mars is in Taurus, a zodiac sign ruled by Venus, while Venus is in Aries, a sign ruled by Mars. This energetic exchange creates a strong bond between the two planets, who are ready to help each other out in any transactions that may take place.

The net result is thus that there is a strong and positive connection between risk-taking and reaping the rewards associated with those risks during the weeks following this Lunar Return. While much of the market action may be overshadowed by the impact of the February solar eclipse, this Lunar Return horoscope creates a clear impression that we can expect positive outcomes in the markets and a generally bullish atmosphere for trading during the final weeks of March and the beginning of April.

April 7, 2017

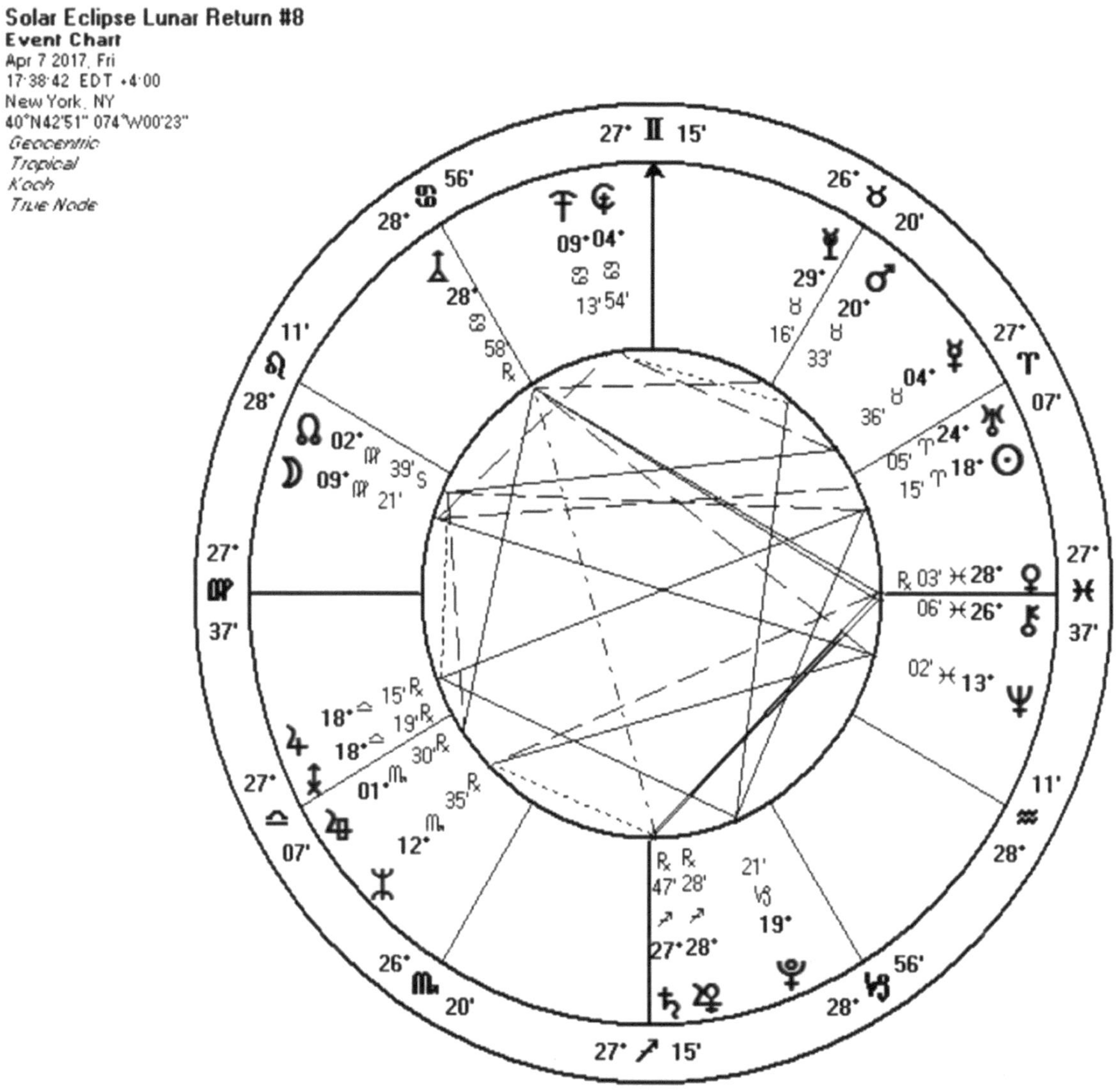

The solar eclipse Lunar Return horoscope for April 7 is particularly striking because all of its planetary alignments to chart angles. The conjunction of Saturn and Cupido is tightly aligned with the Nadir, at the bottom of the chart wheel, while the conjunction of Venus and Chiron sits astride the Descendant in the Lunar Return chart.

This emphasis on angularity through these particular planets creates a sharp focus on inhibiting factors in the financial realm. Note that Venus is the ruler of the second house of financial assets, while Saturn rules the fifth house of speculation. These two planets are not only angular; they are aligned in a stressful square, which is intensified by the fact that Venus is in retrograde motion, and thus is applying to the 90° aspect to strengthen the force of the planetary configuration.

During the previous Lunar Return we observed the potential impact of a Venus/Mars mutual reception. This Lunar Return chart also ultimately resolves itself with a mutual reception. In this case, however, it is a mutual reception between Venus and Jupiter which holds sway. Jupiter is very powerful in this chart, but it's expansive potential can create some potential friction, as is evidenced by its conjunction to Zeus and its engagement in a stressful T-square pattern with the Sun and Pluto. At the very least this is a strong indication that we can expect enormous trading volume during the final three weeks of April, with large blocks of capital dominating market movements in dramatic ways.

That dynamic should make for some very interesting trading. But with Saturn as the planetary ruler of the fifth house in this chart, our expectation is that the net outcome will be a negative one, with the bears dominating the trading environment for most of the month. Savvy traders would do well to watch for big sales of significant blocks of stock by the firms and funds that have been long-term holders of large positions. The reactions to those kind of moves could color the overall trading environment in important ways.

May 4, 2017

The final Lunar Return horoscope that we will consider in this sequence following the solar eclipse of September 2016 comes on May 4, 2017. At this point in the cycle the impact of the September solar eclipse has begun to weaken considerably, and the influence of the February solar eclipse is on the rise. With that fact in mind, it's worth noting that Mars in this Lunar Return horoscope forms a square to the Moon to create a T-square pattern with the February 26 eclipse point.

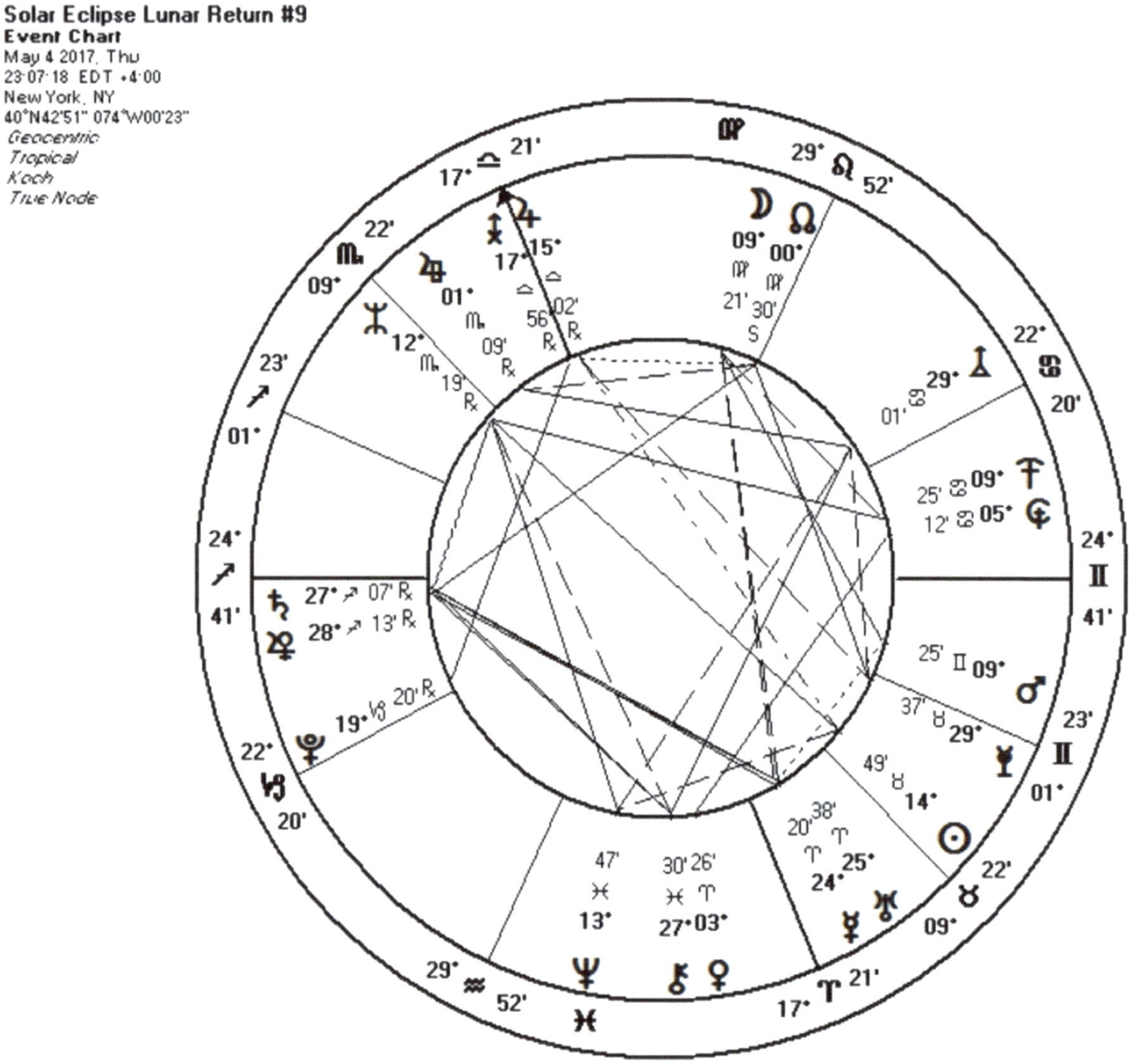

One of the major focal points for this chart is the Midheaven, which is framed by the conjunction of Jupiter and Zeus. This powerful combination suggests an expansionary thrust to the market activity at this time, with a weak square to Pluto adding to the potential for big trading volume.

The horoscope is disposited by a mutual reception between Mercury and Mars. This is an indication that while trading opportunities may seem abundant, the natural tendency for many traders will be to get stuck in analytical loops which in some cases may ultimately fail to lead to effective trading activity.

This is not a case of the typical "analysis paralysis" situation, however. We are just as likely to see trades executed, and then regretfully analyzed after the fact, as we are to see detailed analysis in play which delays trading activity so long that potentially profitable opportunities disappear.

It is likely to be an uncertain time in the markets as we close out this Lunar Return cycle, but the bias seems to be fairly bearish overall. While Jupiter is prominent at the Midheaven, it is also the ruler of the 12th house of hidden fears and apprehensions, so the potential for reactionary moves is quite strong. Venus, the ruler of the fifth house of speculation, has returned to direct motion, but is applying to a square with Hades, adding to the potential for market pessimism at this time.

The Eclipse Point, Antiscion, and Two-Eclipse Midpoint

In anticipating the potential effects of the September 2016 solar eclipse, we can work not only with upcoming transits to the eclipse point and its antiscion at 20° 39' Libra and with Lunar Returns for the eclipse horoscope, but also with transits in celestial longitude and in declination to the positions of the planets, Chiron, and the transneptunians in the solar eclipse horoscope.

We also want to be aware of 08° 46' Sagittarius as a sensitive point, since it is the zodiacal midpoint of the September solar eclipse and the next solar eclipse on February 26, 2017. This two-eclipse midpoint is often a key factor in triggering changes in market trends.

Typically when we review these sensitive points in eclipse horoscopes, we look at the transiting dynamics in the fourth harmonic, which gives us conjunctions, oppositions, and squares to the degrees in question. In this case, however, in order to simplify our observations in a way that can make for more effective trading, our main concern is the second harmonic, so we have just listed the key conjunctions and oppositions with sensitive points in the eclipse horoscope.

Because we have found the parallel and contraparallel aspects in declination to be powerful triggering factors in moving the markets, we have also added these factors to our listing of sensitive points activations.

Although the eclipse we are considering doesn't take place until early September, we have also included the transits throughout the month of August that can potentially activate the September 1 solar eclipse horoscope. Eclipses can cast significant shadows that trigger important events before the eclipses themselves actually occur, and we want to take that effect into account as we lead up to the date of the eclipse. Note as well that for a few months we have also included some of the key transits to the solar eclipse of March 2016, since that previous eclipse is still making its influence felt, although its effect is diminished.

In reviewing these dates for upcoming transits to sensitive points in eclipse horoscopes, pay particular attention to the "clusters" of eclipse activations, when several activations occur on the same day or within a period of two or three days. These occasions have a higher likelihood of being associated with significant geopolitical events, and can also bring extra energy to the market environment, amplifying market dynamics and increasing the potential for trend accelerations, break-outs, or reversals.

August 2 2016	Venus opposition March Eclipse Venus
August 2 2016	Venus opposition August Lunar Eclipse
August 3 2016	Mars opposition September Eclipse Admetos
August 3 2016	Mars contraparallel September Eclipse Kronos
August 3 2016	Mercury opposition March Eclipse Mercury
August 3 2016	Admetos parallel September Eclipse Vulcanus
August 4 2016	Mercury parallel September Eclipse Uranus
August 5 2016	Mercury contraparallel September Eclipse Neptune
August 5 2016	Venus contraparallel August Lunar Eclipse
August 5 2016	Mercury parallel September Eclipse Antiscion
August 5 2016	Mars conjunct March Eclipse Mars
August 6 2016	Mercury opposition March Eclipse Neptune
August 6 2016	Mercury conjunct September Eclipse Point
August 6 2016	Mercury parallel September Eclipse Point
August 7 2016	Mercury opposition September Eclipse Neptune
August 7 2016	Neptune contraparallel September Eclipse Antiscion
August 7 2016	Mercury parallel September Eclipse TN Node
August 7 2016	Mercury contraparallel September Eclipse Zeus
August 8 2016	Venus contraparallel September Eclipse Apollon
August 8 2016	Mercury conjunct September Eclipse TN Node
August 8 2016	Jupiter opposition September Eclipse Chiron

August 10 2016	Jupiter contraparallel September Eclipse Mercury
August 10 2016	Sun contraparallel September Eclipse Poseidon
August 10 2016	Venus opposition March Eclipse Mercury
August 12 2016	Jupiter opposition September Lunar Eclipse
August 13 2016	Venus conjunct September Eclipse Point
August 13 2016	Mercury contraparallel September Eclipse Mercury
August 13 2016	Mercury conjunct March Eclipse Jupiter
August 13 2016	Venus opposition March Eclipse Neptune
August 13 2016	Mercury opposition March Eclipse Point
August 14 2016	Venus opposition September Eclipse Neptune
August 14 2016	Chiron conjunct September Lunar Eclipse
August 14 2016	Venus parallel September Eclipse Uranus
August 15 2016	Venus contraparallel September Eclipse Neptune
August 15 2016	Mercury contraparallel September Lunar Eclipse
August 15 2016	Venus parallel September Eclipse Antiscion
August 15 2016	Venus conjunct September Eclipse TN Node
August 15 2016	Mercury opposition March Eclipse Chiron
August 16 2016	Mercury conjunct March Eclipse TN Node
August 16 2016	Mercury parallel September Eclipse Jupiter
August 16 2016	Venus parallel September Eclipse Point
August 16 2016	Mercury parallel September Eclipse Chiron
August 16 2016	TN Node contraparallel September Eclipse Zeus
August 18 2016	Venus parallel September Eclipse TN Node
August 18 2016	Venus contraparallel September Eclipse Zeus
August 18 2016	Mercury opposition September Eclipse Chiron
August 18 2016	Sun opposition March Eclipse Venus
August 18 2016	Penumbral Lunar Eclipse
August 19 2016	March Solar Eclipse Lunar Return
August 19 2016	Mercury contraparallel September Eclipse Venus
August 19 2016	Chiron parallel September Eclipse Jupiter
August 19 2016	Mercury opposition September Lunar Eclipse
August 19 2016	Mercury parallel September Eclipse Venus
August 20 2016	Venus conjunct March Eclipse Jupiter
August 20 2016	Venus opposition March Eclipse Point
August 22 2016	Venus opposition March Eclipse Chiron
August 22 2016	Mars conjunct Sept/February 2-Eclipse Midpoint
August 22 2016	Sun contraparallel September Eclipse Apollon
August 22 2016	TN Node contraparallel September Eclipse Zeus
August 23 2016	Mercury contraparallel September Eclipse Chiron
August 23 2016	Mercury contraparallel September Eclipse Jupiter
August 23 2016	Venus conjunct March Eclipse TN Node

August 24 2016	Venus opposition September Eclipse Chiron
August 24 2016	Mars conjunct September Eclipse Saturn
August 25 2016	Venus contraparallel September Eclipse Mercury
August 25 2016	Mercury parallel September Lunar Eclipse
August 25 2016	Venus opposition September Lunar Eclipse
August 25 2016	Jupiter contraparallel September Lunar Eclipse
August 25 2016	Vulcanus parallel September Eclipse Admetos
August 26 2016	Mercury conjunct September Eclipse Jupiter
August 26 2016	Admetos conjunct September Eclipse Admetos
August 27 2016	Admetos parallel September Eclipse Admetos
August 27 2016	TN Node contraparallel September Eclipse Zeus
August 27 2016	Venus contraparallel September Lunar Eclipse
August 28 2016	Mercury conjunct September Eclipse Mercury
August 28 2016	Venus conjunct September Eclipse Jupiter
August 28 2016	Venus parallel September Eclipse Jupiter
August 28 2016	Sun opposition March Eclipse Mercury
August 29 2016	Venus parallel September Eclipse Chiron
August 29 2016	Venus conjunct September Eclipse Mercury
August 30 2016	Sun parallel September Eclipse Uranus
August 31 2016	Sun contraparallel September Eclipse Neptune
August 31 2016	Venus contraparallel September Eclipse Venus
September 1 2016	Annular Solar Eclipse
September 1 2016	Sun opposition March Eclipse Neptune
September 2 2016	Sun opposition September Eclipse Neptune
September 3 2016	Mercury conjunct September Eclipse Jupiter
September 3 2016	Jupiter parallel September Eclipse Chiron
September 3 2016	Venus contraparallel September Eclipse Chiron
September 4 2016	Jupiter conjunct September Eclipse Mercury
September 4 2016	Venus contraparallel September Eclipse Jupiter
September 4 2016	Zeus contraparallel September Eclipse TN Node
September 4 2016	Sun conjunct September Eclipse TN Node
September 4 2016	Sun parallel September Eclipse TN Node
September 4 2016	Sun contraparallel September Eclipse Zeus
September 4 2016	Mars conjunct March Eclipse Saturn
September 5 2016	Venus parallel September Lunar Eclipse
September 6 2016	TN Node conjunct September Eclipse TN Node
September 6 2016	TN Node parallel September Eclipse TN Node
September 7 2016	Mercury parallel September Lunar Eclipse
September 7 2016	Venus parallel September Eclipse Mercury
September 7 2016	Venus conjunct March Eclipse Antiscion

September 8 2016	Mercury contraparallel September Eclipse Jupiter
September 9 2016	Mercury opposition September Lunar Eclipse
September 9 2016	Mercury contraparallel September Eclipse Chiron
September 9 2016	Mercury opposition September Eclipse Chiron
September 10 2016	Sun conjunct March Eclipse Jupiter
September 11 2016	Sun opposition March Eclipse Point
September 11 2016	Mercury conjunct March Eclipse TN Node
September 11 2016	TN Node parallel September Eclipse TN Node
September 11 2016	TN Node conjunct September Eclipse TN Node
September 11 2016	Mercury parallel September Eclipse Venus
September 12 2016	Mercury contraparallel September Eclipse Venus
September 12 2016	Venus conjunct September Eclipse Zeus
September 12 2016	Mercury opposition March Eclipse Chiron
September 13 2016	Sun opposition March Eclipse Chiron
September 13 2016	Venus conjunct March Eclipse Zeus
September 13 2016	Cupido conjunct September Eclipse Cupido
September 13 2016	Sun contraparallel September Eclipse Mercury
September 14 2016	Venus parallel September Eclipse Zeus
September 14 2016	Venus contraparallel September Eclipse TN Node
September 14 2016	Mercury parallel September Eclipse Chiron
September 14 2016	Mercury parallel September Eclipse Jupiter
September 14 2016	Sun conjunct March Eclipse TN Node
September 14 2016	Venus opposition March Eclipse Uranus
September 14 2016	Mercury opposition March Eclipse Point
September 15 2016	Mercury conjunct March Eclipse Jupiter
September 15 2016	Mercury contraparallel September Lunar Eclipse
September 15 2016	Sun opposition September Eclipse Chiron
September 15 2016	Venus opposition September Eclipse Antiscion
September 16 2016	Venus contraparallel September Eclipse Point
September 16 2016	Penumbral Lunar Eclipse
September 16 2016	March Solar Eclipse Lunar Return
September 16 2016	Sun contraparallel September Lunar Eclipse
September 16 2016	Venus contraparallel September Eclipse Antiscion
September 17 2016	Venus parallel September Eclipse Neptune
September 17 2016	Mercury contraparallel September Eclipse Mercury
September 18 2016	Sun parallel September Eclipse Jupiter
September 18 2016	Venus contraparallel September Eclipse Uranus
September 18 2016	Venus opposition September Eclipse Uranus
September 18 2016	Sun parallel September Eclipse Chiron
September 18 2016	TN Node conjunct September Eclipse TN Node
September 18 2016	TN Node parallel September Eclipse TN Node

September 19 2016	Jupiter contraparallel September Eclipse Venus
September 19 2016	Mars conjunct September Eclipse Cupido
September 20 2016	Sun conjunct September Eclipse Jupiter
September 21 2016	Sun conjunct September Eclipse Mercury
September 22 2016	Sun contraparallel September Eclipse Venus
September 22 2016	Jupiter conjunct September Eclipse Venus
September 22 2016	Sun parallel September Eclipse Venus
September 22 2016	Jupiter parallel September Eclipse Venus
September 22 2016	Mars conjunct March Eclipse Cupido
September 23 2016	Venus conjunct September Eclipse Apollon
September 23 2016	Venus parallel September Eclipse Apollon
September 24 2016	Admetos parallel September Eclipse Vulcanus
September 24 2016	Venus conjunct March Eclipse Apollon
September 25 2016	Sun conjunct September Eclipse Venus
September 26 2016	Sun contraparallel September Eclipse Chiron
September 26 2016	Sun contraparallel September Eclipse Jupiter
September 26 2016	Venus parallel August Lunar Eclipse
September 28 2016	Sun parallel September Lunar Eclipse
September 28 2016	September Solar Eclipse Lunar Return
September 28 2016	Mercury conjunct March Eclipse Jupiter
September 29 2016	Mercury opposition March Eclipse Point
September 30 2016	Uranus contraparallel September Eclipse Neptune
September 30 2016	Mercury opposition March Eclipse Chiron
October 1 2016	Mercury conjunct March Eclipse TN Node
October 1 2016	Sun parallel September Eclipse Mercury
October 2 2016	Venus parallel September Eclipse Poseidon
October 2 2016	Venus conjunct September Eclipse Poseidon
October 2 2016	Mercury opposition September Eclipse Chiron
October 2 2016	Neptune conjunct March Eclipse Neptune
October 2 2016	Mars opposition March Eclipse Hades
October 3 2016	Venus conjunct March Eclipse Poseidon
October 3 2016	Sun conjunct March Eclipse Antiscion
October 3 2016	Mercury opposition September Lunar Eclipse
October 4 2016	Mercury contraparallel September Eclipse Mercury
October 6 2016	Mercuryconjunct September Eclipse Jupiter
October 6 2016	Mercury contraparallel September Lunar Eclipse
October 6 2016	Mercury conjunct September Eclipse Mercury
October 6 2016	Mars opposition September Eclipse Hades
October 7 2016	Mercury parallel September Eclipse Jupiter
October 7 2016	Mercury parallel September Eclipse Chiron

October 8 2016	Jupitercontraparallel September Eclipse Chiron
October 8 2016	Mercury conjunct September Eclipse Venus
October 9 2016	Mercury contraparallel September Eclipse Venus
October 9 2016	Neptune contraparallel September Eclipse Uranus
October 9 2016	Sun conjunct September Eclipse Zeus
October 9 2016	Sun parallel September Eclipse Zeus
October 9 2016	Mars opposition March Eclipse Kronos
October 10 2016	Sun conjunct March Eclipse Zeus
October 10 2016	Zeus conjunct March Eclipse Zeus
October 10 2016	Sun contraparallel September Eclipse TN Node
October 10 2016	Mercury parallel September Eclipse Venus
October 10 2016	Jupiter contraparallel September Eclipse Jupiter
October 11 2016	Mercury contraparallel September Eclipse Chiron
October 11 2016	Chiron opposition March Eclipse TN Node
October 11 2016	Sun opposition March Eclipse Uranus
October 12 2016	Mercury contraparallel September Eclipse Jupiter
October 12 2016	Sun contraparallel September Eclipse Point
October 12 2016	Mars opposition September Eclipse Kronos
October 13 2016	Mercury parallel September Lunar Eclipse
October 13 2016	Sun contraparallel September Eclipse Sun
October 13 2016	Mars parallelSeptember Eclipse Mars
October 13 2016	Sun opposition September Eclipse Antiscion
October 13 2016	Sun contraparallel September Eclipse Antiscion
October 13 2016	Mercury conjunct March Eclipse Antiscion
October 14 2016	Sun parallel September Eclipse Neptune
October 14 2016	Mercury parallel September Eclipse Mercury
October 14 2016	Venus contraparallel September Eclipse Vulcanus
October 14 2016	Venus contraparallel September Eclipse Admetos
October 15 2016	Sun contraparallel September Eclipse Uranus
October 15 2016	Venus parallel September Eclipse Saturn
October 16 2016	Sun opposition September Eclipse Uranus
October 16 2016	Venus opposition March Eclipse Admetos
October 17 2016	Mercury conjunct March Eclipse Zeus
October 17 2016	Mercury conjunct September Eclipse Zeus
October 17 2016	Jupiter parallel September Lunar Eclipse
October 17 2016	Uranus parallel September Eclipse Antiscion
October 18 2016	Venus opposition September Eclipse Admetos
October 18 2016	Venus parallel September Eclipse Pluto
October 18 2016	Mercury opposition March Eclipse Uranus
October 19 2016	Venus conjunct March Eclipse Mars
October 19 2016	Mercury parallel September Eclipse Zeus

October 19 2016	Mercury contraparallel September Eclipse TN Node
October 19 2016	Mercury opposition September Eclipse Antiscion
October 19 2016	Mars conjunct September Eclipse Pluto
October 19 2016	Venus parallel Sept/February 2-Eclipse Midpoint
October 20 2016	Mercury contraparallel September Eclipse Point
October 20 2016	Mercury contraparallel September Eclipse Sun
October 21 2016	Mercury contraparallel September Eclipse Antiscion
October 21 2016	Pluto conjunct September Eclipse Pluto
October 21 2016	Mercury opposition September Eclipse Uranus
October 21 2016	Mercury parallel September Eclipse Neptune
October 21 2016	Mercury contraparallelSeptember Eclipse Uranus
October 22 2016	Venus contraparallel September Eclipse Hades
October 22 2016	Uranus parallel September Eclipse Sun
October 22 2016	Venus parallel September Eclipse Cupido
October 22 2016	Mars conjunct Pluto
October 23 2016	Sun conjunct September Eclipse Apollon
October 23 2016	Sun parallel September Eclipse Apollon
October 24 2016	Venus contraparallel September Eclipse Kronos
October 24 2016	Mercury conjunct September Eclipse Apollon
October 24 2016	Sun conjunct March Eclipse Apollon
October 25 2016	Mercury conjunct March Eclipse Apollon
October 25 2016	September Solar Eclipse Lunar Return
October 25 2016	Venus conjunct Sept/February 2-Eclipse Midpoint
October 25 2016	Mercury parallel September Eclipse Apollon
October 26 2016	Venus conjunct September Eclipse Saturn
October 26 2016	Sun parallel August Lunar Eclipse
October 27 2016	Mercury parallel August Lunar Eclipse
October 29 2016	Saturn conjunct September Eclipse Mars
October 29 2016	Venus conjunct September Eclipse Mars
October 29 2016	Saturn opposition March/Sept 2-Eclipse Midpoint
October 29 2016	Venus opposition March/Sept 2-Eclipse Midpoint
October 31 2016	Jupiter conjunct March Eclipse Antiscion
October 31 2016	Venus conjunct March Eclipse Saturn
October 31 2016	Neptune opposition September Eclipse Point
October 31 2016	Mercury conjunct September Eclipse Poseidon
October 31 2016	Mercury parallel September Eclipse Poseidon
November 1 2016	Jupiter parallel September Eclipse Mercury
November 2 2016	Mars contraparallel September Eclipse Kronos
November 2 2016	TN Node opposition September Eclipse Neptune
November 3 2016	Sun conjunct September Eclipse Poseidon

November 3 2016	Sun parallel September Eclipse Poseidon
November 5 2016	Mars parallel September Eclipse Cupido
November 6 2016	Venus parallel September Eclipse Mars
November 6 2016	Mars contraparallel September Eclipse Hades
November 7 2016	Venus conjunct September Eclipse Cupido
November 8 2016	Mars opposition September Eclipse Vulcanus
November 9 2016	Mercury contraparallel September Eclipse Vulcanus
November 9 2016	Mercury contraparallel September Eclipse Admetos
November 9 2016	Mars parallel Sept/February 2-Eclipse Midpoint
November 10 2016	Mercury parallel September Eclipse Saturn
November 11 2016	Hades conjunct September Eclipse Hades
November 11 2016	Saturn parallel September Eclipse Pluto
November 11 2016	Uranu parallel September Eclipse Point
November 12 2016	TN Node parallel September Eclipse Point
November 12 2016	Mars parallel September Eclipse Pluto
November 12 2016	Mercury parallel September Eclipse Pluto
November 12 2016	Mercury opposition September Eclipse Admetos
November 13 2016	Mercury parallel Sept/February 2-Eclipse Midpoint
November 14 2016	Mercury contraparallel September Eclipse Hades
November 15 2016	Mercury parallel September Eclipse Cupido
November 16 2016	Mercury contraparallel September Eclipse Kronos
November 16 2016	TN Node parallel September Eclipse Sun
November 16 2016	TN Node conjunct September Eclipse Point
November 16 2016	Mars parallel September Eclipse Saturn
November 17 2016	Venus opposition September Eclipse Hades
November 17 2016	Kronos parallel September Eclipse Kronos
November 18 2016	Mars contraparallel September Eclipse Admetos
November 18 2016	Kronos conjunct September Eclipse Kronos
November 18 2016	Mars contraparallel September Eclipse Vulcanus
November 18 2016	Mercury conjunct Sept/February 2-Eclipse Midpoint
November 18 2016	TN Node parallel September Eclipse Antiscion
November 19 2016	Mercury conjunct September Eclipse Saturn
November 20 2016	Chiron contraparallel September Eclipse Venus
November 20 2016	Venus opposition September Eclipse Kronos
November 21 2016	Mercury conjunct September Eclipse Mars
November 21 2016	Sun contraparallel September Eclipse Vulcanus
November 21 2016	September Solar Eclipse Lunar Return
November 21 2016	Sun opposition September Eclipse Admetos
November 21 2016	Sun contraparallel September Eclipse Admetos
November 22 2016	Venus parallel September Eclipse Mars
November 23 2016	Sun parallel September Eclipse Saturn

November 24 2016	Venus conjunct September Eclipse Pluto
November 25 2016	Mercury parallel September Eclipse Mars
November 27 2016	TN Node contraparallel September Eclipse Neptune
November 27 2016	Sun parallel September Eclipse Pluto
November 29 2016	Mercury conjunct September Eclipse Cupido
November 30 2016	Sun conjunct Sept/February 2-Eclipse Midpoint
November 30 2016	Sun parallel Sept/February 2-Eclipse Midpoint
December 1 2016	Sun conjunct September Eclipse Saturn
December 1 2016	TN Node parallel September Eclipse Uranus
December 3 2016	Jupiter conjunct September Eclipse Zeus
December 4 2016	Sun contraparallel September Eclipse Hades
December 4 2016	Uranus conjunct September Eclipse Antiscion
December 5 2016	Venus contraparallel September Eclipse Kronos
December 5 2016	Sun conjunct September Eclipse Mars
December 6 2016	Sun parallel September Eclipse Cupido
December 6 2016	Venus parallel September Eclipse Cupido
December 7 2016	Venus opposition September Eclipse Vulcanus
December 7 2016	Mercury opposition September Eclipse Hades
December 7 2016	Venus contraparallel September Eclipse Hades
December 9 2016	Mars parallel September Eclipse Poseidon
December 9 2016	Neptune opposition September Eclipse Point
December 9 2016	Mercury parallel September Eclipse Mars
December 10 2016	Venus parallel Sept/February 2-Eclipse Midpoint
December 11 2016	Sun contraparallel September Eclipse Kronos
December 11 2016	Mercury opposition September Eclipse Kronos
December 11 2016	Venus parallel September Eclipse Pluto
December 13 2016	Mars conjunct August Lunar Eclipse
December 14 2016	Venus parallel September Eclipse Saturn
December 15 2016	Venus contraparallel September Eclipse Admetos
December 15 2016	Venus contraparallel September Eclipse Vulcanus
December 16 2016	Sun conjunct September Eclipse Cupido
December 17 2016	Mars parallel August Lunar Eclipse
December 18 2016	Saturn parallel Sept/February 2-Eclipse Midpoint
December 18 2016	Mercury conjunct September Eclipse Pluto
December 18 2016	Hades parallel September Eclipse Hades
December 19 2016	September Solar Eclipse Lunar Return
December 19 2016	Mercury contraparallel September Eclipse Kronos
December 19 2016	Mercury conjunct September Eclipse Pluto
December 20 2016	Mercury parallel September Eclipse Cupido
December 21 2016	Mercury contraparallel September Eclipse Hades

December 22 2016	Mars parallel September Eclipse Apollon
December 24 2016	Mercury parallel Sept/February 2-Eclipse Midpoint
December 24 2016	Jupiter parallel September Eclipse Zeus
December 24 2016	Jupiter contraparallel September Eclipse TN Node
December 25 2016	Mercury parallel September Eclipse Pluto
December 26 2016	Mercury opposition September Eclipse Kronos
December 27 2016	Vulcanus parallel September Eclipse Vulcanus
December 27 2016	Vulcanus conjunct September Eclipse Vulcanus
December 27 2016	Neptune contraparallel September Eclipse Uranus
December 27 2016	Sun opposition September Eclipse Hades
December 28 2016	Venus parallel September Eclipse Poseidon
December 28 2016	Jupiter opposition September Eclipse Antiscion
December 29 2016	Mercury opposition September Eclipse Hades
December 30 2016	Venus conjunct August Lunar Eclipse
December 31 2016	Mercury parallel September Eclipse Saturn
December 31 2016	Sun contraparallel September Eclipse Kronos
December 31 2016	Sun opposition September Eclipse Kronos
December 31 2016	Mars opposition September Eclipse Point
January 1 2017	Mars contraparallel September Eclipse Uranus
January 2 2017	Mars parallel September Eclipse Neptune
January 2 2017	Mars conjunct September Eclipse Neptune
January 2 2017	Venus parallel August Lunar Eclipse
January 2 2017	Vulcanus parallel September Eclipse Admetos
January 3 2017	Mars contraparallel September Eclipse Antiscion
January 3 2017	Mercury contraparallel September Eclipse Admetos
January 4 2017	Mercury contraparallel September Eclipse Admetos
January 4 2017	Mars contraparallel September Eclipse Point
January 4 2017	Chiron contraparallel September Eclipse Venus
January 5 2017	Mars opposition September Eclipse TN Node
January 5 2017	Sun conjunct September Eclipse Pluto
January 5 2017	Sun parallel September Eclipse Cupido
January 5 2017	Venus parallel September Eclipse Apollon
January 7 2017	Sun contraparallel September Eclipse Hades
January 7 2017	Mars contraparallel September Eclipse TN Node
January 7 2017	Mars parallel September Eclipse Zeus
January 8 2017	Mercury parallel September Eclipse Saturn
January 10 2017	Pluto parallel September Eclipse Pluto
January 11 2017	Sun parallel Sept/February 2-Eclipse Midpoint
January 11 2017	Venus contraparallel September Eclipse Uranus
January 12 2017	Venus opposition September Eclipse Point

January 12 2017	Venus parallel September Eclipse Neptune
January 12 2017	Venus contraparallel September Eclipse Antiscion
January 13 2017	Venus conjunct September Eclipse Neptune
January 13 2017	Sun parallel September Eclipse Pluto
January 13 2017	Venus contraparallel September Eclipse Point
January 14 2017	Mercury parallel September Eclipse Pluto
January 15 2017	September Solar Eclipse Lunar Return
January 15 2017	Venus opposition September Eclipse TN Node
January 15 2017	Venus contraparallel September Eclipse TN Node
January 15 2017	Venus parallel September Eclipse Zeus
January 17 2017	Mercury parallel Sept/February 2-Eclipse Midpoint
January 18 2017	Mars parallel September Eclipse Mercury
January 18 2017	Sun parallel September Eclipse Saturn
January 19 2017	Sun contraparallel September Eclipse Admetos
January 19 2017	Mars conjunct September Eclipse Chiron
January 19 2017	Sun contraparallel September Eclipse Vulcanus
January 19 2017	Sun opposition September Eclipse Vulcanus
January 20 2017	Mercury opposition September Eclipse Hades
January 20 2017	Mars conjunct September Lunar Eclipse
January 22 2017	Mars parallel September Lunar Eclipse
January 22 2017	Uranus conjunct September Eclipse Antiscion
January 22 2017	Venus parallel September Eclipse Mercury
January 22 2017	Mercury contraparallel September Eclipse Hades
January 23 2017	Mercury opposition September Eclipse Kronos
January 23 2017	Mars contraparallel September Eclipse Jupiter
January 24 2017	Mars contraparallel September Eclipse Chiron
January 25 2017	Venus parallel September Lunar Eclipse
January 25 2017	Mars opposition September Eclipse Jupiter
January 26 2017	Venus contraparallel September Eclipse Jupiter
January 26 2017	Mars opposition September Eclipse Mercury
January 26 2017	Venus conjunct September Eclipse Chiron
January 26 2017	Venus contraparallel September Eclipse Chiron
January 27 2017	Mercury conjunct September Eclipse Pluto
January 27 2017	Venus conjunct September Lunar Eclipse
January 28 2017	Mars parallel September Eclipse Venus
January 29 2017	Venus parallel September Eclipse Venus
January 29 2017	Mars contraparallel September Eclipse Venus
January 30 2017	Neptune parallel September Eclipse Neptune
January 30 2017	Venus contraparallel September Eclipse Venus
January 31 2017	Mercury contraparallel September Eclipse Hades
January 31 2017	Mars opposition September Eclipse Venus

February 1 2017	Venus opposition September Eclipse Jupiter
February 1 2017	Neptune conjunct September Eclipse Neptune
February 2 2017	Venus opposition September Eclipse Mercury
February 2 2017	Venus parallel September Eclipse Chiron
February 2 2017	Venus parallel September Eclipse Jupiter
February 3 2017	Mars parallel September Eclipse Chiron
February 3 2017	Mars parallel September Eclipse Jupiter
February 4 2017	Venus contraparallel September Lunar Eclipse
February 4 2017	Saturn conjunct September Eclipse Cupido
February 5 2017	Mercury parallel Sept/February 2-Eclipse Midpoint
February 5 2017	Mars contraparallel September Lunar Eclipse
February 6 2017	Venus contraparallel September Eclipse Mercury
February 6 2017	Sun parallel September Eclipse Poseidon
February 7 2017	Mercury opposition September Eclipse Vulcanus
February 7 2017	Venus opposition September Eclipse Venus
February 7 2017	Mercury parallel September Eclipse Pluto
February 9 2017	Mars contraparallel September Eclipse Mercury
February 9 2017	Uranus parallel September Eclipse Point
February 10 2017	Mercury parallel September Eclipse Saturn
February 10 2017	Penumbral Lunar Eclipe
February 11 2017	Mercury contraparallel September Eclipse Admetos
February 11 2017	Mercury contraparallel September Eclipse Vulcanus
February 12 2017	September Solar Eclipse Lunar Return
February 14 2017	Sun parallel August Lunar Eclipse
February 14 2017	Sun conjunct August Lunar Eclipse
February 14 2017	Venus contraparallel September Eclipse Zeus
February 14 2017	Venus parallel September Eclipse TN Node
February 17 2017	Venus parallel September Eclipse Point
February 17 2017	Sun parallel September Eclipse Apollon
February 18 2017	Neptune contraparallel September Eclipse Antiscion
February 18 2017	Venus parallel September Eclipse Sun
February 18 2017	Venus parallel September Eclipse Antiscion
February 19 2017	Venus contraparallel September Eclipse Neptune
February 20 2017	Mars opposition September Eclipse Zeus
February 20 2017	Venus parallel September Eclipse Uranus
February 20 2017	Mars contraparallel September Eclipse Zeus
February 20 2017	Mars parallel September Eclipse TN Node
February 22 2017	Neptune contraparallel September Eclipse Sun
February 22 2017	Mercury parallel September Eclipse Poseidon
February 23 2017	Mercury conjunct August Lunar Eclipse

February 23 2017	Chiron conjunct September Eclipse Chiron
February 24 2017	Mars parallel September Eclipse Point
February 25 2017	Mars parallel September Eclipse Sun
February 25 2017	Mars conjunct September Eclipse Antiscion
February 25 2017	Mars parallel September Eclipse Antiscion
February 25 2017	Sun contraparallel September Eclipse Uranus
February 26 2017	Mars contraparallel September Eclipse Neptune
February 26 2017	Mercury parallel August Lunar Eclipse
February 26 2017	Sun parallel September Eclipse Neptune
February 26 2017	Annular Solar Eclipse
February 27 2017	Sun contraparallel September Eclipse Antiscion
February 27 2017	Mars parallel September Eclipse Uranus
February 27 2017	Sun opposition September Eclipse Point
February 27 2017	Sun opposition September Eclipse Sun
February 27 2017	Sun contraparallel September Eclipse Sun
February 28 2017	Uranus parallel September Eclipse Sun
February 28 2017	Sun contraparallel September Eclipse Point
February 28 2017	Mercury parallel September Eclipse Apollon
February 28 2017	Sun conjunct September Eclipse Neptune

March 1 2017	Mars conjunct September Eclipse Uranus
March 2 2017	Sun opposition September Eclipse TN Node
March 2 2017	Sun contraparallel September Eclipse TN Node
March 2 2017	Mercury opposition September Eclipse Point
March 2 2017	Sun parallel September Eclipse Zeus
March 3 2017	Mercury conjunct September Eclipse Neptune
March 3 2017	Uranus parallel September Eclipse Antiscion
March 4 2017	Venus contraparallel September Eclipse Apollon
March 4 2017	Mercury contraparallel September Eclipse Uranus
March 4 2017	Mercury opposition September Eclipse TN Node
March 4 2017	Mercury parallel September Eclipse Neptune
March 5 2017	Mercury contraparallel September Eclipse Antiscion
March 5 2017	Mercury contraparallel September Eclipse Sun
March 5 2017	Mercury contraparallel September Eclipse Point
March 6 2017	Mercury contraparallel September Eclipse TN Node
March 6 2017	Mercury parallel September Eclipse Zeus
March 8 2017	Chiron conjunct September Lunar Eclipse
March 9 2017	Mars contraparallel September Eclipse Apollon
March 10 2017	Mars opposition September Eclipse Apollon
March 10 2017	Mercury conjunct September Eclipse Chiron
March 10 2017	Mercury parallel September Eclipse Mercury

March 10 2017	Mercury conjunct September Lunar Eclipse
March 11 2017	September Solar Eclipse Lunar Return
March 11 2017	Sun parallel September Eclipse Mercury
March 12 2017	Mercury parallel September Lunar Eclipse
March 12 2017	Mercury contraparallel September Eclipse Jupiter
March 12 2017	Mercury opposition September Eclipse Jupiter
March 12 2017	Mercury contraparallel September Eclipse Chiron
March 13 2017	Mercury opposition September Eclipse Mercury
March 13 2017	Sun conjunct September Eclipse Chiron
March 14 2017	Mercury parallel September Eclipse Venus
March 14 2017	Sun parallel September Lunar Eclipse
March 14 2017	Sun conjunct September Lunar Eclipse
March 14 2017	Mercury contraparallel September Eclipse Venus
March 14 2017	Neptune contraparallel September Eclipse Point
March 14 2017	Mars contraparallel August Lunar Eclipse
March 15 2017	Jupiter contraparallel September Eclipse TN Node
March 15 2017	Mercury opposition September Eclipse Venus
March 15 2017	Jupiter parallel September Eclipse Zeus
March 16 2017	Sun contraparallel September Eclipse Jupiter
March 16 2017	Mercury parallel September Eclipse Chiron
March 16 2017	Mercury parallel September Eclipse Jupiter
March 16 2017	Sun contraparallel September Eclipse Chiron
March 16 2017	Mercury contraparallel September Lunar Eclipse
March 17 2017	Uranus contraparallel September Eclipse Neptune
March 17 2017	Venus contraparallel September Eclipse Apollon
March 17 2017	Jupiter opposition September Eclipse Antiscion
March 18 2017	Mercury contraparallel September Eclipse Mercury
March 18 2017	Sun opposition September Eclipse Jupiter
March 19 2017	Sun opposition September Eclipse Mercury
March 19 2017	Sun parallel September Eclipse Venus
March 20 2017	Chiron parallel September Eclipse Chiron
March 20 2017	Sun contraparallel September Eclipse Venus
March 21 2017	Mercury contraparallel September Eclipse Zeus
March 21 2017	Mercury parallel September Eclipse TN Node
March 22 2017	Mercury opposition September Eclipse Zeus
March 23 2017	Mercury parallel September Eclipse Point
March 23 2017	Sun opposition September Eclipse Venus
March 23 2017	Mercury parallel September Eclipse Antiscion
March 23 2017	Mercury contraparallel September Eclipse Neptune
March 24 2017	Sun parallel September Eclipse Chiron
March 24 2017	Mercury parallel September Eclipse Uranus

March 24 2017	Mars contraparallel September Eclipse Poseidon
March 24 2017	Sun parallel September Eclipse Jupiter
March 24 2017	Mercury conjunct September Eclipse Antiscion
March 25 2017	Mars opposition September Eclipse Poseidon
March 26 2017	Sun contraparallel September Lunar Eclipse
March 26 2017	Mercury conjunct September Eclipse Uranus
March 27 2017	Venus parallel September Eclipse Uranus
March 27 2017	Mercury contraparallel September Eclipse Apollon
March 28 2017	Venus opposition September Eclipse Venus
March 28 2017	Venus contraparallel September Eclipse Neptune
March 29 2017	Sun contraparallel September Eclipse Mercury
March 29 2017	Neptune opposition September Eclipse TN Node
March 29 2017	Chiron parallel September Eclipse Jupiter
March 29 2017	Venus parallel September Eclipse Antiscion
March 29 2017	Mercury contraparallel August Lunar Eclipse
March 30 2017	Venus parallel September Eclipse Point
March 31 2017	Mercury opposition September Eclipse Apollon

April 2 2017	Venus parallel September Eclipse TN Node
April 2 2017	Venus contraparallel September Eclipse Zeus
April 4 2017	Uranus parallel September Eclipse Uranus
April 4 2017	Mercury contraparallel September Eclipse Poseidon
April 5 2017	Venus opposition September Eclipse Mercury
April 6 2017	Sun opposition September Eclipse Zeus
April 6 2017	Sun contraparallel September Eclipse Zeus
April 6 2017	Sun parallel September Eclipse TN Node
April 7 2017	Venus opposition September Eclipse Jupiter
April 7 2017	September Solar Eclipse Lunar Return
April 7 2017	Uranus conjunct September Eclipse Uranus
April 9 2017	Sun parallel September Eclipse Point
April 10 2017	Sun conjunct September Eclipse Antiscion
April 10 2017	Sun parallel September Eclipse Antiscion
April 11 2017	Sun contraparallel September Eclipse Neptune
April 12 2017	Sun parallel September Eclipse Uranus
April 12 2017	Venus contraparallel September Eclipse Mercury
April 13 2017	Sun conjunct September Eclipse Uranus
April 14 2017	Mercury contraparallel September Eclipse Poseidon
April 15 2017	Jupiter conjunct September Eclipse Zeus
April 18 2017	Mars parallel September Eclipse Vulcanus
April 18 2017	Mars parallel September Eclipse Admetos
April 18 2017	Venus contraparallel September Lunar Eclipse

April 19 2017	Mars contraparallel September Eclipse Saturn
April 20 2017	Sun opposition September Eclipse Apollon
April 20 2017	Sun contraparallel September Eclipse Apollon
April 20 2017	Mercury opposition September Eclipse Apollon
April 20 2017	Mercury contraparallel August Lunar Eclipse
April 21 2017	Mars conjunct September Eclipse Admetos
April 23 2017	Mercury contraparallel September Eclipse Apollon
April 23 2017	Venus parallel September Eclipse Jupiter
April 23 2017	Venus opposition September Eclipse Jupiter
April 23 2017	Sun contraparallel August Lunar Eclipse
April 24 2017	Chiron contraparallel September Lunar Eclipse
April 25 2017	Mars contraparallel September Eclipse Pluto
April 25 2017	Venus opposition September Eclipse Mercury
April 28 2017	Mars contraparallel Sept/Feb 2-Eclipse Midpoint
April 29 2017	Mercury parallel September Eclipse Uranus
April 30 2017	Mercury contraparallel September Eclipse Neptune

May 1 2017	Sun opposition September Eclipse Poseidon
May 1 2017	Sun contraparallel September Eclipse Poseidon
May 1 2017	Mercury parallel September Eclipse Antiscion
May 1 2017	Venus parallel September Eclipse Jupiter
May 2 2017	Mercury parallel September Eclipse Point
May 3 2017	Mars parallel September Eclipse Hades
May 3 2017	Venus opposition September Eclipse Venus
May 4 2017	September Solar Eclipse Lunar Return
May 4 2017	Mars opposition Sept/February 2-Eclipse Midpoint
May 5 2017	Mars contraparallel September Eclipse Cupido
May 5 2017	Mars opposition September Eclipse Saturn
May 8 2017	Venus contraparallel September Lunar Eclipse
May 9 2017	Mars parallel September Eclipse Kronos
May 11 2017	TN Node contraparallel September Eclipse Apollon
May 11 2017	Mars opposition September Eclipse Mars
May 13 2017	Mercury parallel September Eclipse Point
May 15 2017	Mercury parallel September Eclipse Antiscion
May 15 2017	Venus contraparallel September Eclipse Mercury
May 16 2017	Mercury contraparallel September Eclipse Neptune
May 16 2017	Mercury opposition September Eclipse Apollon
May 17 2017	Mercury parallel September Eclipse Uranus
May 20 2017	Sun parallel September Eclipse Vulcanus
May 20 2017	Sun conjunct September Eclipse Admetos
May 20 2017	Sun parallel September Eclipse Admetos

May 22 2017	Sun contraparallel September Eclipse Saturn
May 23 2017	Venus opposition September Eclipse Zeus
May 24 2017	Mercury contraparallel September Eclipse Apollon
May 25 2017	Chiron opposition September Eclipse Jupiter
May 26 2017	Mercury opposition September Eclipse Poseidon
May 27 2017	Sun contraparallel September Eclipse Pluto
May 27 2017	Mercury contraparallel August Lunar Eclipse
May 27 2017	Venus conjunct September Eclipse Antiscion
May 27 2017	Mars opposition September Eclipse Cupido
May 28 2017	Venus contraparallel September Eclipse Zeus
May 28 2017	Venus parallel September Eclipse TN Node
May 29 2017	Sun opposition Sept/February 2-Eclipse Midpoint
May 29 2017	Sun contraparallel Sept/February 2-Eclipse Midpoint
May 30 2017	Venus conjunct September Eclipse Uranus
May 31 2017	Sun opposition September Eclipse Saturn
May 31 2017	Mercury contraparallel September Eclipse Poseidon

Eclipse Trading Opportunities

While it's interesting to review the history of past eclipses and to speculate about the overall impact that the eclipse of March 8, 2016 will have on the market in general, it's also useful to identify specific trading opportunities in individual equities that are linked to the eclipse.

In reviewing potential candidates for eclipse related trades, we are first of all concerned with identifying those stocks whose First-Trade horoscopes are significantly impacted by the eclipse itself. When a solar eclipse conjoins the First-Trade Sun or the First-Trade Midheaven, experience has shown that we are more likely to see that particular stock appreciate in value during the months following the eclipse.

In some cases, there will be an opportunity to take profits in these stocks when the Sun squares the eclipse point or when it conjoins the two-eclipse midpoint. In cases where the trade has turned profitable, however, it may be advisable to take some money off the table at one or both of those occasions, while leaving a portion of the position open for possible future price appreciation. That kind of decision, of course, is left up to the discretion of the individual astro-trader.

It's important to note that an activation of the First-Trade horoscope by a solar eclipse is not sufficient in and of itself to warrant indiscriminate buying of the stock. In all of our stock selections we are concerned not only about the astrological dynamics at work, but also about corporate fundamentals and about the technical picture presented by the stock's trading history. When an eclipse activates significant planetary pictures or midpoint structures in the First-Trade horoscope, we are far more likely to consider that stock as a possible trading candidate.

Here are four individual stocks that offer some potential for price appreciation following the solar eclipse on September 1, 2016. In each case, our trading strategy will be to put on a long position soon after the eclipse takes place. This is typically within a couple of weeks following the eclipse (in some cases waiting for price pull-backs where appropriate for optimum purchasing opportunities).

Our plan is to set an initial stop on each trade to minimize risk exposure, to trail a stop if a trade turns profitable, and then, if we are still in the trade, to reevaluate our positions around November 30, 2016, when we will get the Sun's conjunction and parallel with the September/February two-eclipse midpoint, as well as the transiting Sun square the September Eclipse Point.

ABIOMED, Inc. (NASDAQ - ABMD)

ABIOMED, Inc. engages in the research, development, and sale of medical devices to assist or replace the pumping function of the failing heart. It also provides continuum of care to heart failure patients. The company offers Impella 2.5 catheter, a percutaneous micro heart pump with integrated motor and sensors for use in interventional cardiology; Impella CP that provides partial circulatory support using an extracorporeal bypass control unit; Impella 5.0 catheter and Impella LD, which are percutaneous micro heart pumps with integrated motors and sensors for use primarily in the heart surgery suite; and Impella RP, a percutaneous catheter-based axial flow pump. It also manufactures and sells AB5000 circulatory support system for temporary support of acute heart failure patients in profound shock, including patients suffering from cardiogenic shock after a heart attack, post-cardiotomy cardiogenic shock, or myocarditis. In addition, the company engages in the research, development, prototyping, and the pre-serial production of a percutaneous expandable catheter pump, which enhances blood circulation from the heart with an external drive shaft. It sells its products through direct sales and clinical support personnel in the United States, Canada, Europe, and Japan. ABIOMED, Inc. was founded in 1981 and is headquartered in Danvers, Massachusetts. The planetary price lines in our trading chart are for geocentric Venus and Kronos in the fourth harmonic.

ABMD
New York, NY
Aug 31 1992
9:30:00 AM EDT

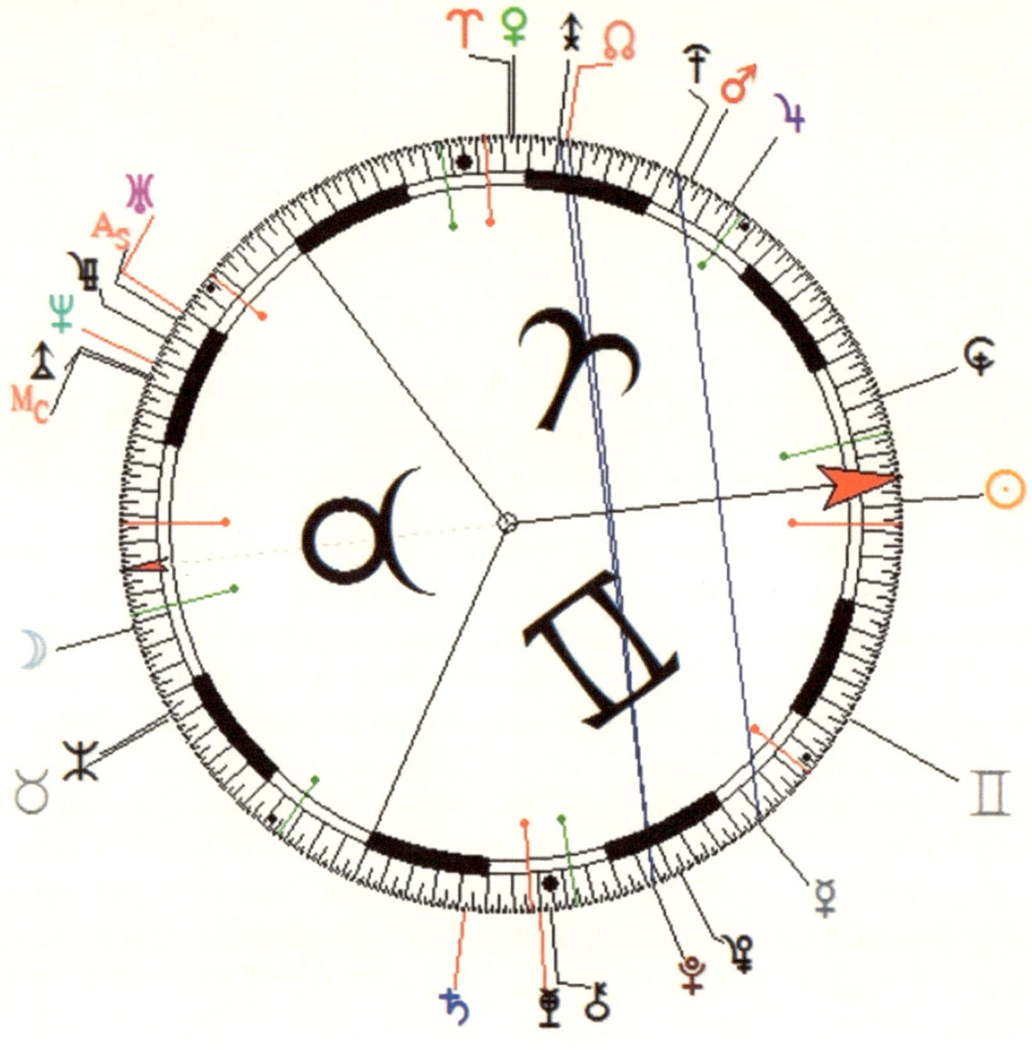

The September solar eclipse activates the Mercury/Kronos midpoint, the Pluto/True Lunar Node midpoint and the Pluto/Zeus midpoint in the ABMD First-Trade horoscope.

Amphastar Pharmaceuticals, Inc. (NASDAQ - AMPH)

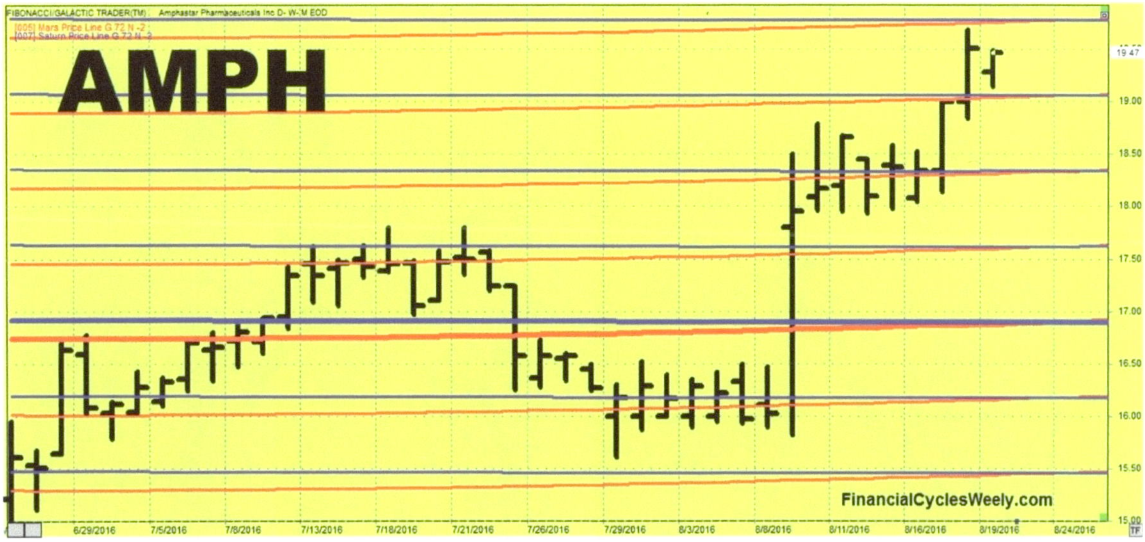

Amphastar Pharmaceuticals, Inc., a specialty pharmaceutical company, develops, manufactures, and markets generic and proprietary injectable, inhalation, and intranasal products. It operates in two segments, Finished Pharmaceutical Products and Active Pharmaceutical Ingredients. The company's products include Enoxaparin, a low molecular weight heparin that is used as an anticoagulant for prevention and treatment of deep vein thrombosis; Cortrosyn, a lyophilized powder for use as a diagnostic agent in the screening of patients presumed with adrenocortical insufficiency; Amphadase, a bovine-sourced hyaluronidase injection for the dispersion and absorption of other injected drugs; and Lidocaine jelly, a local anesthetic product used primarily for urological procedures. It also provides Lidocaine topical solution; phytonadione injection for newborn babies; syringe products, which include critical care drugs, such as morphine, atropine, calcium chloride, dextrose, lidocaine, naloxone, and sodium bicarbonate for emergency use; and epinephrine in vial form; and lorazepam injection, a sedative for surgery and medical procedures. In addition, the company develops Primatene Mist HFA, an over-the-counter epinephrine inhalation product for the temporary relief of mild symptoms of intermittent asthma; and active pharmaceutical ingredients, such as recombinant human insulin and porcine insulin. Further, it has a pipeline of 21 generic and proprietary product candidates in various stages of development for various indications. The company was established in 1996 and is headquartered in Rancho Cucamonga, California. In tracking this stock with planetary price lines, we're using geocentric Mars and Saturn in the fifth harmonic.

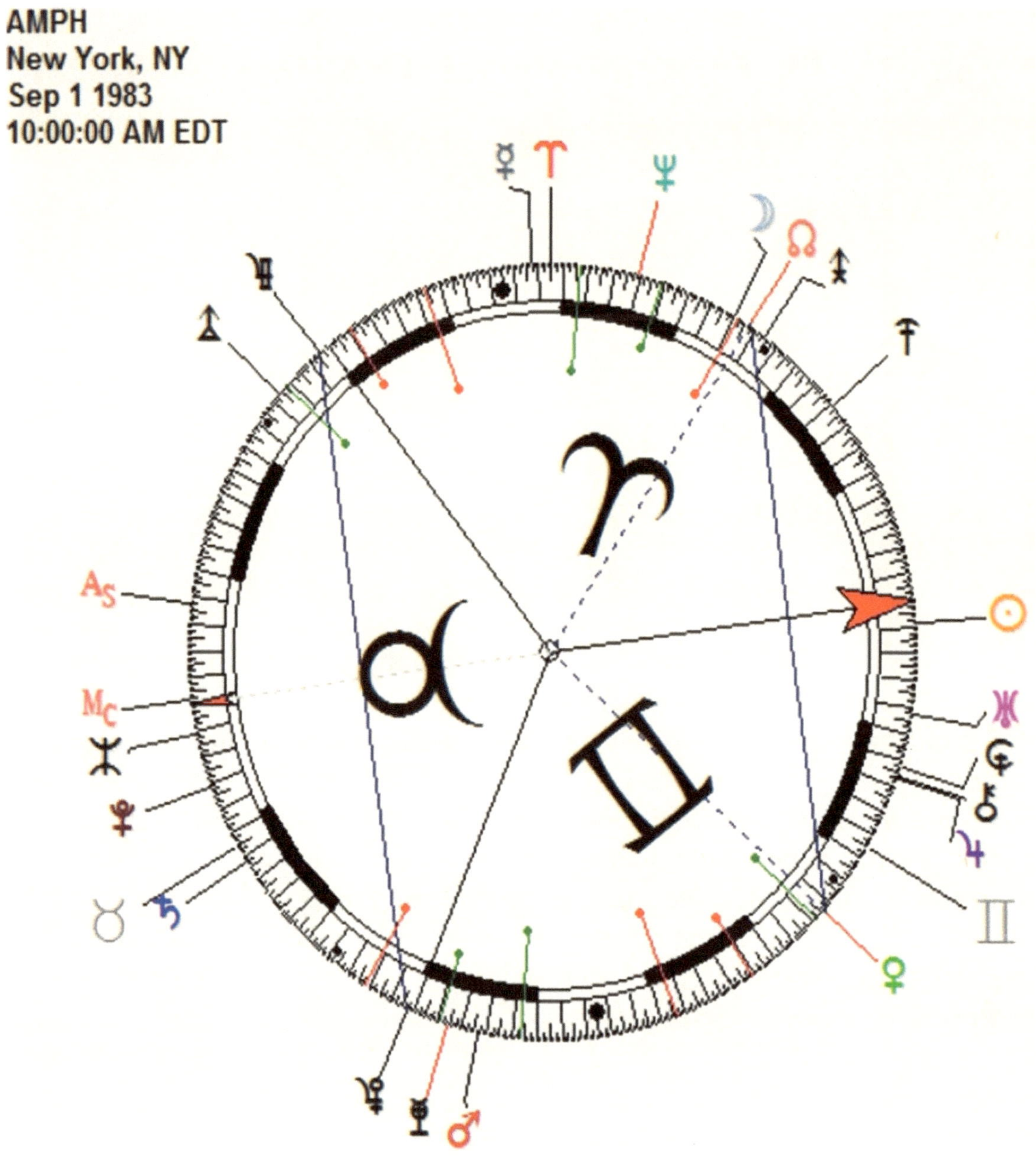

The solar eclipse in Spetember activates the Midheaven, as well as both the Venus/True Lunar Node midpoint and the Cupido/Apollon midpoint, in the AMPH First-Trade horoscope.

PolyOne Corporation (NYSE - POL)

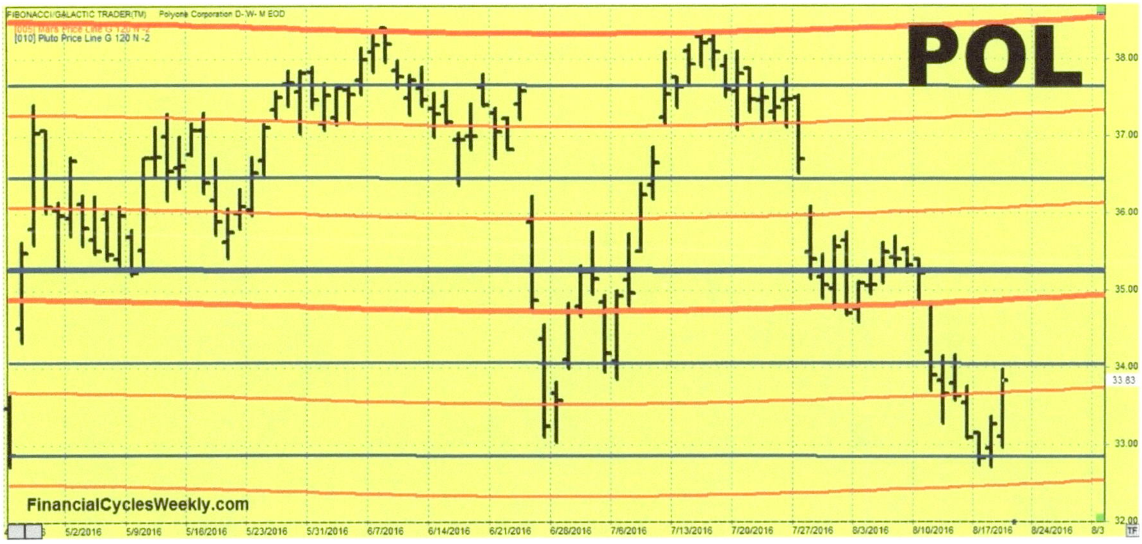

PolyOne Corporation provides specialized polymer materials, services, and solutions with operations in specialty polymer formulations, color and additive systems, plastic sheet and packaging solutions, and polymer distribution. Its Color, Additives and Inks segment provides specialized color and additive concentrates in solid and liquid for thermoplastics; and dispersions for thermosets, as well as specialty inks, plastisols, and vinyl slush molding solutions. The company's Specialty Engineered Materials segment offers specialty polymer formulations, services, and solutions for designers, assemblers, and processors of thermoplastic materials. Its Designed Structures and Solutions segment provides various solutions in engineered polymer structures, rigid barrier packaging, and specialty cast acrylics to produce portfolio of sheets, custom rollstock and specialty films, laminates, and acrylic solutions. This segment also offers stock and custom packaging solutions for various industry processes that are used in the food, medical, and consumer markets. The company's Performance Products and Solutions segment provides vinyl molding and extrusion processors to various manufacturers of plastic parts and consumer-oriented products. The company's PolyOne Distribution segment distributes approximately 3,500 grades of engineering and commodity grade resins to custom injection molders and extruders. PolyOne Corporation sells its products worldwide through direct sales personnel, sales agents, and distributors. The company was founded in 1927 and is headquartered in Avon Lake, Ohio. We track the price action for this stock with geocentric planetary price lines for Mars and Pluto in the third harmonic.

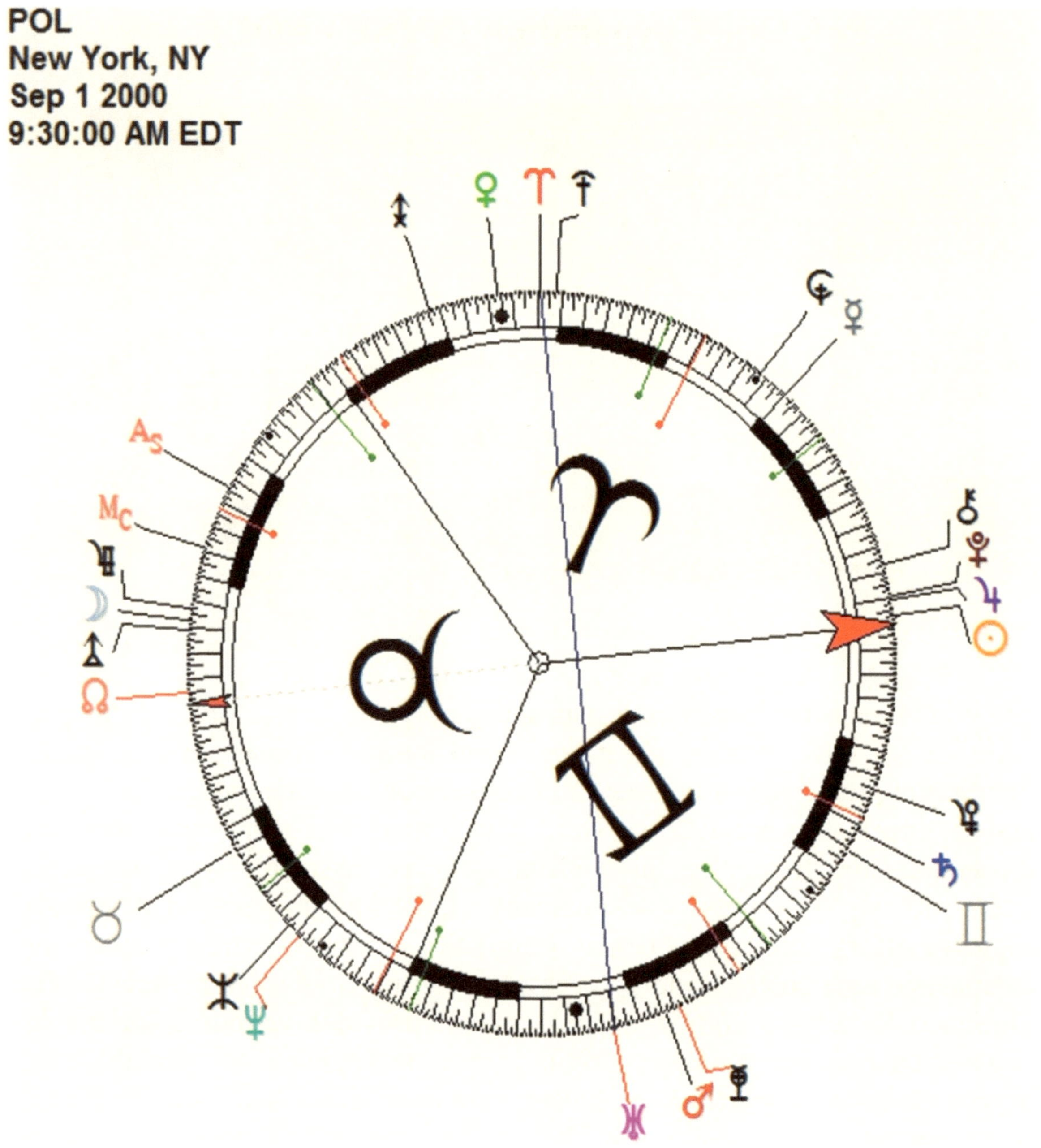

The POL First-Trade horoscope picks up the September solar eclipse effects through the True Lunar Node and the Uranus/Aries Point midpoint.

Westar Energy, Inc. (NYSE - WR)

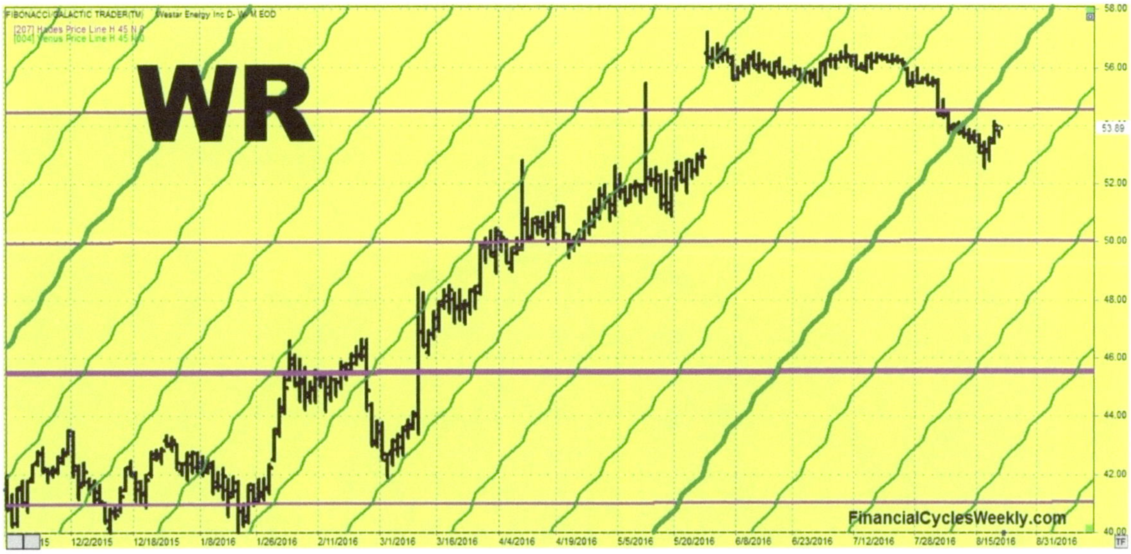

Westar Energy, Inc., an electric utility company, generates, transmits, and distributes electricity in Kansas. The company has 6,267 megawatts of electric generation capacity that produces electricity through various fuel types, including coal, uranium, natural gas, diesel, wind, and landfill gas. It also owns approximately 6,400 miles of transmission lines, 24,000 miles of overhead distribution lines, and 4,900 miles of underground distribution lines. It retails electricity to residential, commercial, and industrial customers, as well as for lighting public streets and highways; and is involved in electricity wholesale to electric cooperatives, municipalities, other electric utilities, and regional transmission organizations. The company provides its services in central and northeastern Kansas, including the cities of Topeka, Lawrence, Manhattan, Salina, and Hutchinson, as well as in south-central and southeastern Kansas, including the city of Wichita. It serves approximately 700,000 customers. Westar Energy, Inc. was founded in 1924 and is headquartered in Topeka, Kansas. We track its trading with heliocentric eighth-harmonic price lines for Venus and Hades.

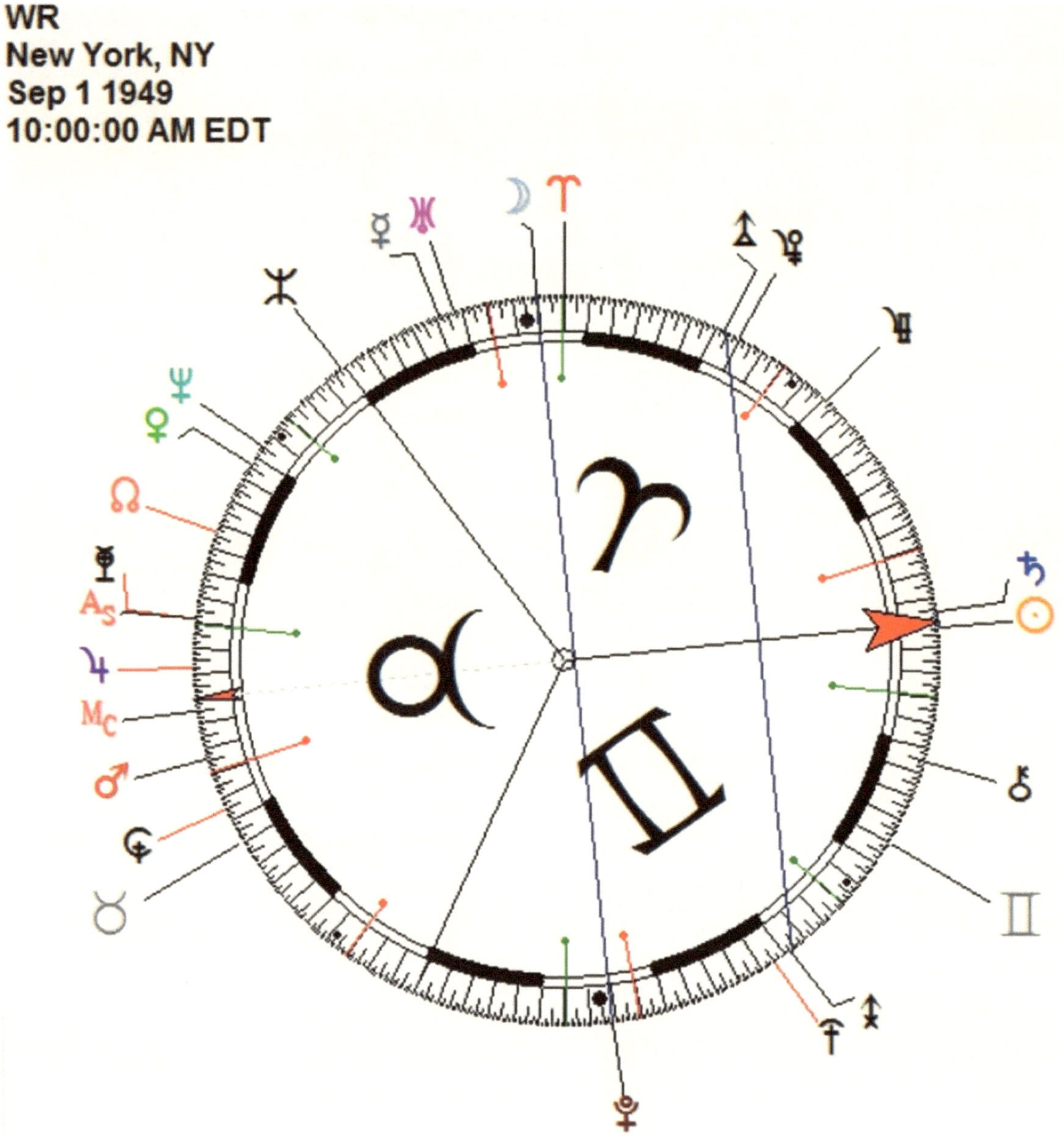

The September solar eclipse triggers the WR Jupiter/Midheaven midpoint, the Zeus/Vulcanus midpoint, and the Moon/Pluto midpoint structures.

DISCLAIMER

Beyond The Shadows: Divergence and Opportunity **is a general interest publication which has been prepared from astrological information, news reports, cycle projections, and market observations which are believed to be accurate and reliable, but which cannot be guaranteed. Even with accurate information, past performance is no guarantee of future results. Speculation in securities and commodities involves considerable financial risk, and readers who plan to invest or speculate in securities or commodities mentioned in** ***Beyond The Shadows: Divergence and Opportunity*** **agree to assume complete personal responsibility for making themselves fully aware of all the risks involved before they invest. The authors of this report may at various times have positions in the securities and commodities discussed in this publication, and the information in** ***Beyond The Shadows: Divergence and Opportunity*** **should in no way be understood or construed as a solicitation or an offer to buy or sell any products or securities, nor should the material published herein be considered buy/sell advice.**

APPENDIX

The Geopolitical Dynamics of the Solar Eclipse of September 1, 2016

Additional Commentary By
Jim Cummins

A Note On The Appendix

Eclipses have many facets, and they inevitably affect our personal lives, the activities of the markets, and global affairs in many different ways.

Different astrologers bring a variety of skills and experiences to their understanding and interpretation of solar eclipses, and it's useful to have those differing perspectives in gaining the maximum advantage in tapping into the resources that eclipses offer us.

With that in mind, we're pleased to present these additional perspectives from our colleague, Jim Cummins.

– *Tim Bost*

The Geopolitical Dynamics of
The Solar Eclipse of September 1, 2016

by Jim Cummins

Part I

This is Part I of a two-part report. I shall present Part II in person at the Heart of the Lion Astro-Trading Symposium, in Bradenton, Florida on September 26-27, 2016.

Figure 1 is a diagram of a Solar Eclipse:

Solar eclipses happen when the Moon moves between Sun and Earth, blocking the Sun's rays and casting a shadow on Earth

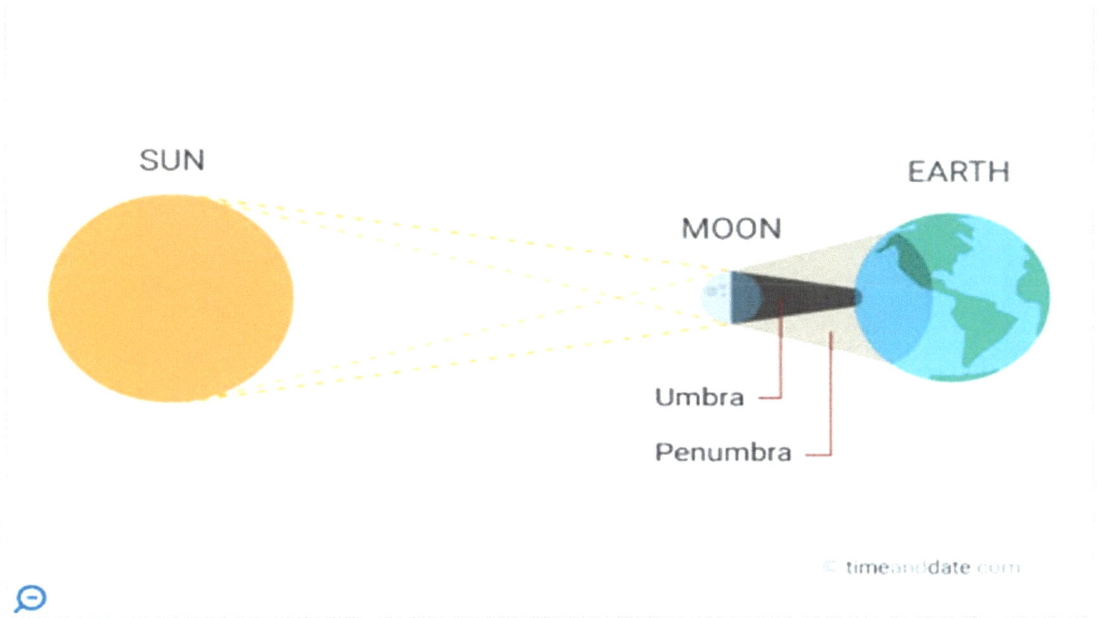

Total Solar Eclipse: The Moon's umbra blocks the sun's rays from reaching a small area on Earth, while the penumbra causes a Partial Solar Eclipse in a larger area. (Not to scale)

Fig. 1

As the Earth turns on its axis, the primary, or central shadow cast by the Moon (Umbra) becomes a darkened Path upon the Earth's surface. Someone standing in the center of that Path will not be able to see the Sun at all, because the Moon blocks it out. That is what is meant by a Total Eclipse of the Sun. The Sun is obscured, or eclipsed from the view of an observer standing in that shadowed Path (Umbra) cast upon the Earth.

However, anyone standing in the larger, less shaded area (Penumbra) will be able to see some portion of the Sun during the eclipse. The percentage of the Sun that will be visible to an observer standing in the larger, but less darkened area will depend on how near the observer is to the central Path of Totality.

The term, "Path of Totality" is hugely important. It describes the narrow band across the Earth that is totally deprived of the Sun's life-giving light, energies and rays during the course of the Eclipse.

By proportion, the same is true of the wider, or larger area (Penumbra) that is less shaded, but nonetheless still within the shadow of the Solar Eclipse.

The difference is that the further an observer is from the Path of Totality, from either side of that central darkened Path, the more of the Sun will be visible to that observer, and therefore the less potency or effect will the eclipse have upon that area in which the observer is then standing, or upon the observer who is standing there. It's a matter of percentage, or degree, of the eclipse's shadow.

Figure 2 on the following page, from Fred Espenak, illustrates this point.

Fig 2.

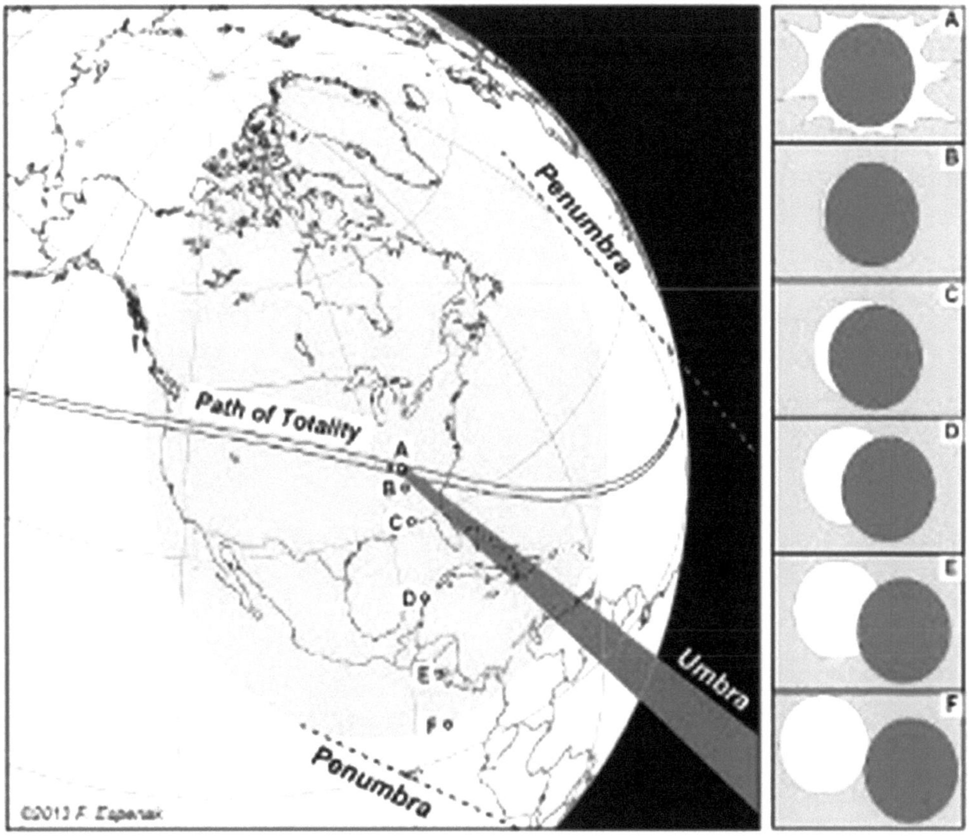

Figure 1-3 illustrates the path of totality for the total solar eclipse of 2017 Aug 21. The appearance of maximum eclipse from six different geographic locations on the map (labeled A through F) is shown in the side bar. The total eclipse is visible from position A because it lies in the path of totality.

History has taught us that wherever the shadow of an eclipse falls, that geographical area will be considerably sensitized for months to come following the advent of the eclipse. That geographical area, especially along the Path of Totality, is deprived of the Sun's life-giving energies and rays during the tenure of that particular eclipse. The same is true all across whatever area its larger shadow (Penumbra) falls, only to a lesser degree, depending on how close, or far one is from the central darkened Path of Totality.

For example, Figure 2 shows the Path of Totality (during the Total Solar Eclipse of August 21, 2017), as well as the larger, less dark, but nonetheless shadowed (Penumbra) areas of the Earth on that date. This particular Total Solar Eclipse, on August 21, 2017, will darken ALL of the United States, and much of Canada to our north, and Mexico and Central America to our south. Its Path of Totality will cut right across our Great Land, directly overhead three of America's most potentially sensitive geological areas: Yellowstone National Park, the New Madrid fault zone, and Charleston, South Carolina.

An in-depth discussion of the implications of that particular Solar Eclipse (August 21, 2017) will have to wait for Part II of this report. Our focus here must be on the Solar Eclipse that comes next: September 01, 2016. Its Path of Totality (Umbra) and wider shadow (Penumbra) coverage is illustrated in Figure 3.

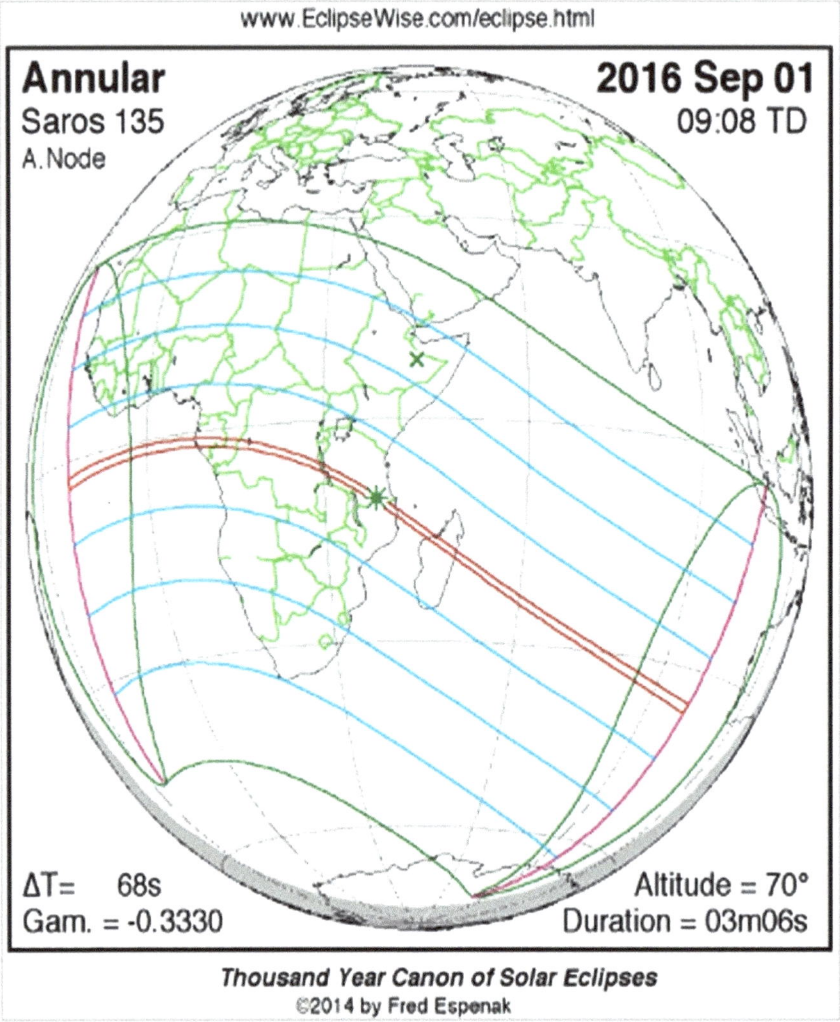

Fig. 3.

On the following page Figure 4 shows another way of seeing the geographical reach of the Solar Eclipse of September 01, 2016.

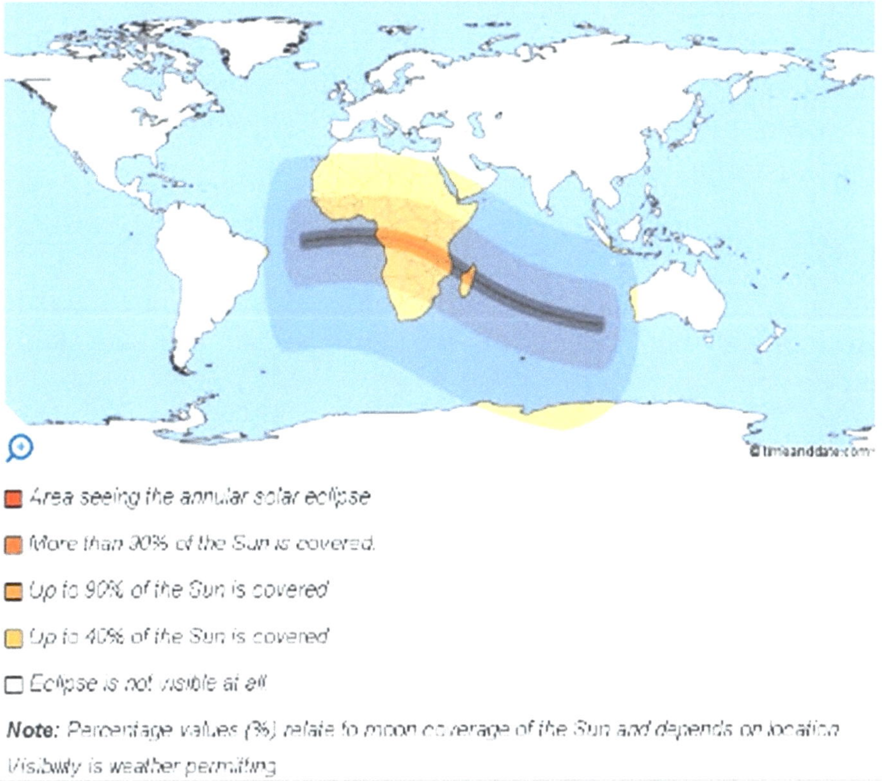

Fig. 4

Yet another illustrative diagram to show where on Earth the shadows of the Solar Eclipse of September 01, 2016 fall is Figure 5 below:

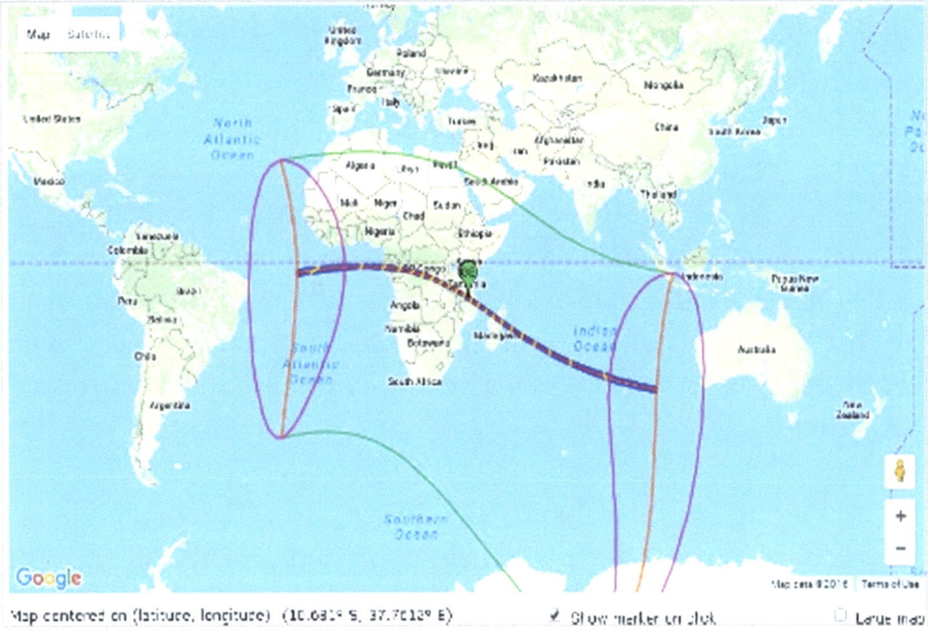

Fig. 5.

Obviously, very nearly the entire continent of Africa is covered by the shadows of the Solar Eclipse of September 01, 2016. So is part of the South Atlantic Ocean, and the island of Madagascar, and a large enough sector of the vast Indian Ocean that the edges of this Eclipse's shadow are also cast on parts of Indonesia, Australia, and Antarctica.

Remember the note, on page 129, that "wherever the shadow of an eclipse falls, that geographical area will be considerably sensitized for months to come following the advent of the eclipse." The keyword here is "sensitized."

Depending on the then prevailing alignments of the rest of the solar system at the moment of the eclipse, the nature and depth of those affected areas' sensitivity can trigger all manner of disturbances within those areas, from political upheaval to geologic, climatic, economic and/or significant social turmoil during the period of that Solar Eclipse's trailing effects.

Solar Eclipse leave lingering, "trailing" effects – some as long as 2-3 years. Considering that there are at least two Solar Eclipses each year, sometimes more, the effective imprint and impact of each Solar Eclipse must be considered to apply, at the very minimum, six months.

Eclipses come and go in patterns, and like ripples in a pond, they certainly overlap in their effectiveness. My personal observation through the years is that a basic minimum effective period for each Solar Eclipse is definitely a year, and in most instances, 18 months to 2 years. Solar Eclipses tend to re-ignite the energies of those which preceded them, and to pave the way, so to speak, for those which follow.

The best way to see the varying relationships between each of the other bodies in our local solar system at the moment of the Solar Eclipse, and what impact they may or may not have on the severity, or intensity, or placidity of that particular eclipse, is to draw an astrological chart for the moment of the eclipse's exactness.

That chart can be calculated, or drawn from anyplace on Earth, of course. Figure 6 shows our local solar system, with all its prevailing astronomical/astrological geometric interactions between the various planets, as well as their respective alignments with the Zodiacal position of the Solar Eclipse itself.

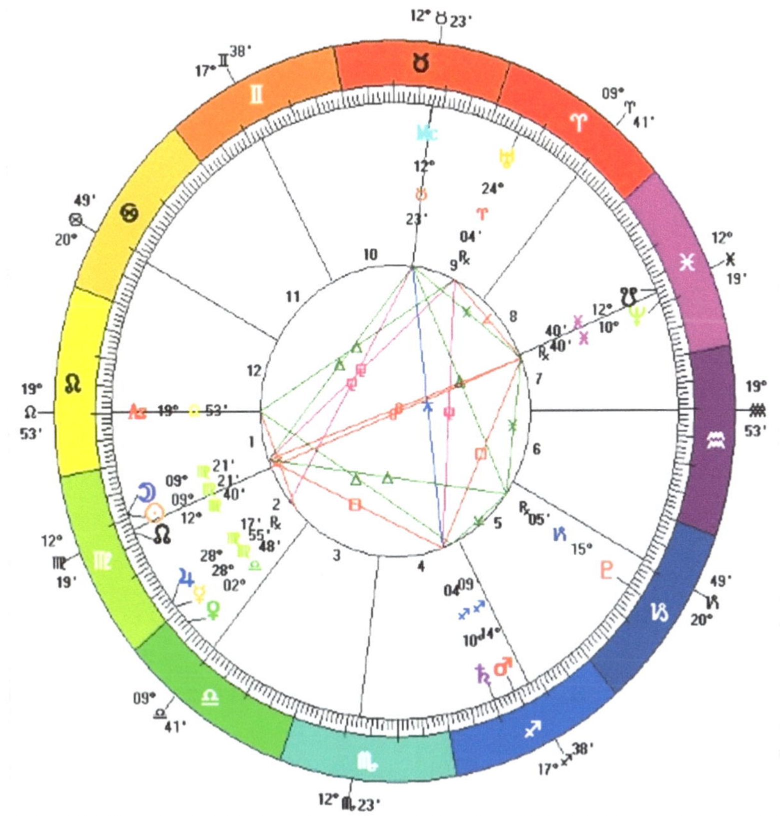

Fig. 6. Solar Eclipse of September 01, 2016. Location: White House, DC. 05:04:04 EDT.

This chart was drawn for the White House in Washington, D.C. It shows that the Solar Eclipse takes place at 09 degrees Virgo 21 minutes. While the Sun and Moon, each at that degree and minute within the Sign of Virgo, and close to a conjunction to the Moon's North Node, opposing them is Neptune, conjunct the Moon's South Node in Pisces, at 10 and 12 degrees, 40 minutes of Pisces, respectively.

Immediately, the "double T-square," involving Saturn and Mars, both in Sagittarius, challenging the Moon conj Sun Solar Eclipse, and its closeness to the Moon's North Node on the one side, and simultaneously squaring Neptune, and the Moon's South Node on the other, jumps to the fore.

Each of the planets involved are in Angular Houses, adding urgency, emphasis, and activity to the placements (although Neptune is not usually a symbol of activity – at least outwardly.)

Before going any further with an analysis of this chart, it is important to note that this Solar Eclipse indicates a stressful time ahead for all upon whom it will have bearing – especially those millions in Africa (who already have enough difficulties to bear). I shall discuss this theme more fully later in this report.

The prevailing squares between the Eclipse's Saturn and the Eclipse point have an outlet in a mutual double sesquiquadrate (135 degrees) to the planet Uranus in Aries.

In astrology, a sesquiquadrate aspect (angle) is often termed a "release of tension." However, the release of tension is somewhat akin to a heavily pressured torrent of water trying to come through a hose with a small nozzle – like a fireman's hose. That can be difficult to handle, if one is not properly prepared for it.

Uranus in Aries is definitely a revolutionary. Thankfully, it is Retrograde in this chart – indicating that some degree of the intensity which would propel those under this Eclipse's shadow to rebel, might be mitigated – or withheld.

On the other hand, some circumstance beyond their control could also be preventing them from rebelling, or finding flight when their lives are at stake, because of the holding-back indicator of a Retrograde Uranus.

This chart, drawn for the White House in Washington, DC (Fig 6) indicates extreme volatility – long-standing feuds and deep-seated animosities, even hatreds. It is guerrilla fighting – dashing in and out – lightning fast, deadly contacts, driven by fatalistic idealism behind which to cloak the most disturbing and destructive behaviors.

I shall return to a more explanatory analysis of these indicators in Part II of this report.

As shown on the following page, Figure 7 is the chart for the September 01, 2016 Solar Eclipse relocated to Port-Gentil, Gabon, the point at which the Path of Totality enters the African continent. The same angular relationships between the respective planets remain, but in this chart, they are in different Houses. That makes all the difference here.

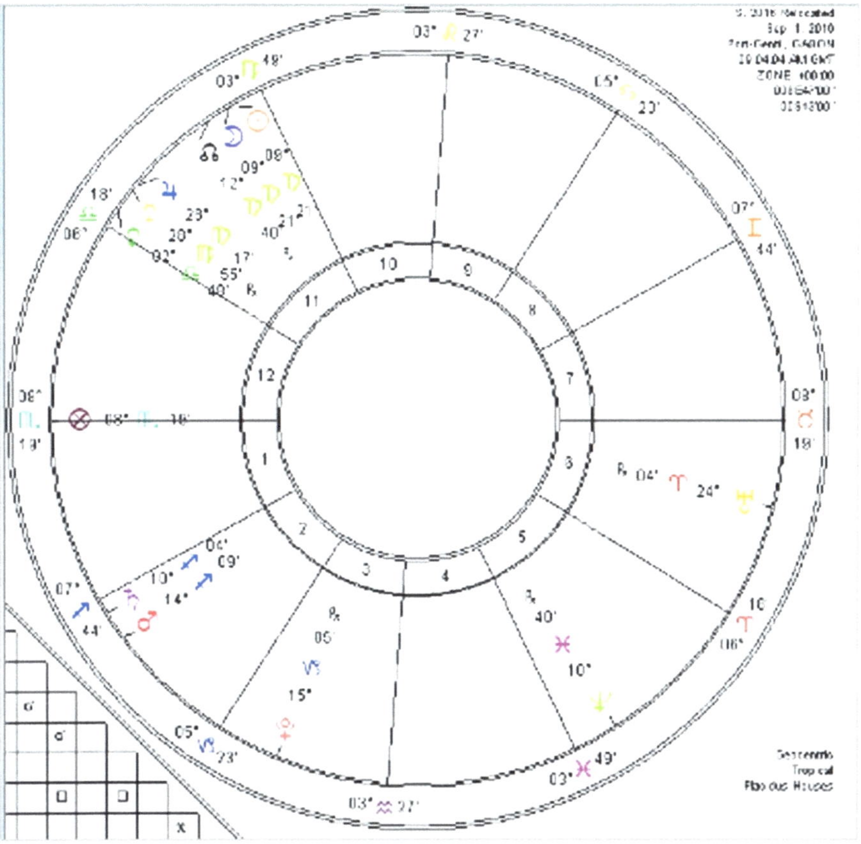

Fig. 7 SolEcl 9-1-2016 relocated for Port-Gentil, Gabon

The Solar Eclipse in this chart falls into the 11th House, of the Parliament, and business corporations.

Of all the nations in Africa, Gabon is one of the more peaceful, and prosperous. Its main industries are oil and timber.

Investors from Hong Kong, Singapore, and India work closely in joint-venture arrangements with President Ali Bongo Ondimba, who is up for re-election on August 27, 2016 to his second 7-year term. President Ondimba and U.S. President Barack Obama are close friends, incidentally.

Gabon boasts an 83.5% literacy rate, but since the richest 20% of the population earn more than 90% of the income, more than a third of the people live in poverty.

The 11th House placement for this Solar Eclipse in this chart indicates advancement for the nation during the term of this eclipse's duration (remember, at least a year or more) with friends and allies of the nation, and an improved economic condition overall.

The prevailing multiple "T-squares" against that Eclipse position, however, definitely indicate that there will be considerable corruption – so what comes into the Treasury, may just as quickly be siphoned out the back into some unscrupulous hands – again to the detriment of the population.

The IMF or World Bank may find cause to look into this matter later this year.

Pluto in this chart, being in the 3rd House of all means of transportation, and communications, including roads, bridges, automobiles, traffic in general, etc., signifies this to be a trouble spot for the nation.

Although Pluto is not precisely squared here, Uranus, which is herein retrograde, will be coming back to within orb of being square to that Pluto in December, after Mars has squared it in late October, indicating there could be considerable tensions in these sectors, as well as with neighboring nations.

Of all the nations neighboring her, Gabon may be the "adult" in the community. She is relatively stable, especially when compared to her Nigeria, with Boko Haram in her northeastern corner of Borno, or the Democratic Republic of Congo, with its perennial tribal violence…each only one small country removed from the relative stability of the West African nation of Gabon.

Figure 11, shown on the next page, is the Solar Eclipse chart relocated to Masasi, Tanzania. [Note that in this edition of Part I of this report, Figures 8, 9, and 10 have been omitted. I will be reviewing them as a part of my presentation during Part II at the Heart of the Lion Astro-Trading Symposium.]

This location in Tanzania is near to where the Eclipse will be at its maximum. Here we find Saturn and Mars straddling the Ascendant, while Neptune and the South Node in the 4th House hold opposition to the Solar Eclipse itself very close to the MC. The "T-square" configuration inherent in this chart is front and center here – announcing major shifts in who holds power, or how that power is wielded during the tenure of this Solar Eclipse.

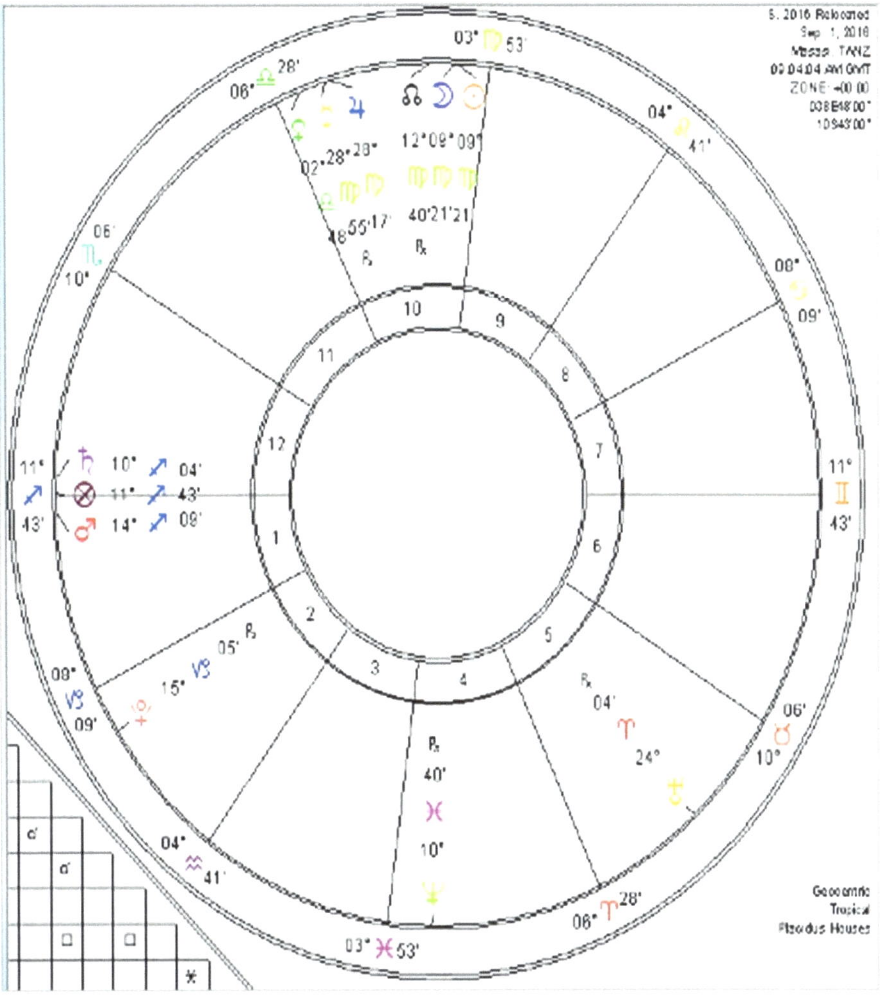

Fig. 11 SolEcl 9-1-2016 relocated for Masasi, Tanzania

The double-release-of-tension Uranus is in the 5th House here, repository of all forms of speculation and gambling – whether the nation's stock exchange, or an individual's incurable habit, at the loss of others in positions of responsibility.

There is a race going on between Kenya and Tanzania – as to which one will become East Africa's biggest port. Tanzania plans to develop Bagamoyo into one of the largest ports in sub-Saharan Africa. The Kenyan port of Mombassa and Tanzanian port of Dar es Salaam have long been competitors for the region's businesses. However, the Kenyan government is now planning a new port at Lamu as Tanzania develops Bagamoyo.

Either of these ports will be larger than any other port in sub-Saharan Africa when they are completed – which will take decades, not just years, incidentally.

They will also be the centers of even bigger developments via proposed Industrial Zones being laid out, and plans for intensive farming being proposed. Tanzanian authorities believe that Bagamoyo will be able to handle 20 million containers per year, which is 25 times larger than the port of Dar es Salaam. Kenya's planned Lamu port is expected to be just as big.

Early work on Bagamoyo, which is to begin by the end of this year, has already displaced more than 2,000 people from their homes, farmlands and properties – for which Tanzania has promised compensation. The Tanzanian and Kenyan governments will also be competing for businesses from the land-locked nations of East Africa. Neither Lamu, nor Bagamoy have been used for more than a century, but once they were rivals for the lucrative East Africa slave trade.

Financing for Bagamoyo will be by China Merchant Holding International, and the State General Reserve Fund, which is at Omani Sovereign Wealth Fund. Preliminary work has already begun on Lamu, even before the funding is finalized.

The Tanzanian port of Tanga is also being refurbished and upgraded. The government convinced Uganda to route its planned oil export pipelines through this port, rather than take a chance on being attacked by Somali Islamists, Al Shabaab group, which situation might happen should they go through Lamu, a port that is closer to Somalia. Additionally, a new railroad to run parallel to the oil pipeline to connect with ferry services on Lake Victoria is being built.

Kenya has stayed with state ownership. Kenyan Port Authority continues to own and manage its port of Mombassa, while Tanzania operates its Dar es Salaam port with Tanzania International Container Terminal Services, an offshoot of Hong Kong's Hutchison Whampoa. Bagamoyo will be operated by China Merchant Holdings; Lamu is being developed by China Communications Construction Company, with the Kenya Ports Authority still being in control.

The two countries are also boosting their rail infrastructure, connecting themselves to the inner continent by long distance railways. The old colonial rails, now in disrepair, need much upgrading, even replacing. One such new railway now being constructed, with Chinese funding, goes from Mombassa to Nairobi.

Fig. 12

Figure 12 outlines Kenya/Tanzania rail lines, and seaports, mostly funded by China.

Considering the Solar Eclipse chart as an overlay to these projects, one can only imagine the amount of perseverance and determination that must be wielded to further the aims and goals the Chinese have laid out.

However, such tenacity is potentially evident in this chart, i.e. Saturn and Mars conj. the Ascendant, in square to the Eclipse point near the MC (supported by the North Node, Jupiter, Mercury and Venus, all so highly placed…but possibly undermined by Neptune/South Node in the 4th, may only indicate swamp lands or marshes to be overcome in the building process.

Will the money be there on time?

No. Pluto in the 2nd is retrograde, and Saturn, its dispositor is kept under tight wraps in the 12th, even though Jupiter is in the 10th…that just goes to keeping a good face on whatever setbacks they encounter.

The last bit of land this eclipse passes over is Madagascar, the world's fourth largest island, which is famous for its ring-tailed lemurs, and other exotic wildlife (because of its relative isolation), as well as being the world's favorite source for vanilla.

Madagascar has long had political difficulties – and very trying weather conditions, especially torrential rains and floods. The relocation chart for this Solar Eclipse over Madagascar promises more of the same…difficult weather along the coastlines, conflicts from long-established political hacks against anyone wanting to improve such things as schools, hospitals, or other public service institutions. The inherent "T-squares" in this chart augur incessant mentation in any discussion about anything. "All talk – no action," as Donald Trump might say. This is a *spinning one's wheels* sort of chart.

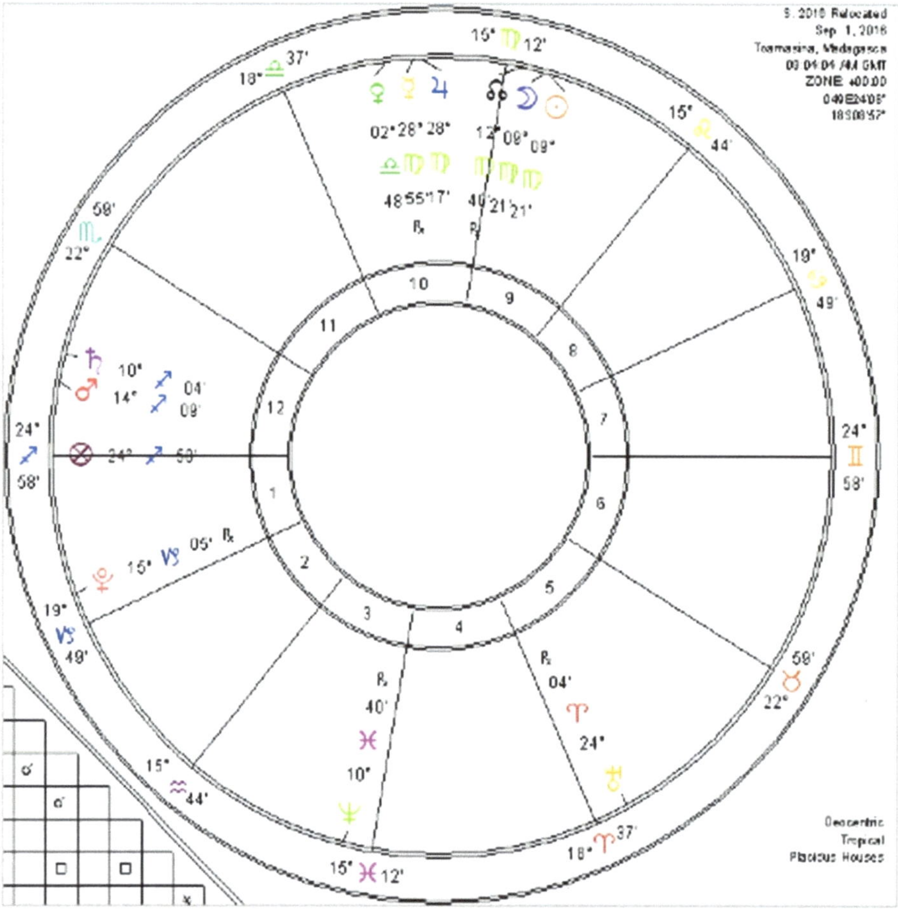

Fig 13 SolEcl 9-1-2016 relocated for Toamasina, Madagascar

Oh, well, if one wants to just enjoy being laid back, without a lot of either want or need to accomplish much, other than to discuss ad nauseam whatever is the going topic of the moment, with whomever is available for such a going-nowhere discussion; and no need to make bold decisions or take definite actions, then this could be just the chart for such an individual.

It reminds me of the many years I spent in as a piano entertainer in lounges around the world watching the folks at the long bar talk around and over each other, none ever really hearing the other…but it didn't matter, each just loved to talk for the sake of carrying on a conversation with themselves.

Houses, Dispositors, and Rulers of the Sign on the cusps of Houses make all difference.

At least, with these planets placed here as they are, there is not a hint of real cruelty, as they would indicate in certain other House placements.

Let's revisit China's involvement, and investments in Africa for a moment.

China has long pursued the mineral resources of Africa. Back in 2008, for instance, two firms, China Railway and Sinohydro, bankrolled (invested approx. $1.8 Billion USD) in a copper and cobalt project (a joint venture with local partners) in the ever-volatile Democratic Republic of Congo, in return for a regular supply of key minerals at a time when global prices are soaring, or the minerals are otherwise in short supply.

The DR Congo holds 10% of the world's copper reserves, and at least one-third of its cobalt supplies.

On July 23, 2016, the China Daily reported: "Sino-Africa Co-op To Go On, Despite Global Economic Slowdown." China maintains that its move to expand its own domestic market will strengthen Africa's export sector, especially Africa's agricultural products, thereby promoting the continent's industrialization ambitions.

Speaking on the sidelines of the recently concluded Africa Union Summit in Kilgali, Rwanda, Erasus Mwencha, Deputy Chairman of African Union Commission said that commitments made by the two partners, (Africa and China) on the Forum on China- Africa Cooperation (FOCAC) meeting in December (2015) gave this bid the needed impetus.

"The economic slowdown in China will not derail these plans," Mr. Mwencha said. In the next two weeks (this was being spoken on 23 July 2016), there will be an FOCAC ministerial meeting (in Beijing,China) to follow up on the agreement that was made in Johannesburg, South Africa. The Deputy Chairman of the AUC is confident that the partnership between Africa and China will continue in their unified pursuit of industrialization, infrastructure development, and poverty eradication, among other objectives.

During the FOCAC summit in December 2015, President Xi Jinping announced a $60 Billion USD investment into development projects in Africa, which included $10 Billion USD to the China-Africa Fund for Production Capacity Cooperation.

A 10-plan strategy was also proposed that included: (1) industrialization; (2) agricultural modernization; (3) infrastructure; (4) financial services; (5) green development; (6) trade and investment facilitation; (7) poverty reduction and public welfare; (8) public health; (9) people-to-people exchanges and (10) security.

President Jinping noted that this amount (USD $60 Billion) is equal to 1.5 times the Silk Road fund on the Belt and Road Initiative. It is broken down as follows: USD $5 Billion in outright grants and 0 interest loans; USD $35 Billion in loans and more favorable terms; an export credit line; and USD $20 million added to the fund for development of the China-Africa Fund for Production Capacity Cooperation.

Notes On Terrorism

This is a far less pleasant subject for discussion, but this Solar Eclipse, shadowing nearly all the entire continent of Africa, brings the issue front and center. It cannot be ignored. During the course of this Eclipse's tenure, it will rise up far more often, and deadly than civilized people everywhere can fathom, or tolerate.

In F*oreign Affairs* magazine, March/April 2016, we read the headline: "Isis Goes Global."The article is subtitled: "Fight the Islamic State by Targeting Its Affiliates." The writer contends that "...the downing of a Russian passenger plane over Egypt's Sinai Peninsula last October (2015) for which the Islamic State (ISIS) claimed responsibility may ultimately prove more consequential than the horrific attacks in Paris, San Bernadino, Orlando,..”

He writes that Western security officials had long been worried that their own citizens would conduct attacks after returning home from Iraq, or Syria or strike out as “lone wolf” terrorists…or even worse, second generation home-grown individuals radicalized via the Internet, etc., are ever harder to spot before they engage in their dastardly deeds.

All 224 people on that Russian passenger plane were killed. This multiple murder was caused by a “different beast: neither a lone wolf, nor ISIS itself, but an ISIS affiliate that had pledged his loyalty to Abu Barkr al-Baghdadi, ISIS’s self-declared Caliph.”

Such individuals, and/or groups expand ISIS’s geographic scope – vastly!

One example is the militant Islamist extremist group Boko Haram, headquartered in Nigeria’s northeast province of Borno.

According to the Council on Foreign Relations, the Nigeria Security Tracker (NST), is a project of the Council on Foreign Relations Africa Programme, which documents and maps violence in Nigeria that is motivated by political, economic, and social grievances. Different groups in Nigeria resort to violence, but Boko Haram is the most dangerous. Violence among ethnic groups, farmers, herdsmen sometimes acquires religious overtones. But a new generation of Niger Delta militants threatens war against the state; government soldiers kill civilians indiscriminately; police are notorious for extra-judicial murder.

Sounds like a lovely place, doesn’t it?

Boko Haram is most active in Borno, the northeastern corner of Nigeria. They alone are believed to have been directly responsible for 25,514 media-documented deaths between May 2011 and July 2016.

The Council on Foreign Relations (CFR) African Security Tracker (AST), which maps the violence in sub-Saharan Africa, which is made up of 48 countries, and is home to approximately 1 Billion people (ALL of whom will be directly impacted by the September 01, 2016 Solar Eclipse).

Sub-Saharan Africa does not include Algeria, Libya, Morocco, or Tunisia (although portions of each of these nations will also experience the edges of the shadows of this Solar Eclipse).

Continuing political violence in sub-Saharan Africa certainly causes untold misery, and impedes political, economic and social development. From January 1, 2011 through April 16, 2016, Nigeria had 34,091 reported deaths; 6,665 reported incidents of violence; while Sudan had 21, 651 reported deaths, and 5,096 reported violent incidents, etc, according to CFR-AST. In every nation in Africa, one may be confronted with such horrific realities.

Some might point to our own city of Chicago, Illinois, as an example, to counter that such volatile situations and deplorable social conditions are not exclusive to Africa.

My point is that the Solar Eclipse of September 01, 2016, shadowing nearly every square mile of Africa indicates that matters such as these are only going to be aggravated, and made much worse for Africa during the course of this Eclipse's tenure, and especially for the sub-Saharan nations, and most severely those through which the Path of Totality traverses.

When one considers further the depths to which Al Qaeda, Al Shabaab, ISIS, and their many Radical Islamic affiliates have planted their roots throughout Africa, and then realizes how much these entities are now on the move throughout the world, the extended reaches and powerful impacts of this Solar Eclipse's effects are all the more obvious and ominous – no matter who you are, or where you live.

"We are in a world war, but very few Americans recognize it, and fewer still have any idea how to win," write Lt. General Michael T. Flynn and Michael Ledeen in their concise and precise book, *The Field of Fight*, now available in bookstores everywhere.

General Flynn spent more than thirty-three years in Army intelligence, serving all over the world, becoming the Director of the Defense Intelligence Agency and Senior Military Intelligence Officer in the Department of Defense.

Michael Ledeen, the author of more than thirty-five books, is the Freedom Scholar at the Foundation for the Defense of Democracies, and served as Special Adviser to the Secretary of State, and consultant to the National Security council during the Reagan Administration.

In their book, *The Field of Fight*, these uniquely qualified men reveal to us in detail the international alliances structure of the world of Radical Islam, which is far more pervasive and extensive than most of us could have possibly known, and explain to us in clear and precise language that global alliances' fanatical, militant determination to usher in their version of Armageddon in the hopes of destroying all Western Civilization, leaving only a fundamentalist Islamic Sharia-law based Caliphate to rule the entire world in its place.

The September 01, 2016 Solar Eclipse, as it carves its Path of Totality across all of Africa, becomes a clarion call to all Radical Islamist terrorist Muslims and like-minded affiliates and sympathizers throughout the world. A dark shadow indeed arises from the Dark Continent, Africa. We can neither ignore, nor escape its challenge.

End Part I

Jim Cummins will present the second part of his detailed eclipse analysis, including a review of the geopolitical impact of the major summer solar eclipse of 2017, during the Heart of the Lion Astro-Trading Symposium in Bradenton, Florida on September 26 and 27, 2016. For more information about this event, go to: http://bit.ly/HOTLATSeb

More Information on the Astro-Trading Advantage

http://FinancialCyclesWeekly.com

http://HarmonicResearchAssociates.com

http://ProjectRegulus.com

http://bit.ly/HOTLATSeb

www.ingramcontent.com/pod-product-compliance
Lightning Source LLC
LaVergne TN
LVHW072313210926
848482LV00020B/201